The Pinecone

THE PINECONE

*The Story of Sarah Losh,
forgotten Romantic heroine – antiquarian,
architect and visionary*

JENNY UGLOW

faber and faber

First published in 2012
by Faber and Faber Limited
Bloomsbury House
74–77 Great Russell Street
London WC1B 3DA

Typeset by Faber and Faber Ltd
Printed and bound by TJ International Ltd, Padstow, Cornwall

A CIP record for this book
is available from the British Library

ISBN 978-0-571-26950-1

2 4 6 8 10 9 7 5 3 1

For Clara

Contents

CONTENTS

III MAKER

I preferred the Gothic pine cones . . . I would stroke the pine cones. They would bristle. They were attempting to persuade me to do something. In the tenderness of their shells, in their geometric giddiness, I sensed the rudiments of architecture whose demon has accompanied me all my life.

OSIP MANDELSTAM, Journey to Armenia, 1933[1]

The Losh Family, a short family tree

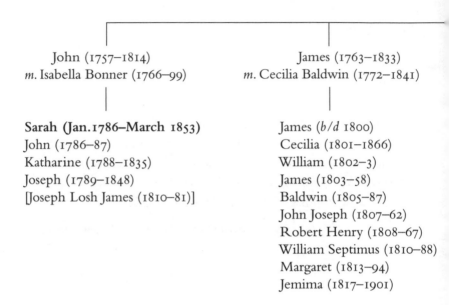

John Losh, 'the Big Black Squire' (c.1723–89)

John (1757–1814) *m.* Isabella Bonner (1766–99)	James (1763–1833) *m.* Cecilia Baldwin (1772–1841)

Sarah (Jan.1786–March 1853) John (1786–87) Katharine (1788–1835) Joseph (1789–1848) [Joseph Losh James (1810–81)]	James (*b/d* 1800) Cecilia (1801–1866) William (1802–3) James (1803–58) Baldwin (1805–87) John Joseph (1807–62) Robert Henry (1808–67) William Septimus (1810–88) Margaret (1813–94) Jemima (1817–1901)

Note: Sarah's cousins' marriages, if not mentioned above, were as follows:
JAMES'S CHILDREN: Cecilia *m.* William Gale (1820); Baldwin *m.* Gertrude Harding (1856); Margaret *m.* Edmund Townley (1836); Jemima *m.* Richard Postlethwaite (1841)
GEORGE'S DAUGHTERS: Mary *m.* James Kemmis (1817); Frances *m.* Francis Hutchinson (1820); Georgina *m.* Thomas Cussans (1834)
WILLIAM'S DAUGHTERS: Alice *m.* James Crosby Anderson (1822, *d.* 1837), then (2) Henry Player; after Spencer Boyd's death Margaret *m.*(2) Rev. Henry Mayhew (1836)

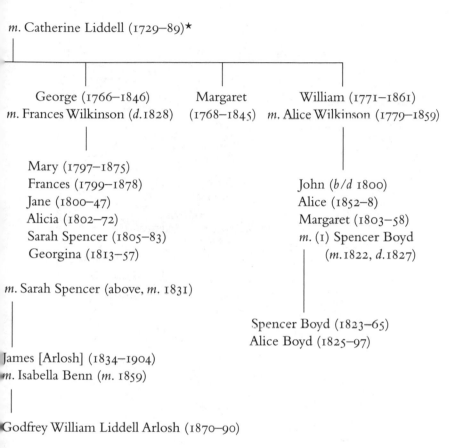

m. Catherine Liddell (1729–89)★

George (1766–1846)   Margaret   William (1771–1861)
m. Frances Wilkinson (*d.*1828)   (1768–1845)   *m.* Alice Wilkinson (1779–1859)

Mary (1797–1875)
Frances (1799–1878)   John (*b/d* 1800)
Jane (1800–47)   Alice (1852–8)
Alicia (1802–72)   Margaret (1803–58)
Sarah Spencer (1805–83)   *m.* (1) Spencer Boyd
Georgina (1813–57)   (*m.*1822, *d.*1827)

m. Sarah Spencer (above, *m.* 1831)

                                       Spencer Boyd (1823–65)
                                       Alice Boyd (1825–97)

James [Arlosh] (1834–1904)
m. Isabella Benn (*m.* 1859)

Godfrey William Liddell Arlosh (1870–90)

★ Four sons died young: William (1758–68), Joseph (1760–84), Thomas
(*b/d* 1766), Robert (1768–87)

[xi]

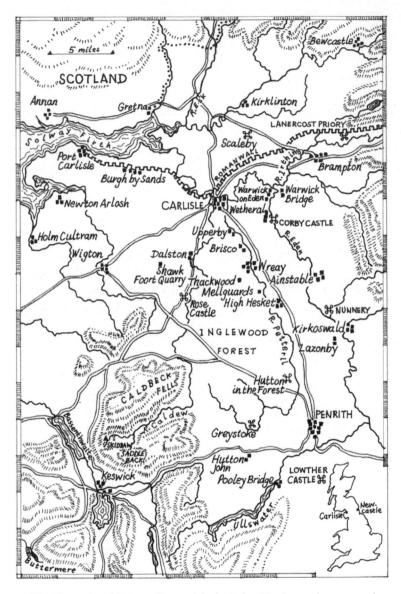

The Petteril and Eden valleys, with the Lake District to the west and Pennines to the east.

Prologue

The village of Wreay, or 'Rhea', as the locals say, to rhyme with 'near', lies five miles south of Carlisle. Four country roads meet at the village green, shaded by trees, and across the way is the church. It looks like a small Romanesque chapel from northern Italy, a long oblong with an apse. What is it doing in this northern village, with the mountains of the Lake District to the west, and the Pennines to the east? The closer you get, the odder it seems. The gargoyles are turtles and dragons. Instead of saints and prophets, the window embrasures are carved with ammonites and coral, poppies and wheat, caterpillar and butterfly. Inside, the light is filtered through strange stained glass, bright leaves on black backgrounds, kaleidoscopic mosaics, alabaster cut-outs of fossils. The pulpit is a hollow tree trunk made from black oak, dug from the bog. An eagle and stork of ferocious energy hold up the lectern and reading desk and on the altar table, instead of a cross, are two candlesticks in the shape of the lotus, immortal flower of the East.

This exuberant building was created in 1842 by a local woman, Sarah Losh. Around it she fashioned a whole landscape of memory, equally personal: a Celtic cross and a mausoleum – 'a Cell in the druidical fashion' one contemporary gazetteer called it – and a chapel copied from ruins centuries old, uncovered among Cornish dunes. Around the village she built wells, cottages and schools, all of them in her own highly individual style. Architectural critics from Rossetti, who hailed her as a genius, to Simon Jenkins, who called her 'a Charlotte Bronte in wood and stone', have described her work as unique, personal, unorthodox. When Nikolaus Pevsner visited Wreay in the 1960s, touring the county for his monumental *Buildings of Britain*, he was dumbfounded at her originality. Asking which was the finest Victorian church in Cumberland, he wrote, aware of the oddity of the claim, 'The first building to call out, one introduces with hesitation; for it is a crazy building without any doubt, even if it is a most impressive and in some ways amazingly forward-pointing building: the church at Wreay.'[2]

Sarah – who signed herself Sara when young – and her sister Katharine – often called Catherine, or Katherine – came from an old Cumbrian family, but her father and uncles set out across the country to make their fortunes in the new industries on the Tyne, like many men from these parts. They were radicals and freethinkers, scientific experimenters, friends of the Lake poets, campaigners against slavery and for toleration and reform. Heir to all this, Sarah was unusual in many ways – as a woman intellectual, antiquarian and architect – yet she was also typical of her age in combining a concern for the present with an equally strong preoccupation with the past. She destroyed many of her papers and others have been lost, although the Carlisle doctor Henry Lonsdale included extracts from her travel journals in his *Worthies of Cumberland* in 1873 and the vicar of Wreay, Richard Jackson, copied her forthright notes on the school and the church into his parish notebook. Here and in the manuscript diaries of her uncle James Losh, Sarah's presence is strong. But it is in her buildings that we have to look for her: she left stones and wood, not letters, for us to read.

She foreshadowed Ruskin and Morris in her use of local materials and appreciation of local craftsmen, while her style anticipated the Arts and Crafts movement by half a century. If the structure of her church is simple, the symbolic language is rich, drawing on a wealth of sources and cultures. And everywhere among those symbols there are pinecones, carved on the walls, on the roof beams and even the graves in the churchyard. The pinecone is an ancient symbol of regeneration, fertility and inner enlightenment: pinecones, carved in stone, decorated a Roman tombstone found at Gallows Hill near Carlisle in Sarah's day. But the pinecone was also a graphic embodiment of what Sarah, a fine mathematician, would have called the 'Sacred Geometry' of nature. The cone's bracts swirl in opposing directions from the base, following the spiralling Fibonacci sequence, a mathematical wonder since the thirteenth century, a simple sequence that comes from adding to each number the one that came before it – 1, 2, 3, 5, 8, 13 – which achieves a unique ratio, the Golden Mean. The pattern is found throughout nature from the seeds of a sunflower to the whirls on a snail shell, and – although Sarah Losh would not have known this – it is there in the twists of DNA and the wheels of galaxies. It is the geometry of life.

As I pieced together Sarah's story, I found that it too spiralled outwards, in overlapping curves. It is the tale of a pioneering, imaginative woman, but also of a colourful extended family and of the changing life of a village. It tells of ancient stones and Celtic crosses but also of the struggle of Carlisle weavers, the growth of Tyneside industries, the coming of the railways and the long fight for reform, and the fate of a soldier in the passes of Afghanistan. It shows how the industrial revolution made some women independent and how they burned to make their mark. Her story is intensely local but it opens on to many aspects of late Georgian and early Victorian England, driven by the energy and ideas that flowed through the age. Sarah Losh's buildings are Romantic in their powerful expression of sympathy between the human and natural world, yet Victorian in embodying the layers of history beneath the present, the findings of geology that shook conventional faith, and the concern with death, mutability and transience. Her favourite symbol, the pinecone, with its promise of rebirth, is also the way into her life and her work – as you enter the church and close the oak door behind you, the door-latch is two overlapping cones, carved in wood, touching and swinging apart.

I

DAUGHTER

1 The Walk

In mid-March the Cumbrian skies are sometimes a clear, cutting blue. At noon, the sun holds a faint touch of warmth, but it is cold, half a season behind the southern counties. Snowdrops are still out and wild daffodils just in bud. Sitting on the low wall with its rounded arches, around the enclosure of family graves, on a March day in 1850, Sarah Losh could feel snow in the breeze as she listened to the children's voices from the school across the road that she and her sister Katharine had built long ago. From here Sarah could survey her kingdom. At her back was her church and in front of her the broad green oval on the slope of the hill was ringed with her works. The buildings with their ancient forms looked now like part of the landscape, as if they had always been here. On the brow of the hill, she could see the wall of the new cemetery that she had given to the village, the mortuary chapel, standing out against the skyline, and the sexton's cottage beside it. Then the road dipped back to the churchyard, past the little dame school down to the cottages and the blacksmith's shop and the Plough Inn, before plunging towards the river Petteril in the valley.

Her first task, when she began to plan her church, had been to move the lane that cut across the north of the churchyard to the other side, so that it circled the whole domain. The process was slow, following set customs. First she had to gain the agreement of the Twelve Men of Wreay, the landowners and farmers who had

run village affairs since the Restoration, using the rents of parish land to pay the schoolmaster, administering local charities and
acting as guardians of the poor. Every Candlemas Eve, before the
quarter day that falls on 2 February, they met at the Plough at six in
the evening to conduct their business, then paid a shilling for their
supper of bread, cheese, oatcake, butter and ale, lit their churchwarden pipes and filled their tankards before they told tales, sang
ballads and recited poetry. They were 'the Township', and convivial
or not, they took their role seriously. In notes and petitions in the
early eighteenth century the men asked for the schoolmaster to be
made a deacon so that he could administer baptisms and visit the
sick.[1] Sarah's great-grandfather, William Losh, was one of the signatories to this petition, and in the year of her birth the list of the
Twelve Men included both her grandfather and her father.

The vicar, William Gaskin, who had lived with her family before
his marriage, when he was a young curate, had recorded the meetings of the Twelve Men in his leather-bound notebook since 1786,
when she was born. In her own notes describing the building of
the church Sarah explained that the plot of land on which it stood
was 'anciently part of the common belonging to the Township'
and when Wreay Common was enclosed in 1778, 'this was hedged
in to form a cow grassing' for the parish clerk. The original church
on the common was a long, low building dating back to the time
of Edward II: in 1319 the bishop allowed a chaplain here.[2] The
district was known as the Chapelry of Wreay, a sub-parish of St
Mary's abbey in Carlisle, and villagers always referred to the church
simply as 'the chapel'. In 1739 it was reconsecrated as St Mary's
of Wreay and since 1750 burials had been allowed here, relieving
the families of the arduous custom of carrying the corpse to the
mother church in Carlisle.

When Sarah persuaded the Twelve Men to hand the land over
to her in 1836, their action, she said, enabled her 'to improve the
appearance of the place by planting it with evergreens and also to

rebuild, with a little additional space, the wall of the chapel yard, which had almost wholly disappeared'. It seemed a reasonable and modest exchange, a gracious act by a local benefactor. But more was to come. 'June twentieth, 1836', the minutes declared in a looping hand, 'Resolved unanimously that leave be granted to Miss Losh to divert the Road to the West end of the Chapel yard'. But moving the road, although no one noted this at the time, also left her room to build a new church.

For many years the villagers remembered Sarah in her black cloak and bonnet, walking from the church to her home at Woodside, a good mile away. At the brow of the hill, where she could lean on the gate to the sexton's cottage, Wreay lay behind her in a sheltered curve on the side of the ridge that blocked the view to the west. To the east, though, the view suddenly widened: across the valleys of the Petteril and the Eden, the long shoulders of the Pennines sloped northwards from the heights of Cross Fell, still covered in snow, towards Carrock Fell, the small town of Brampton and the Newcastle road. She knew the name of every field she passed, for she owned them all, over six hundred acres on both sides of the road, as far as the hamlets of Brisco and Upperby, almost up to Carlisle.

The old road, known as Waygates, ran straight as an arrow. Before the enclosures of the late eighteenth century – from which the Loshes gained considerably – this had been a track across common land, crossing others at right angles with no need to circle awkwardly round private property. It was unusually wide, so that haycarts could pass, avoiding ruts and boggy patches. One half of it was paved and the other half was left as common. Canon Hall, the vicar of Wreay in the early twentieth century, remembered this wide margin as 'a wild tangle of gorse, sallows, brambles, honeysuckle, and dog roses, with meadow sweet, peppermint, orchids, and other flowers below'. In spring there were

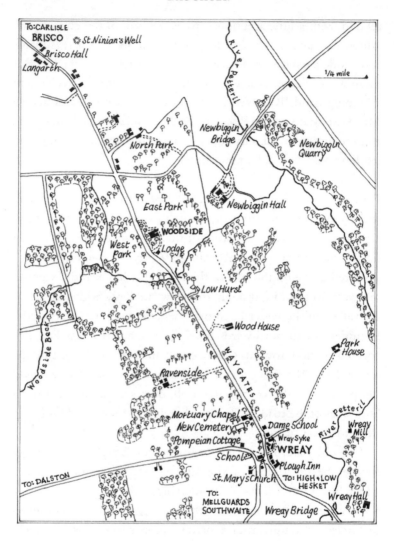

violets and dog's mercury, in autumn it was red with haws and hips, and in winter the snow lay deep and frozen.

The road ran past the farms of Wood House and Low Hurst, then down through a small wood, across the beck and up the hill to Woodside. The old house, set at right angles to the road, stood on a spur of land with views to all points of the compass. The effect of an airy plateau was strengthened by the way the grass was banked up to the top of the wall so that the road was hidden and the eye passed straight across to the fields and trees of the West Park: on a clear day you could see the Caldbeck Fells and the back of Saddleback, northern sentinel of the Lakes. Across the hidden ditch of the ha-ha, the view stretched across the pond and clumps of trees in the North Park to the hazy land of the borders; to the east lay the Pennines, and to the south Woodside's windows gazed across terraced lawns to the heights of Cross Fell.

A leisurely walk on the Woodside lawns, in Hutchinson's *History of Cumberland*, published in 1794, when Sarah was eight.

The Loshes had lived at Woodside for generations and her grandfather John had turned the old house into a Georgian mansion, with sweeping lawns and open views. A sundial stood in the garden, marked '1757', two years after his marriage. When her parents John and Isabella married in 1785, her grandparents moved to a house in Fisher Street in Carlisle, leaving Woodside to them. Sarah was born on New Year's Day 1786, and baptised six days later in St Cuthbert's, Carlisle. This was where all the family worshipped when they were in the city, where her parents had married and where her grandparents were buried within a week of each other in April 1789 – Catherine dying first and the Squire tumbling after.

Sarah was three when her grandfather died, but stories abounded of this huge, rumbustious man, twenty stone or more, with a roaring voice and bellowing laugh, fair-haired and red-faced, known as the Big Black Squire after the black stallion he rode. The Loshes were not among the grandest landowners but they were friends with all the powerful local families: the Blamires of Thackwood, a few miles away; the Hudlestons of Hutton John to the south; the Aglionbys of Nunnery, and the three branches of the Howard family, at Greystoke Castle, Corby and Naworth. They knew the Christians of Cockermouth and the magnates of the coast, like the Curwens of Workington Hall, who combined collieries with farming, the Senhouses of Netherhall, who had developed the fishing village of Maryport into a thriving port, and the Spedding families of Whitehaven and Bassenthwaite. Beyond this the marriages of the Squire's sisters brought connections with other well-known local names which would be marked in the margins of Sarah's life: Parkers, Bells and Wilsons.[3]

The Squire married pretty, charming Catherine Liddell, a woman less than half his size. She came from Burgh-by-Sands – or 'Bruff' in local speech – where the flat lands and creeks at the mouth of the Eden merged into the misty wastes of the Solway Firth. They were a sociable couple and they and their children were great favourites in Carlisle society. John was born in 1757, the eldest of nine children, eight boys and a girl, Margaret. The Loshes had their share of family tragedies: one of a pair of twins died within a week and their second son, William, died aged ten, after a fall from a tree while bird-nesting. Then just before John married, his brother Joseph, a young dragoons officer, died in Gloucester: there were lasting rumours of a duel, but his violent fever seems to have stemmed not from wounds but from heatstroke in the fierce July sun. Three years later Margaret's twin brother Robert collapsed in Newcastle when he was nineteen, after a walking match 'which, however, he won'.[4] These shadows hovered over Sarah's childhood. But when she was growing up her aunt Margaret and her uncles James and George, still in their twenties, and another William, who was fourteen when she was born, were vibrantly alive.

Their world was far from cut off in the late 1780s, however much their family friend Kitty Senhouse might lament that travel was so difficult: 'The mail being overturn'd does not surprise one as I believe accidents often happen to it unknown to anyone but those who have the misfortune of sharing in them – for the obvious reason that if it was known nobody would be foolhardy enough to trust so dangerous a conveyance.'[5] The Loshes had a house in London and business interests in Newcastle and Edinburgh and their sons travelled the world. The Squire was interested in new scientific ideas and friendly with the intellectuals of the cathedral close. His plans for his sons followed a standard pattern for the landed gentry: the eldest, John, would inherit the land; the next, James, would go into the church; the third – the ill-fated Joseph – into the army. The younger sons, Robert, George and William, would make their way in trade. As far as that was concerned, there were already good openings in Newcastle. Their mother Catherine had useful family connections with the Liddells of Ravensworth, powerful coal owners and merchants who were prominent in the politics of the Tyne.

John and his brothers had a radical, adventurous streak and looked far beyond Carlisle. All were talented linguists, studying abroad in France and Germany and the Low Countries, lovers of literature, filling the old house with books. They were born into a new age of improvement, science, law, industry and reform. Like

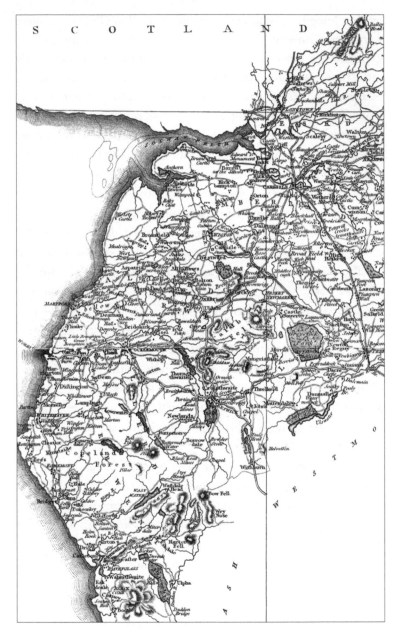

Cumberland, from the Lyson brothers' *Magna Britannia*, 1816

many Cumbrians of their generation, their futures lay on the quays of Newcastle as much as in the markets of Carlisle.

After his father died, John was head of the family, technically responsible for his younger brothers – although in the event it was James, the second son, who worried about their lives and sorted out their problems. Until they were sixteen James and John were both taught at home by the curate William Gaskin, whom James summed up as a man of 'considerable powers of mind', who had studied law and was a good classical scholar, despite being uncouth in his manners and abrupt in his speech.[6] From Wreay they went to be tutored by John Dawson, a brilliant, self-taught doctor and mathematician who took private pupils at Sedbergh, on the edge of the Yorkshire dales. Dawson's story became part of local lore: the poor boy from Garsdale in Yorkshire who walked to Edinburgh with his savings sewn into his coat to train as a doctor and eventually became a noted tutor at Cambridge, studying the orbit of the moon and correcting calculations of the distance of the earth from the sun. Mathematics, Dawson showed, could describe the world and open new vistas.

Both John and James Losh went on to Cambridge. James took his degree in 1786, the year of Sarah's birth. He began, as planned, by studying for the church but at Cambridge he became an admirer of Joseph Priestley, a Unitarian and avowed republican; no longer eligible for the church, he enrolled at Lincoln's Inn and was called to the Bar. His home, though, was still Woodside, and in his twenties, when Sarah and Katharine were girls, he cut a striking Rousseau-esque figure, distinctly at odds with the farmers around him, elegantly dressed, his dark, shining hair hanging over his shoulders. George and William went to school briefly at Hawkshead, where William lodged with Anne Tyson at the same time as William Wordsworth and his younger brothers John and Christopher, and the Spedding brothers.[7] George, always confrontational or 'disputacious' as James called him, was destined for commerce and studied in France and Germany, while William went to college in Erfurt in the centre of Germany, where he met and became a lifelong friend of the great naturalist and explorer Alexander von Humboldt. The two brothers spent time in Sweden, a centre of new discoveries in chemistry and, with Russia, one of Newcastle's great trading partners for timber, tar and bar-iron. George also went to Russia, astounding the locals by walking out without a topcoat, and both brothers travelled to Italy, perhaps taking their sister Margaret with them.[8]

George Losh, looking fine in his green silk waistcoat – the only known portrait of any of the four surviving Losh brothers as dashing young men.

Sarah's father, John, was carefree, 'handsome in person, and highly generous, fond of the beautiful in woman as well as art and nature', as Henry Lonsdale tactfully put it.[9] A gregarious soul, he was 'studious to please everybody, and as ready to entertain a peasant as a peer ... cock of the walk, and one of the most popular of men'. In the girls' childhood he was seen at all county gatherings, riding a black mare as highly strung as his father's, and was known for his love of country sports, following the hounds, wrestling and cock-fighting. Her mother, Isabella, was ten years his junior, only eighteen when they married. Small and elegant, with a classical profile, she was easy-going, affectionate and impulsive, fiercely defensive of her family, her husband and her children. She was not a local girl but came from Callerton Hall, near Newcastle. Her family, like the Loshes, cherished their history and stuck to their radical principles: one forebear, Thomas Bonner, had held out as a Puritan mayor in royalist Newcastle in 1649, and Cromwell, who was deeply unpopular in the region, was reputed to have hidden in the Hall. By contrast, when Isabella's brother, Robert Bonner, inherited his uncle's estate of Warwick Hall, east of Carlisle, and changed his name to Warwick in 1792, he moved into a devoutly Catholic enclave. The Warwicks were Catholics and Jacobites, like their neighbours, the Howards of Corby Castle: if Cromwell stayed at Callerton, Bonnie Prince Charlie slept at Warwick Hall. Woodside itself was the birthplace of Christopher Robinson, a Catholic priest who preached in defiance of the laws of Elizabeth I and was hanged, drawn and quartered in Carlisle in 1597. Tolerance and religious liberty, Sarah came to believe, were the only ways forward.

The Losh babies came fast. When Sarah was one her new brother John died at the age of five weeks; a year later, in early February 1788, Katharine was born, and last of all Joseph, the longed-for male heir. The children shared the nursery, looked after by their nurse and their mother. The girls thrived, began to read, took trips to Carlisle, paid calls on neighbours, visited their Losh and Warwick relations, and went to dancing lessons in Dalston a few miles away.[10] But Joseph was slow, and it was soon clear that something was wrong with him: he grew up to be severely backward, so much so that he could never look after himself and had to be cared for all his life. The hope of Woodside lay, after all, with the girls.

2 City and Strife

From childhood on, Sarah knew the great and good of Carlisle, the powerful men of the church, the politicians and the dignitaries. She absorbed many ideas from them, about faith, about history, about science, but she knew them as individuals with flaws as well as representatives of old institutions and she consistently made her own judgements.

After her grandparents died the Carlisle house was let and eventually sold, but the life of the Loshes still revolved around the city as well as Woodside and Wreay. Carlisle, whose cathedral's nave was demolished in the civil wars, had once been the vital centre of defences against the Scots but by now it had reverted to its role as a cathedral city and market town, admired for its wide streets and 'modern and elegant' houses, with twice-yearly hiring fairs and a Great Fair lasting two whole weeks.[1] New roads linked it to Whitehaven in the west and Newcastle in the east, and stagecoaches ran south over the treacherous heights of Shap Fell, taking three days to reach London. It was also a port, with ships loading and unloading at Sandsfield along the Solway and carts or packhorses carrying goods into the city. The poor of the city, for good or ill, had a dispensary to serve them as well as a cockpit and plenty of inns, selling beer from the breweries by the Irish Gate.

There were plenty of poor by the 1780s, as people streamed in to work in the new textile industry. This had begun forty years before, with a woollen business run by German immigrants, followed in 1761 by the first of the calico printers. One branch of the Losh family, Sarah's distant second cousins, quickly became involved: in the mid-1770s Thomas Losh established Losh & Co.'s Cotton Stampery on the millrace at Denton Holme while his brothers also traded as calico and cotton printers. Years later Robert Anderson, 'The Cumbrian Bard', remembered how as a boy he was apprenticed to a pattern drawer, and in 1783, he wrote, 'I cheerfully commenced the study of that business, under a truly respectable concern, T. Losh & Co., Denton Holme, near Carlisle; where I enjoyed all the happiness an industrious youth could hope for, being treated with every mark of esteem.'[2]

Mills and warehouses spread along the low plain to the south and west of Carlisle, cut off from the city by the river Caldew and the high medieval walls, and yet more were built in the outlying villages. One local man wrote to his son in Manchester in December 1791 mentioning two new mills in Dalston, one in Carlisle, and 'another going forwards at Warwick Bridge . . . we shall be nothing but cotton factories in the North in a short space of time'.[3] These were all spinning mills, using new machines, but in Carlisle – much longer than most other districts – the weaving was still done by out-workers on looms in their own homes with the whole family involved, taking their 'piece' to the factory once a week to pick up their supply of yarn; those working for Carlisle firms radiated out a hundred miles, even to Ireland. Wages were good: in the boom years of the 1790s a weaver could earn over a pound a week, twice as much as a farm labourer. After that other processes followed: stamping, dyeing, printing. Near to Woodside, Sarah's father John found a good source of extra income in leasing land at Woodbank, down by the Petteril near Brisco, for a new bleaching works, with a 'dye house for six coppers, a large three-storey printing house adjoining with a large water wheel, a large drying house and about forty-two acres of bleaching grounds', where the cloth was laid out in the sun to fix the colours.[4] The poet Robert Anderson went on to work here too, celebrating Woodbank's fine colours – 'Black, red, purple, blue, yellow, green' – in his song 'The Bonny Stampt Gown'.[5]

Carlisle's population doubled and then trebled, with immigrants arriving from Scotland and Ireland, prompting loud and depressingly familiar complaints about 'the numerous hordes of the idle and unsettled', arriving 'with one fixed idea – that we are compelled to maintain and support them'. In 1797, when Joseph Milner visited his brother Isaac, Dean of Carlisle, he felt the city had need of Isaac's powerful preaching. 'The people here are a well-behaved, simple people,' he wrote;

the refinement, shall I say, or the lewdness and impudence, of the southern part of our island, they know not. They have the sample, I take it, of the manners of the whole country, in the time of James I. But they are withal, very ignorant in religion; they wander as sheep without a shepherd. They seem, however, open to conviction, they have conscience. There are, here, some Methodist and Dissenting interests, but feeble and of little weight, nor is there a Dissenter here of any popularity, or, as it should seem, of any religious zeal. What a fine field for a pastor, steady, fervent, intelligent, and charitable.[6]

For the county elite with their country estates and town houses in English Street, Castle Street and Fisher Street the cathedral was a focal point, and one of the Losh family's favourite guests was the Yorkshire-born Archdeacon William Paley. Short and square, with bushy eyebrows, Paley was that odd but very British type, a conservative radical, arguing for toleration and rational enquiry and elaborating his own argument of the existence of God from design. The Loshes collected his books, even after he left Carlisle in 1793: *The Principles of Moral and Political Philosophy* in 1785, the *View of the Evidences of Christianity* in 1794, countering Hume's scepticism about miracles, and *Natural Theology* in 1802, with its famous opening thesis that if we see an ingeniously made watch,

Carlisle in 1822, showing the city still huddling within its walls, with the
Castle (A) and Cathedral (B) to the north and the Citadel (E) forming
the gateway to the south.

'the inference, we think, is inevitable, that the watch must have had a maker: that there must have existed, at some time, and at some place or other, an artificer or artificers who formed it for the purpose which we find it actually to answer; who comprehended its construction, and designed its use': so from the complexity of the world we infer an intelligent creator with a definite design.[7] The book was an immediate success, going through nine editions before Paley's death in 1805, and his message and method lingered in Sarah's own thinking all her life.

Paley was also a dazzling mathematician and keen scientific observer. Forceful and clear, he argued, like Joseph Priestley, that people came to know God through studying nature, citing his own investigations: the stones and plants he brought home from his walks, the bone structures of the fish or chickens or game he ate. He was blunt, humorous and funny, and down to earth. In the summers, which he always spent at his Dalston vicarage, he fished, farmed, gardened and visited neighbours, including the Loshes. A genial father of eight children, and a great dinner companion, at Woodside Paley was '*en accord* with mine host, enjoyed his joke and bit of pleasantry, and never failed as a trencherman'.[8]

This large personality was matched by the dean, Isaac Milner. His story too was remarkable – he had been apprenticed as a weaver until his elder brother paid for his education, but rose to become president of Queens' College, Cambridge, Lucasian professor of mathematics and a notable experimental chemist. Evangelical in his leanings, bulky in his physical presence, Milner was hardly a clerical figure, uproarious in company and known for dashing nude through the gardens at Queens'. He was a great friend of the Wreay curate William Gaskin, who himself 'belonged to that old school of country parsons who could enjoy a fox-hunt and cock-fight as well as his Greek Testament'.[9] In later years Gaskin would find his way home after a heavy evening by collapsing unsteadily into his trap and letting the pony have its head. But he too was a fine mathematician and classical scholar who scattered his conversation with Latin quotations. He was quite capable of beating Milner in argument, although he complained of his late hours 'and of his inability to contend with the learned Dean at two o'clock in the morning, inasmuch as his brandy potations were not so potent in argument as the Dean's opium taking!' (Milner took his opium for a heart condition, and was often in pain, allegedly due to inhaling 'noxious gas' during a youthful experiment.) He and Gaskin – both genial, argumentative men – were regulars at John Losh's dinners, which were never light on the brandy.

The experience of these Carlisle men also took in other lands, other ways of life, other histories. Two of the Spedding sons, John and William, who were close friends of George and William, went overseas to try to rescue the family fortunes, one to the West Indies, the other to Calcutta. John's friend Joseph Gilpin – brother of the writer William and the artist Sawrey – was a dashing man about town, who had been an army medical officer in the American War of Independence and in the West Indies: he was knighted for his work in an epidemic at Gibraltar and was four times mayor of Carlisle. Another friend, the son of a local doctor, was the Rev. Joseph Carlyle, who christened Sarah in 1786: he learned Arabic from an Iraqi friend at Cambridge, succeeded Paley as archdeacon in 1793 and two years later became professor of Arabic at Cambridge, publishing translations and *Specimens of Arabic Poetry*.[10]

While friends travelled across the seas John Losh stayed at home and took his place in the village as head of the Twelve Men as his forebears had done. The tasks were small, but vital to the people of Wreay. One minute reads: 'Feb. 2 1792. Joseph Dodd agrees to take Jane Moor and supply her with food and clothes on the following conditions: to receive from the parish of Wreay £5.15.0. per annum, to have her work, find her with tobacco, and to return her at the year's end (if that be necessary) in the same condition in

regard to clothing as he found her'.[11] These tough men were pre-
pared to deal in detail: Jane's clothes, a later entry specifies, were
to include two petticoats, one shift, repairing shoes, 'a brat apron',
a bedgown, and a neck cloth. She stayed as Dodd's servant until
she died a few years later.

The Twelve Men cared for the roads, the fences and the church
as well as the people. The same minute that sent Jane Moor to
Joseph Dodd has another entry, resolving that a house should be
built in the enclosure round the chapel, which had been appointed
for the use of the parish clerk. This came to nothing: the following year's note reads 'The above mentioned house is not yet built,
unsurmountable difficulties having arisen'. It was never built,
leaving the land clear a generation later for Sarah's church. In
the mid-1780s the old bridge needed repairing and they all subscribed, but only a shilling or sixpence each, so the damage was
clearly minor. Then a decade later a new bridge needed building
across Woodside Beck, and a few years after that new pews had to
be made for the chapel. This was a delicate matter, a mapping of
status. Every land-holding was entitled to a pew and families who
worshipped regularly were to be 'allowed their seats as usual' if
they paid a proportion of the expenses. Two men were appointed
'to take the trouble of allotting and setting out the pews and
sittings in such manner as shall appear to them fair, proper and
reasonable'. John Losh had a pew in the front and another in the
twelfth row, for his servants.[12]

John's interests, however, spread beyond the village to the
city, the region and the nation. In Sarah's early years the house
resounded with talk of politics. The Loshes were firm Whigs, and
in 1780 John Losh was on a committee, with his uncle Joseph
Liddell and Humphrey Senhouse, to promote a petition noting
the 'calamitous and impoverished' condition of the country after
the recent wars. But their main focus was opposition to the magnate Sir James Lowther, 'Wicked Jimmy', 'Jimmy Grasp-all, Earl of

Toadstool' or simply 'the Bad Earl'. One of the wealthiest men in England, by the age of twenty-one Lowther had inherited estates across Cumberland and Westmorland, as well as collieries on the west coast and the booming port of Whitehaven.[13] He was a man of violent temper, tyrannical to his tenants and employees: Wordsworth's father worked as his land agent for years and never had his expenses paid – Wordsworth was eventually reimbursed by Lowther's heir, long after his father's death. Aiming at political power Lowther manoeuvred his way to become mayor of Carlisle, filled the corporation with his nominees and bought seats in the House of Commons, spending thousands at each election. In 1784 he was created first Earl of Lonsdale by a grateful William Pitt. Lonsdale had handed Pitt his first parliamentary seat, at Appleby in Westmorland, and also promised that 'his' MPs, collectively dubbed 'Sir James's ninepins', would support Pitt in the Commons. John Losh and his friends were aghast at Lonsdale's tactics. Fearing he might lose one of his Carlisle seats he persuaded the corporation to create nearly twelve hundred new freemen, all with the power to vote: over five hundred of these came from Lonsdale's own collieries. When his cousin, John Lowther, won the seat, this 'mushroom' vote was overturned after a petition in favour of John Losh's friend John Christian (who caused a considerable stir when he eloped with his heiress cousin Isabella Curwen in 1782, adding her name to his in 1790).[14]

All the Loshes' friends were Whigs and chief among them was Charles Howard of Greystoke Castle, who preceded John Christian Curwen as a Carlisle MP before moving to the House of Lords on becoming Earl of Surrey and Duke of Norfolk. Years later, at the height of the Napoleonic wars, Howard risked everything when he gave a toast at a great political dinner at the Crown and Anchor in the Strand, to 'Our Sovereign's health – the majesty of the people'. A drinking companion of John Losh, he was a large, clumsy figure, a great womaniser, and so unkempt that it was said the only way his servants could get him to wash was to hose him down when he was drunk. But if his speech was slurred his wit was sharp, and it was his idea to put on a parodic anti-Lowther satire that left a lasting impression on Wreay. After dinner at Woodside (and a deal to drink), gossip about Carlisle corporation apparently 'gave such a zest to the walnuts and wine that it was agreed to dramatise the said municipal body', to accompany the annual Wreay cock-fight.[15] Howard, the Losh brothers and their uncle Joseph Liddell met at the Plough, where they elected their own corporation prefaced by a letter, 'professedly directed from the great bashaw of Lowther Castle'. Howard was mayor, John Losh and his brother James were sword-bearer and recorder, Liddell was town clerk and other officials followed. Wearing the Whig, anti-Lowther blue sash, Howard was chaired around the village, as in Hogarth's satirical print, *The Election*. For nearly a century this charade became a Shrove Tuesday show, with the new mayor being carried along the green 'to the accompaniment of "See the Conquering Hero Comes"', being pelted with oranges the while'.[16]

This enactment was typical of the world in which Sarah grew up. She was a child of the Regency, when manners were broader, wit harder and when women, even among the gentry, were raised to know their own mind.

With the French revolution in 1789, politics took a sharper turn. The fall of the Bastille in July that year was greeted with widespread delight in Britain as showing that the French people were throwing off the shackles of absolutism and moving nearer, so it was thought, towards the British parliamentary rule. But over the next two years opinion became divided. While many young enthusiasts, the British Jacobins, dashed to Paris to support the cause, the anti-Jacobins – supported by an increasingly nervous government – gathered their forces. By 1791 the argument was intense. Burke's *Reflections on the Revolution in France*, published in November 1790, provoked a host of replies, including Mary Wollstonecraft's *A Vindication of the Rights of Men* and Tom Paine's *Rights of Man* of 1791. William Paley, rattled by the French terror and Paine's popularity – he once threw a copy of the *Rights of Man* angrily on the fire – now showed his conservative side, writing pamphlets and reprinting one of his Dalston sermons, *Reasons for Contentment, Addressed to the Labouring Part of the British Public*, suggesting that the labourers' lot was happy compared to that of the anxious rich.[17]

The corridors of Woodside were touched by these debates. There had long been 'patriotic clubs' in the region and the French Jacobin Marat – who spent three years in Newcastle in the 1770s – had visited those in Carlisle and Penrith. In May 1791, there were 'Church and King' riots across the country against allegedly dangerous radicals like Joseph Priestley of Birmingham, and in the same year a warrant was put out for the arrest of John and James Losh and four others 'for being unlawfully, riotously and routously assembled together and disturbing the peace of our Lord the King'.[18] Nothing seems to have come of this, but James in particular advocated anti-war views and joined the republican Patriotic Club of Carlisle.

His younger brother William had been in the French capital, studying chemistry with Lavoisier, when the revolution broke out. Now, in 1792, James crossed to Paris. France was already at war with Austria and Prussia and fervour was high: that July it became compulsory for men to wear the tricolour cockade and in August came the storming of the Tuileries, when Louis XVI and his family were taken into custody. James went to meetings of the Convention when Danton, the new minister of justice, was at his most eloquent, and he also allegedly had a narrow escape from being strung up by a mob who took him for an aristocrat. In the first week of September, when France was braced for a Prussian invasion, counter-revolutionaries were massacred in the prisons of Paris. By 10 September, James was back in Southampton, 'but not without considerable perils by land and water'.[19] A letter arrived at Wood-side. James doubted, he said, that the Prussians would reach Paris: 'the zeal of the People is astonishing, they crowd by thousands to the Frontiers'. But in his view the revolution was doomed. 'A furious party', led by Robespierre, was 'throwing everything into confusion and probably ruining their country in order to gratify a wild rage for impracticable schemes'. Having spent two days 'witnessing the most dreadful barbarities' James abandoned his clothes and books and fled the city by taking over a diligence that previous passengers had deserted, for fear, they said, of being murdered at the barriers. After driving through a stormy night to Le Havre he sailed home in 'a perfect hurricane', crammed into a small packet boat with seven or eight Englishmen and over fifty French priests. James was unnerved, but did not shed his idealism. He would be a reformer all his life.

In family memory, as a small child Sarah was 'lively, talkative and intelligent, and not without some petulancy of temper, aris-ing from undue sensitiveness to any interference with her own wishes'.[20] In other words, rather spoilt. Although she learned to keep her temper, the wilfulness and determination endured. Katharine was always milder. If we could watch them in 1792, what would we see? When their uncle James came riding north to Woodside, shaken, full of news, Sarah was six and Katharine four. They stood in the hall, Sarah already protective, holding her sister's hand as large men stamped through the door, shouting for help in pulling off their boots, patting the girls absent-mindedly on the head. Both girls had light brown hair and grey eyes, Sarah taller and leaner, Katharine pinker, rounder. In summer they wore mus-lin gowns with square necks and high waists, just short enough to run in but not to show their linen bloomers, edged with lace. In winter they were squeezed into warm woollens, with muf-flers against the Woodside draughts. They ate in the nursery, plain children's food, but they could smell the beef and duck, the hams and gooseberry tarts being cooked for their father's guests, and see the bottles of claret on the sideboard, ready for the long evenings when the men sat and argued about politics and other things beyond their world.

They heard stories. That Uncle George had been to Russia and brought home bearskins; that William had been in Germany and had saved a famous explorer's life in a storm; that James had escaped from a howling mob. In spring, they went out with their father, scooped up on his horse or running beside him to keep up with his stride, to see the new plantations, green against dark earth. In summer they played on the lawns with hoops and balls, screaming as the ball ran over the ha-ha, and exploring the tangle of brushwood round the beck. In the mornings, upstairs in their schoolroom, they read the little books printed by Thomas Slack, a Wreay man who had left for Newcastle a generation ago, but whose family still lived in the village.[21] There were alphabets with A for apple and B for bird, drawn in small squares, and stories of Little Red Riding Hood and Goody Two Shoes. As one of the nearby Blamire family remembered: 'Our books were limited but much read and loved – *Evenings at Home*, Miss Edgeworth's *Tales*, Sandford & Merton, *Robinson Crusoe* – *The Blond Child* etc. Illustrated papers had scarcely appeared.'[22] And their mother told tales of border raids and reivers and read aloud to them, perhaps, the manuscript poems of Susanna Blamire, the aunt of Sarah's friend Jane.

Joseph would never read fluently, let alone become an intellectual. Sarah took the place of the scholar son, learning stories of Greek gods and Roman republican heroes, reading Mrs Marcet's books on science and the Edgeworths' tales. On rainy days the girls might look at their father's collection of minerals, gathered from the fells, and fossils found in the quarries and mines. And on Sundays, the family and their servants went to Wreay, to the old church, to hear Mr Gaskin's sermons.

3 Foundations

When she made her notes about the building of the church in 1842, Sarah recorded that when the workmen were clearing the ground they discovered 'at no great depth, a series of broad, thick, white flagstones, forming two angles of a considerable building, of which no other trace has been left'.[1] It might have been possible, she thought, that a square tower had 'anciently' (a favourite adverb) occupied the space, noting that the field next door was still known as 'the guards'. Wreay had been a prosperous village in medieval times. It would have needed defence against the border raids from the north.

This border had always been fluid. The last Norse king, Dunmail, was killed in AD 945, an ending that Wordsworth remembered in his poem 'The Waggoner', where the horses tread cautiously on the steep hill out of Grasmere:

> And now have reached that pile of stones
> Heaped over brave King Dunmail's bones;
> His who had once supreme command,
> Last king of rocky Cumberland;
> His bones, and those of all his power
> Slain here in a disastrous hour!

After Dunmail's death Cumbria was ruled for a century by the Scottish kings, then briefly by the Earls of Northumberland before the coming of the Normans in 1092. William Rufus built a castle at Carlisle and his brother erected a priory. Rule swung back and forth between Scots and English until Edward I began his attacks on Scotland, starting a hundred years of sporadic warfare in which no farm or village, nunnery or abbey, was safe. A formal border was established in 1237 but for almost four hundred years the Scottish marches were a disputed realm and a large tract of land north of Brampton, 'the Debatable Lands', never bowed to either throne; its people obeyed their own laws, sending gangs of reivers across the borders to raid and burn. This was a land of blood where defensive towers were needed. In the mid sixteenth century the Crown officers tried to stand back and let the clans wipe each other out, but they stayed strong until the Union of the Crowns in 1603, when James I abolished the old Border Laws and executed the poorer clan members in a glut of hangings. After that the region seemed calm, although unrest simmered beneath the surface.

Pondering on the existence of the tower, Sarah added that the village had needed protecting not only from the north, but also from the south, since it was 'especially exposed to aggression by its proximity to Inglewood Forest, the noted retreat of desperate outlaws'. This tract of land, 'the Wood of the Angles' stretching from Carlisle to Penrith, had become a royal forest soon after the Norman Conquest, but it remained a land of legend, linked in local minds with King Arthur and Gawain and his search for the Green Knight, or seen as the true haunt of Robin Hood, according to one fifteenth-century chronicle.[2] Its heartland lay around the parishes of Hesket-in-the-Forest and Hutton-in-the-Forest, where manorial courts still took place every June in Sarah's day, when tenants paid their annual dues by a flat table-stone next to an old tree, the Court-Thorn. Local antiquaries liked to point out the spot where an ancient oak had stood near Wragmire Moss, near Wreay, 'the last tree of Inglewood Forest', enduring the storms of six hundred years until it finally toppled in 1823.[3]

Villagers could still remember the tower that had stood until recently at Wreay Hall, guarding the potteries on the bank of the Petteril. Surely, Sarah argued, something similar would have been needed at Wreay, a key stopping point on the road between Carlisle and Penrith. Some people, she noted – as if continuing a recent argument – might suggest that the building had been a hermit's cell, or something else connected to the chapel. But there was no record of that since there was only a monthly service here, performed by a monk from St Mary's priory in Carlisle.

In Sarah's childhood, dedicated antiquarians were busy studying the region's past. Antiquarians, who studied the remnants of the past in stones or household objects, as well as in historical accounts, had a long history, dating back to William Camden's *Britannia*, at the end of the sixteenth century, a county-by-county survey searching out traces of the past in the present landscape. The interest spread after the Society of Antiquaries was re-founded in London in 1717, and given a royal charter in 1751. As well as printing papers in its journal *Archaeologia* the society published volumes of engravings of buildings, monuments and coins. Many artists were involved in its work, like Joseph Farington and Thomas Hearne, who included many beautifully drawn scenes from Cumberland and Westmorland, and careful architectural views, in his *Antiquities of Great Britain*, published in series from the late 1770s onward. The 'antiquaries' were mocked for their fussiness and obsession but they contributed invaluable information and the county histories sprang out of their work, like Hutchinson's *History of Cumberland* of 1794, to which John Losh contributed his knowledge of local fossils, minerals, semi-metals and strata, an impressive mix of scholarship and personal observation.[4]

The antiquarian interest merged with the vogue for the picturesque that flourished during Sarah's childhood, which made people look afresh at the ancient buildings that formed the centrepiece of paintings, prints and descriptions. One of the key figures of that movement, William Gilpin, artist, author and clergyman, and brother of John Losh's friend Joseph, was himself a local man, born at Scaleby Castle north of Carlisle. His *Observations on Westmoreland and Cumberland* was published in 1786. Gilpin loved wildness and hated the 'classical improvements' of nearby Corby Castle, the walks and statues with 'Diana, Neptune, Polyphemus, Nymphs and Satyrs in abundance', preferring the park now that it was decayed, the statues fallen, the temple in ruins, the cascade overgrown.[5]

Reading Gilpin, Sarah found that the familiar churches and castles gained a sharp new focus. At Warwick Bridge, where her uncle had inherited the Hall, Gilpin wrote, 'The antiquarian's eye is immediately caught here by the parish church; the chancel of which, forming the segment of a circle, and being pierced with small lancet windows, shows at once that it is of Norman origin.'[6] Gilpin was unusual in his appreciation of the round-arched 'Norman' style – sometimes called 'Saxon', since some buildings

The Norman apse of St Leonards, Warwick Bridge, engraved in the 1790s

dated from before the Conquest. Most observers considered these buildings with their solid cylindrical pillars to be crude in comparison to the pointed Gothic of the twelfth century. Yet this was the style that Sarah grew up with and loved: the abbeys and small churches of Cumberland and the great cathedrals of Carlisle and Durham.

When she was small and went to visit her great-uncle Joseph Liddell at Burgh-by-Sands, she entered the strange land that Gilpin saw as he rode from the Caldbeck Fells towards Carlisle and then crossed Burgh Marsh, breathlessly repeating his sense of its airy distances: 'a vast, extended plain, flat as the surface of a quiet ocean. I do not remember that land ever gave me before so vast an idea of space.'[7] Although the land had been reclaimed and the cattle grazed here now, there were no hedges, bushes or trees. On both sides of the glinting, muddy Solway the land simply seemed to fade into the mountains: 'Had the plain been boundless, like an Arabian desert, I know not whether it would not have lost the idea of space, which so vast a circumspection gives it.' There are still great areas of 'moss' here, wild spaces of scrub and marsh. It is a place where sounds carry and hang in the air, where perspectives shift and falter, and two boys and a dog half a mile along the shore could be only a hand's touch away.

This is where Sarah's family had come from, generations ago. Going by the name of Arlosh, they were said to be 'grangers' to Holm Cultram abbey, a Cistercian foundation established in 1150 by King David of Scotland on the edge of the windswept salt marsh. (A fire destroyed the roof in 2006 and the abbey is sad and dusty today, but the nave is still echoing and grand, with strong piers soaring to high arches, and a fine Norman doorway sheltering within the elaborate sixteenth-century porch.) The Arlosh family supposedly worked at one of the abbey's five granges, the farms that provided food and income for the monks and where the grain and cattle from outlying lands were kept under the eye of the granger, *granatarius*, manager of the victual. In the nearby village of Newton Arlosh the church tower had thick walls of stone and cobbles, with slit windows and battlements. The defences were needed: Holm Cultram was sacked by Robert the Bruce in 1322, and legends surrounded Losh ancestors, of resistance to Scots raiders and local bandits and of daring sallies across the border.

Holm Cultram's grand western facade, with its eagle above the belfry and Renaissance doorway masking the Norman arch.

The Losh family still owned lands near Holm Cultram. Sarah knew the abbey well and the other great Norman foundations like Lanercost priory beyond Brampton, near to the Roman Wall. It was partly because of the Roman heritage that the north of Cumberland so fascinated antiquaries. The Senhouses of Netherhall had been collecting finds from the Roman fort nearby since the 1580s and had even established their own museum in Maryport. Everywhere new sites were being excavated. Local antiquaries were also fascinated by the pre-Roman sites, like the stone circles of Castlerigg near Keswick and Long Meg and her daughters at Little Salkeld, not far from Wreay. All the different people who had passed through the land had left their mark. On the summit of Carrock Fell, which Sarah could see from Woodside, lay the remains of a vast Celtic hill fort. The Celtic peoples called themselves Combrogi or Cymri, 'Fellow Countrymen' – giving the county its name – and by the sixth century their kingdom of Rheged stretched from Dumfriesshire to Yorkshire. The spirit of the Celtic church was felt in the great stone crosses, like that of Bewcastle, and their name lingered too in sacred wells, like St Ninian's well at Brisco, a mile from Woodside. Bede named St Ninian as one of the earliest missionaries, a Briton who studied in Rome and travelled among the Scottish Picts in the fourth century. As the story was embellished by the sixth-century historian Aelred, he was described as the son of a British chieftain born on the south shore of the Solway, while other writers said that on his way back from Rome Ninian had met St Martin of Tours, who sent masons back with him to help build Britain's first stone church, the 'White House' at Whithorn in Galloway, in 397. In the Eden valley it was believed he had travelled up the old Roman road, resting in the caves by the river Eamont.

Across Cumbria you could follow the path of the Celtic saints, like St Oswald and his brother Oswiu, remembered in names like Kirkoswald, or St Cuthbert, patron saint of Carlisle, St Kentigern of Keswick, and St Bega, the Irish princess of legend. St Bega, so it was said, had crossed the Irish sea to save herself from a terrible marriage and founded the church at St Bees on the most westerly point of Cumbria. Much later, when the monks feared that their estate would be claimed by the Norman lord, they were promised as much land as was free of snow on the day of perambulation to mark the boundary of the property. Sure enough a thick snowfall came, miraculously settling everywhere except upon the priory lands. St Bega's story came from a set of saints' lives that belonged to Holm Cultram abbey in the thirteenth century, by which time a cult had already grown up around her and around her miracle-working bracelet. She may not have existed at all, but in story it was enough that she was a woman, determined to stay single, whose strength of will overcame powerful men and gained her land to build upon.

The Saxons and Danes came, leaving their Viking-age carvings of beasts and warriors and legendary scenes, like the warriors on their boat on the hogback tombstone at Lowther church, and the cross at Gosforth that links Christ crucified with the tale of Ragnarok, the Doom of the Norse Gods. At Bridekirk, the strange square font had caused argument for generations as to whether it was pagan or Christian, since it was marked in runes that seemed to mix Saxon and Danish, perhaps commemorating the conversion of a leader of the Norsemen.[8] The streams and stories of the past flowed together and mingled, and could be hard to read.

At the dissolution of the monasteries, Holm Cultram abbey was disbanded. Often when this happened, local families slowly moved into the buildings, as the Featherstonehaughs moved into the seminary at Kirkoswald, the Dacres into Lanercost priory and the Graymes and then the Aglionbys into the old convent buildings at Nunnery, but at Holm Cultram the cloisters and other buildings were demolished piece by piece, taken for local building stone. Only the abbey church remained, saved by being also the parish church. There was no rich living to be made here now. One branch of the Losh family moved east, making a clearing at 'Inglewoodside', later Woodside. By the sixteenth century Sarah's forebears were landowners of Wreay, paying tithes to the cathedral church in neighbouring Carlisle, marrying into local families like the Slacks and the Robinsons and using their long and short names interchangeably, as on a conveyance of 1627, signed by 'William Arlosh alias Losh, yeoman at Woodside'.[9]

Carlisle seen from the batteries of the Duke of Cumberland, when he was besieging the Jacobite-held city in 1745.

Sarah's grandfather the Big Black Squire was famous for being almost the last man to fight the Scots raiders, the 'moss-troopers', named after the bandit gangs that haunted the marshes, or 'mosses', when the Scots armies were disbanded after the civil wars. The Squire was old enough to remember the Jacobite rising of 1745, when the Young Pretender, Prince Charles Edward, took Carlisle on his way south, forcing the mayor and corporation to stand by while his father was proclaimed king at the market cross. When the prince marched south crowds flocked to watch him go, waving their banners, but a few weeks later Charles turned back at Derby and limped north again through storms and snow. He passed Carlisle, but his garrison remained and the Hanoverian Duke of Cumberland besieged the city until its surrender. The Jacobite prisoners were then packed off to Lancaster and Chester, but after the battle of Culloden in the spring many were brought back and others sent down from Scotland. Nearly four hundred prisoners were packed into the castle and the city gaol, far too many to try, so the grand jury drew lots, selecting one out of twenty. The rest were transported. At the trial ninety-six were sentenced to die, and while two-thirds of the sentences were reduced to transportation, thirty-one prisoners were executed, and some of their heads were set upon the Carlisle yetts, or gates, as a warning.[10]

After the '45 rising the border raids stopped, with sporadic exceptions. But the Squire himself told the story, with evident enjoyment, of one moonlit night when bandits were driving cattle north from Wreay and he stopped them at the dip down to the Woodside beck, roaring between the trees, 'Come on, ye Scotch rascals and I'll give ye a damned good hiding!'[11]

Years later, as she watched the men clear away the old church, the stones that Sarah found spoke to her of such stories. One flagstone was taken away and laid, as an example, at the schoolmaster's gate. She had the rest moved and placed deep in the new foundations, so that the medieval stones would lie beneath the new Victorian church, like the buried strata of history.

4 Fields and Woods

As Sarah and Katharine grew up, the countryside was changing around them. In the early 1820s, riding from Hutton to Woodside, through land now enclosed and planted with new timber, their uncle James found the change so great, he said, that 'I actually lost my way in a district with which I was familiar when a boy'.[1] In the late eighteenth century, agriculture was the biggest source of earnings in Cumberland and Westmorland, where over a fifth of people lived off the land, twice the national average. Landowners fought against unyielding terrain and harsh weather and were hampered by old customary leases, and many of the farms were tiny, no more than five or ten acres, concentrating on oats and potatoes. One hope seemed to lie in cattle, which could be driven long distances along the terrible roads: Irish cattle arrived by ship in the west Cumberland ports and Scots blacks thundered down along the drove route through Carlisle and up the Eden valley, as many as eighty thousand a year.[2] Local landowners, seeing this, searched for more grazing and richer pastures.

The great swathes of open land gradually diminished with act after act of parliamentary enclosure. The areas enclosed were not common fields, as in other areas, but grazing ground like the meadows of the central Eden valley, or moors, mosses and 'wastes', open spaces where people let their stock wander, so that they seemed 'alive with sheep, cows, sterks and calves; horses of all sizes and ages, stags and ponies'.[3] Geese also grazed on the marshy commons, but not to grow fat, for, wrote one Westmorland man, 'there never was a pasturage so bare, so closely shaved, so incessantly nibbled at as this'. Increasingly, people calculated land in terms of the income it would raise, and in 1794 the Northumbrian agriculturalists John Bailey and George Culley, in their *General View of the Agriculture of the County of Cumberland*, looked longingly at the 'improvable lands in the county of Cumberland', judging that around 150,000 acres of commons could bring in great profits as arable fields and sheep pastures.

The big drive to enclose the land came during the Napoleonic wars, when the commons were ploughed up to yield grain for bread. The rector of Morland in Westmorland wrote in 1801 that he was sure the poor there 'must have died of want the last two years if they had not procured bread corn from some wastes cultivated in Cumberland'.[4] At the same time the textile trade brought workers into the local towns: food was needed, prices rose and the farmers cashed in. In 1815 John Christian Curwen remembered the great line of open commons that once stretched from Workington to Carlisle, now all enclosed.[5] But the process of enclosure had already begun, in a small way, during the 1770s. A few progressive men in the Eden valley and on the coastal plains began one by one to turn the arable fields, which took so much effort and manpower in sowing, ploughing, harvesting and carting, over to dairy and beef herds or sheep. Sarah's grandfather the Squire was one of the leaders of these 'improvers'. In 1777 he was one of the signatories to a petition to the House of Commons, explaining 'that within the townships, villages or hamlets of Carleton, Brisco and Wreay in the Manor or Lordship of Botchergate':

There are several Tracts or Parcels of common and waste ground and also several inclosures and improved Lands and Meadows. That your petitioners and others are intitled to Rights of common in and upon the said common and waste ground. And also, if the said lands were divided into specific Allotments and inclosed, a considerable advantage would accrue to your Petitioners and the several other Persons interested therein . . .

They petitioned, therefore, 'that leave may be given to bring in a Bill for dividing and enclosing the said common and waste grounds . . .'[6]

Once the bill was passed, the Loshes' newly enclosed areas were chopped into large fields, squares and rectangles, marked first by boundaries of raised earth and then by quickset hedges or walls. New plantations formed belts of shelter. The pattern of walls and hedges varied, but everywhere the roads were straight and wide, suddenly bending sharply round the end of a field. Alongside them were public limekilns and quarries, or areas for cutting peat and watering cattle, reminders of a land once held in common.

John Losh followed his father in his zeal to improve the estate, being the first, it was said, to introduce 'Italian rye-grass to the county', mixing it with seeds of sainfoin, lucerne and red clover to make rich meadows, and using it as winter fodder, along with turnips. Like his friend Henry Howard from Corby he increased his herds and flocks, buying Scots black and Kyloe cattle, and new breeds of sheep – South Downs and Suffolks, Cheviots from Northumberland and Teeswater merinos – and trying to winter the upland breeds of Herdwicks and 'Lamplugh Mountaineers' in his new enclosures, despite their fervent desire to escape: 'no fence can stop them'.[7]

The sheep had an annoying habit of nibbling new plantations, and this was a drawback, for John Losh's real love was planting trees. In the old woodlands around Wreay the sessile oak so common in the north shared the ground with alder and birch, hazel, wild bird-cherry, elm and rowan, but John planted so many oaks that the Woodside lands could be singled out a century later by these alone. The major change on the Losh estates, however, was the new plantations of larches. These had been introduced to

Britain from Europe in the seventeenth century because their wood was tough and durable and resistant to rot, good for fencing and cladding buildings. The larches liked the sun on the open fells, but they startled old-timers since they lost their needles in winter, their knobbly buds bursting into fans of pale green in spring, surprisingly soft against their wide-ridged, pink-brown bark.

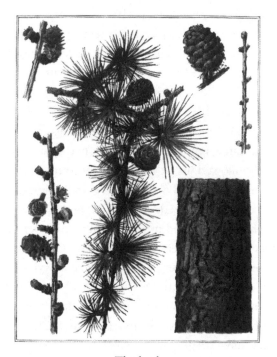

The larch

In 1794, in his *History of Cumberland*, William Hutchinson recorded the history and current size of Wreay, with its 'twenty-one families, sixty men and fifty-four women', but he also wrote that 'Mr Losh of Woodside is making everything smile round him; his garden, his farms, are almost daily under his improving hands, land too barren for tillage he plants with wood.'[8] He noted the tract of poor ground nearby, 'divided but not inclosed, nor cultivated'.

John had bought part of this cheaply, at two pounds ten shillings an acre, and had enclosed and planted it with forest trees, while 'the other proprietors, it appears, have not yet discovered how much it would be to their advantage, either to dispose of their shares to Mr Losh; or follow his example in turning them to profit'. John was, however, joined in these efforts by particular friends. Henry Howard planted larches at Corby and John Christian Curwen – who set up an experimental farm and founded the Workington Agricultural Society, a vital forum for discussion – was said to have planted three million trees on the shores of Windermere. Curwen was a Whig, working on behalf of the common people. In parliament in 1796 he introduced a motion to repeal the game laws, declaring that 'too many have found their way into our prisons from the oppressive nature of these laws', and that they should be erased from the statute book as an insult to the 'first principles of our constitution'.[9] But Curwen, like Losh, was no out-and-out democrat – his call was the classic one of 'liberty and property'. He upheld the interests of his own class even though this sometimes meant trampling on the rights of those he claimed to speak for.

In his zeal for progressive farming and forestry, John Losh went to Scotland, to consult with John Murray, fourth Duke of Atholl, 'the planting Duke', who grew larches and Norway spruce on a grand scale on his previously open and treeless estates in Perthshire.[10] John also met Sir John Sinclair, first president of the Board of Agriculture, and author of the astonishing *Statistical Account of Scotland*, a many-volumed survey of historical, social and economic facts about each parish. There were losses as well as gains – Atholl's larches drove out the old Scotch firs, while Sinclair's fervour for new breeds of sheep sparked a minor Highland clearance, banishing tenants to the harsh coastal lowlands. Yet Sinclair was a romantic as well as a ruthless moderniser, weaving a past to suit his dreams of his own land, funding archaeological digs and publishing the 'originals' of the Ossianic poems.[11]

Not everyone admired the new plantations. Thomas de Quincey remembered how for years Wordsworth abused the larches and their planters, and how once, 'finding a whole cluster of birch-trees grubbed up, and preparations making for the installation of larches in their place', he 'was seen advancing to the spot with gathering wrath in his eyes';

> next he was heard pouring out an interrupted litany of comminations and maledictions; and, finally, as his eye rested upon the four or five larches which were already beginning to 'dress the line' of the new battalion, he seized his own hat in a transport of fury, and launched it against the odious intruders.[12]

Years later, Wordsworth was still inveighing against the plantations as a deformity, and against the tree itself: 'peculiar and vivid' in spring, dingy in summer, 'spiritless, unvaried yellow' in autumn, while in winter, the other deciduous trees 'seem only to sleep, but the Larch appears absolutely dead'.[13] As Sarah grew to be a woman, it was if the landscape itself looked forward and back, the enclosures and plantations thrusting it into a 'progressive' new age, while arousing a deep nostalgia for that which was lost.

As girls, Sarah and Katharine went out with their father: Joseph, 'poor Joe', was unlikely to ride out, and would never inherit. The new larches had small cones, often no more than an inch long, soft and flexible, a strange purple colour when young but turning brown in the autumn. They grew in small clusters and looked markedly different from the cones of the old Scots pines on the fellsides, the only British native conifer – the Douglas firs and spruces all came later, after the 1820s. The Scots pinecones were red when new, then pale brown, fat and round, changing as they aged to a pointed oval. Such cones were a wonderful mystery for a child. They helped to forecast the weather, their scales shrinking and opening when dry and closing when the air became damp. They were hard and spiky yet fitted the curve of the hand, warm to the touch, as light as a ball to toss in the air and catch. And each scale with its prickly point made a compact home for its seed. As the cones of the Scots pine opened in the spring, the blackish seeds with their pale brown wings floated on the air.

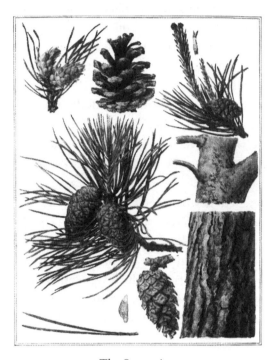

The Scots pine

When they eventually came to inherit the estate, Sarah and Katharine cared for their land, extending its spread by buying up parcels from local landowners when they could. They protected it, and its wildlife too, even from renowned naturalists like Thomas Coulthard Heysham, son of a Carlisle doctor who had been their father's friend. In 1829 Heysham sent his man into their woods, without asking their permission, to procure a rare hawfinch – the only time, he thought, that one had been seen in Cumberland – and then persuaded their gardener to join the hunt. The past season had been 'extremely barren' as regarded rarities, he explained to a correspondent, and this was the only novelty, 'repeatedly seen in the months of Janry and Feby last in the pleasure grounds of a lady, about four miles from the city, who, however, would not allow it to be killed'.[14] Sarah's stubborn resistance ran counter to the main instinct of naturalists of the time, which was to shoot anything unusual that came their way. The sisters put up with the pursuit for some time, as Sarah explained tartly, but put a stop to it when they found 'it was kept up only by the gardener & another person at Woodside who were shooting great numbers of singing birds'. The hawfinch vanished. 'Its able defence', she wrote, made one think it deserved to escape, 'but it must either have been shot or have flown to a distance as it has never since been seen'.[15]

As a sweetener, Heysham sent them a print destined for a new book: the contretemps was smoothed over. The Miss Loshes, wrote Sarah, 'offer their best thanks to Mr Heysham for the great treat that he has afforded them in the inspection of the beautiful work on Humming Birds, which was entirely new to them'. They should 'certainly be further gratified', she added, 'by being allowed to see the remainder of the plates when they arrive'.[16]

5 Springs, Fresh and Salt

Sarah grew up in a land of waters, springs and becks and rivers: the Petteril with its woods and birds and otters; the Caldew that rushed down from its source high on the mountain of Skiddaw; the Eden, sometimes wide and smooth, shining in the broad, green valley, then suddenly narrowing, forging its way through gorges, with swift turns and rapids. At the estate of Nunnery, in her grandfather's time, the owners made new walks beside the Eden to suit the passion for the picturesque, and the rocks by the river were inscribed and carved. A little further downstream the Howards at Corby Castle also created dramatic paths and river terraces. But it was another river and another spring that made the Loshes' fortune and gave Sarah the money to build – the great, grand Tyne and the small and salty Birtley Spring.

The Losh brothers came from a generation for whom natural philosophy, involving scientific experiment, was a fashionable hobby and often a passion. Lecturers toured provincial cities with demonstrations of electricity or magnetism, putting on shows in assembly rooms and inns; small clubs of enthusiasts grew up, devoted to chemistry, the study of birds and insects or the collecting of minerals. With this went an interest in mathematics, horology and engineering, and new books catered for all these tastes, especially Priestley's works on electricity, chemistry and gases, with their vivid descriptions and instructions on making your own equipment and carrying out experiments.

John Losh looked the part of the local squire but he was an avid reader, interested in history, philosophy, and science and its application to industry. In 1786, the year of Sarah's birth, his name appeared, with that of his brother George and other Liddell and Losh relations, in the subscription list for Robert Miln's *Course of Physico-Theological Lectures upon the State of the World*, published in Carlisle. He was also caught up in the industrial ventures of his family and friends. All the Losh brothers and their uncle Joseph Liddell had an interest in Saltwellside mine at Gateshead, and John also inherited Bonner interests in Northumberland mines when Isabella's father died. In Carlisle, he acted as intermediary between Liddell and John Christian Curwen when miners from Liddell's lead mines on the Alston fells headed for Curwen's Workington collieries for better wages.[1]

John's scientific, agricultural and industrial interests overlapped, especially after he met the wayward Archibald Cochrane, ninth Earl of Dundonald, later the author of a *Treatise, Shewing the Intimate Connection that Subsists between Agriculture and Chemistry* (1795). A naval officer, Dundonald was determined to rebuild his family's lost wealth by his inventions, taking out a patent for a cheap way of distilling coal tar which could be used to keep the hulls of ships from being fouled by barnacles, a good idea, promptly developed by the navy as soon as his patent ran out. The two men got on well and the earl came to Woodside when Sarah and Katharine were small, to join the Losh brothers in exuberant experiments in the sheds and outhouses, building furnaces, creating bangs, fumes and smells and causing some panic, it was said, among the locals, who felt, as a later commentator wrote, that 'sum uncanny work o' sum kein was bein' carried out – magic or witchcraft, or sum devil's work o' that sort'.[2]

In these years John was also an entrepreneur, with an eye to profit. In 1792, with his uncle Joseph Liddell and two other part-

ners, he started a bank in the centre of Carlisle, next to the Crown
and Mitre in Castle Street, at the shop of the linen draper and
factory owner Alexander Wilson.[3] Two years later he was ready
to invest in another venture, linked to his experiments, this time
on the Tyne. The river downstream from Newcastle was crammed
with ships, anchoring off the staithes, the long projecting jetties
where they could unload their goods and load up again with
coal, or waiting in mid-channel for the keel boats to bring their
cargoes. The great sailing ships and smaller vessels negotiated the
long bar and the Black Midden rocks at the estuary mouth, working their way up on the tide, watching out for treacherous currents, narrow channels and twisting bends. The most dangerous of
these bends, until the promontory was removed in the 1850s, was
at Bill Point above Hebburn, 'jutting into the river like the beak
of a bird', so high that vessels on opposite courses could not see
round it and occasionally collided or ran aground.[4] It was on this
headland that the Loshes' future interests lay.

The hinterland and river banks hummed with industry. As
well as the collieries, there were the salt-pans at North and South
Shields, the cones and chimneys of the glassmakers who had clus-
tered here since the mid seventeenth century, the kilns of potters,
the furnaces of lead and iron works and the steaming vats of the
soap-makers, a relatively new industry established in the late 1770s.
In between these lay the shipbuilders' yards, noisy with hammer-
ing. To judge from his letters, Dundonald came here hoping to
find a tar works near an iron foundry, and happened upon one run
by Surtees and Liddell, close connections of the Loshes.[5] He set up
here, but as he looked at the glass-cones and soap factories nearby,
he recognised another route to wealth, the making of alkali.

The glass-makers had chosen the Tyne because of the cheap
coal, but they also needed alkali, which was not so easily available.
Their glass was made by fusing silica-rich sand or crushed flint
with lead oxide and alkali – potash or soda or a mixture of both

– at a ferociously high temperature, producing a molten, syrup-like substance that could then be worked and shaped. The Tyne soap-makers also used alkali, mixed with fat, to make soap, and the Carlisle textile firms, too, needed alkali for bleaching. At the time, this came from different sources. One was potash (potassium carbonate), the residue from burning vast quantities of timber, imported from the Baltic forests at a steep price: Russian potash sold for £40 a ton on Tyneside in 1802.[6] Another was the seashore plant barilla, imported from Spain and the south of France, but this was even more expensive, at around £45 per ton. A cheaper, local source, though less rich in alkali content, was ash from kelp collected and burnt on the Northumberland coast and in the west of Scotland, and when barilla supplies were cut off at the start of the French wars, the price of local kelp soared. A small amount of alkali could be reclaimed from the scum from the top of the glass pots themselves, or from the local soap works, known respectively as sandiver and soapers' salts. But these, though useful, were not enough. The hunt was on for a man-made substitute. If the partners could find one, their fortunes would be made.

Others had tried before them, and it was generally agreed that the key to making soda – sodium carbonate – was salt. Since the mid-1760s people had been trying to produce alkali by the reaction of salt with lime or coal. In Birmingham James Watt, of steam-engine fame, and the chemist James Keir had been working on this, and Keir had established a large soap manufactory. On the Tyne it was whispered that the Fordyce brothers, George and Alexander, were making discoveries: in 1781 James King, of South Shields Glassworks, wrote to Sir John Delaval about their experiments in 'decomposing marine acid [hydrochloric acid] and rendering it an alkali'. But while some sort of alkali was being used in glass-making, King said, it did not come from Fordyce's works.[7]

Dundonald and John Losh set to work. They began at Bell's Close, above Scotswood Bridge, where Dundonald was already running his coal-tar distillery, and to begin with they took a third partner, Aubone Surtees, a local banker.[8] They knew that in the 1770s the Swedish chemist Carl Wilhelm Scheele had discovered that salt could be decomposed by lead oxide, forming soda. In Bell's Close they tried out Scheele's method, stirring salt and lead oxide into a paste and leaving it for days until caustic soda was formed. For months the experiments continued in secret. In May 1795 Dundonald took out a patent for 'Treating Neutral Salts to obtain Alkalies'.[9] They then formed the Walker Chemical Company, with the Scottish tycoon and engineer Lord Dundas, for a brief time, as an extra partner. In January 1796 Helen Landell, sister of a local iron-master and banker, told Matthew Boulton at his Soho manufactory:

Lord Dundonald has lived a recluse in Newcastle for many months, and I am told has at last exercised his chemical abilities to advantage and will in all probability make a large fortune by his substitute for Barilla. Our Glass manufacturers are contracting with him and make little doubt of his success.[10]

To make alkali in bulk, however, they needed a good, cheap source for their salt. Then came their great break. John's uncle, Joseph Liddell, had inherited a share in Walker Colliery at Bill Point, further down the Tyne, and here, a few years earlier, Boulton and Watt had installed a famous 'sun and planet' engine, to pump water from one of its pit shafts, the King Pit. But the King Pit was also known for an unusual feature, Birtley Spring. This was a brine spring, 'a salt spring of very great strength and copiousness, capable, it was said, of furnishing salt enough to supply the consumption of the whole kingdom', or so claimed one local manufacturer and historian forty years later.[11] Could they use this salt?

In 1797, when Sarah was eleven, Dundonald and Losh moved their works to premises in Walker on an optimistic twenty-one-year lease. There were still farmhouses, corn mills and windmills here, following the line of the Roman Wall, and woods running down to the water's edge, but Bill Point marked the place where the Newcastle Corporation decreed that ships must dump their ballast of stone and chalk before heading further up the Tyne, and the six shallow valleys on the headland were now almost levelled. Everywhere pits and works were beginning to take over: it was an ideal spot for a bold new venture.[12] A year later, Dundonald and Losh signed an agreement with the owners of Walker Pit for their engine to pump out the brine from Birtley Spring through a special lead pipe that would not interfere with the coal works. At the same time, they signed a lease with Newcastle Corporation for sole use of the spring. They still faced one considerable problem: in Britain, salt was heavily taxed, at £36 per ton, and such a tax would wipe out their profit. In Birmingham James Watt had long been lobbying, without success, to get parliament to allow an exclusion, or at least a rebate, of the salt tax for the manufacture of chemicals, and Dundonald had argued the same for ten years.[13] Now he negotiated a deal whereby he would be excused the tax as long as he contaminated the salt with soot and ashes, making it impossible to use domestically (an exciseman even lived on the premises to ensure this was done).

Once the alkali works were up and running, John's younger brother William joined the partnership, and after Dundonald left to pursue other ventures and the Surtees bankers pulled out, the brothers ran the business themselves. As time went on, they became interested in rumours of a new method developed by the French chemist Nicolas Leblanc. At his plant in St Denis outside Paris, Leblanc adapted Scheele's method, but used sulphuric acid to decompose the salt, then mixed it with chalk and charcoal and heated it until the soda evaporated and dried. In 1794, when the revolutionary government in Paris seized Leblanc's works and made his process public, the Losh brothers, travelling back and forth to France, were quick to take note. William returned to France at the Peace of Amiens in 1802, a visit barely disguising his industrial espionage, and four years later the Walker company began using the Leblanc process – the first plant in Britain to do so. After another visit in 1816, when the wars were over, this was the sole method used. Poor Leblanc died a pauper, shooting himself in despair in 1806, but the Loshes made a fortune.

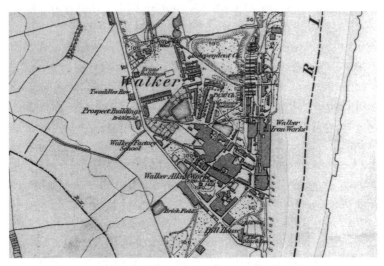

Walker, Newcastle, in the early nineteenth century, showing the alkali works and the iron foundry, the main sources of the Losh family's wealth.

The Loshes' refined soda, known as 'British ashes', compared well with the French alkali. They also made acetic acid, produced charcoal, and smelted lead to produce litharge (lead oxide) and silver. All their products found ready customers. Their advertisement was proud:

Alkaline salts, chrystals of mineral alkali or of soda, dried chrystals of alkali, barilla salts, crystals of dried potash, pearl ashes of unusual strength as are now preparing in large quantities at the works established near Newcastle, from whence plant, flint and crown glass manufacturers and bleachers may be supplied with the article that suits their purpose.[14]

[55]

The Losh girls visited Newcastle, staying with their relatives in the city of ships and merchants, and going out to Walker with its mines and furnaces and evil-smelling vats. Back home, Woodside was filled with earnest exchanges between the Losh brothers on finances and plans for the company. In reality, however, John was always more concerned with his land and his Cumbrian affairs, and it was William who ran the show on Tyneside.

To begin with the amount of soda was small – only ten tons in the first year, sixty-six tons by 1810 and 121 by 1820 – but it was the start of a chemical industry. The workmen were skilled, well paid and loyal. His success won William the title of 'father of soda making on the Tyne' and he moved into a fine house at Point Pleasant nearby. But it was not all good as the plant belched out smoke and fierce hydrochloric acid fumes 'doing considerable damage to vegetation': William might also be called the father of acid rain. By 1800 he had added a new concern, importing Swedish bar-iron and setting up a slitting mill to make nail-rods.

To help with the alkali business, in a deal arranged by his brother James, he took on a manager. This was James Thain, a man with an intriguing past. Thain had been a soldier, selling his services abroad after the American wars were over. Like William and George, he spent time in Sweden, as an officer in the Swedish guards, and was on duty, it was said, when Count Ankarstroem shot King Gustavus at a masked ball at the Stockholm opera in March 1792, and present too when the assassin was strung from a gibbet in the market square.[15] After he returned to England, he joined the volunteer Northumberland Militia at the start of the French wars in 1793. He was currently staying with Dundonald at Scotswood, learning chemistry, but he had a small son and daughter, and badly needed a permanent job. He would be superintendent of the alkali works for many years, embraced within the spreading Losh family. And his son, William, would become part of the story of Sarah and the small church at Wreay.

6 Friendships and Books

The money for Sarah's church, then, came from Newcastle, from the alkali works and later from shares in iron works and railways. In later years this industrial wealth was shepherded for her carefully by her uncle James, who was himself dependent on the Losh partnerships in Hexham Brewery, Tynemain Colliery and other ventures to provide for his family while he established himself in the law. Eventually he became a successful barrister on the northern circuit and a leading member of the Unitarian congregation in Newcastle led by the remarkable William Turner. He helped Turner set up Sunday schools – for adults rather than children – an infirmary and a mechanics institute, and became vice-president of the Newcastle Literary and Philosophical Society, which Turner had founded, and a vehement spokesman for the abolition of slavery. James was a driven man, but he was subject to low moods in which he often accused himself of building castles in the air. He never really felt that he achieved the dreams of his radical youth.

In the 1790s Sarah and Katharine were both drawn into the margins of James's idealistic, republican circles. In these years, many British radicals admired Napoleon, like William Hazlitt, who had the emperor's bust on his mantelpiece; a century later there was still a bust of Napoleon at Woodside. After his return from Paris, while studying for the Bar in London, James was fired by William Godwin's anarchistic *Enquiry Concerning the Principles of Political Justice*, in 1793. If people could be educated to understand their 'natural' duties to society, wrote Godwin, and liberated from the oppression and tyranny of government and law, society would run itself: mind would control matter, disease would fade away. Inspired, James contributed to the drive for freedom of speech by editing a new edition of Milton's *Areopagitica* in 1792, with a passionate preface. In March 1793 he was a steward at a dinner given by the Friends of Liberty of the Press for William Frend, a Unitarian who had been ousted from his fellowship at Jesus College, Cambridge, for publishing *Peace and Union*, a pamphlet criticising the war.[1] (Ironically, Frend's chief persecutor at Cambridge was William Gaskin's argumentative friend, Isaac Milner.) With other Cumbrians like Curwen, James joined the Friends of the People for Parliamentary Reform, and he helped to draw up the first public petition, calling for an inquiry into the current state of the franchise, which was presented to the House of Commons in 1792 by Charles Grey, then a young MP for Cumberland.

Grey's motion for an inquiry was defeated by 248 votes to forty-one. The time had not yet come, and the backlash was severe. There was a punitive clampdown on all open meetings, and when the London Corresponding Society held an open-air meeting at Chalk Farm in north London, thirteen men were arrested and indicted for treason, including the society's founder, Thomas Hardy, the veteran campaigner John Horne Tooke and the fiery orator and writer John Thelwall. James Losh and William Frend, and six more of their Cambridge friends, were on a committee to raise funds for the defendants.[2] In 1794 they were acquitted, thanks to the skill of their barrister, Thomas Erskine, but many radicals were imprisoned, or lost their livelihoods. That winter, Coleridge wrote 'Religious Musings: A Desultory Poem Written on the Christmas Eve of 1794', proclaiming:

The hour is nigh;
And lo! The great, the Rich, the Mighty Men,
The Kings and the Chief Captains of the World
With all that fixed on high like stars of heaven
Shot baleful influence, shall be cast to earth,
Vile and down trodden as the untimely fruit
Shook from the fig tree by a sudden storm.
Even now the storm begins . . .

James Losh was one of those eagerly awaiting the storm, which in Britain, never came. He became a good friend of Godwin, now even more of a hero after his eloquent support of the accused at the treason trials, although he later came to see Godwin's 'school' as too radical. 'Tea at Frend's,' wrote Godwin in his diary for 27 February 1795, 'with Holcroft, Losh, Tweddell, Jonathan Raine, Edwards, Wordsworth, Higgins, French and Dyer'.[3] All these men were outspoken radicals, some notably under threat: Thomas Holcroft, essayist and playwright, had just been released from Newgate after being triumphantly acquitted of treason; George Dyer was the eccentric author of *Complaints of the Poor People of England*; John Tweddell was a Northumbrian, a fellow student of James's at Trinity College, Cambridge, and at Lincoln's Inn, a classical scholar and fierce advocate of reform.[4]

All were James Losh's friends, including the twenty-five-year-old William Wordsworth. The families knew each other and the two men had also met in 1793 when the lawyer Edward Christian brought them both on to an unofficial 'court of enquiry' into the mutiny on the *Bounty*, designed to clear the name of Fletcher Christian, whom they had known as a boy in Cockermouth.[5] It was a dangerous time for radicals, and a tense one for James, who suffered all his life from stress and headaches. In 1795, when his brothers were preoccupied with setting up their works at Walker, he fell ill. Apparently fearing consumption, he went to Bath. But instead of taking the waters, he still spent his time with his radical friends. He heard Coleridge preach, and bought his *Poems on Various Subjects*, containing 'Religious Musings'. He corresponded with Wordsworth, now living with Dorothy at Racedown in Dorset, sending him *The Monthly Magazine*, and books and pamphlets, and when Wordsworth came to Bath in June and July he and James visited mutual friends such as the Spedding sisters, who had brought their ailing mother to take the waters. They dined with the Wedgwoods, paid calls and took walks together. James also worked on his writing. 'That good man, James Losh', Coleridge reported to Thelwall in February 1797, had translated Benjamin Constant's *Observations on the Strength of the Present Government of France.*[6] Quoting from the book, 'Woe to that country', Coleridge wrote, 'where crimes are punished by crimes, and when men murder in the name of Justice.'

James's reading – which he would later pass on to his nieces – was wide and varied, taking in politics, philosophy and science: Mary Wollstonecraft and Paley and Berkeley; Lavoisier and Fourcroy. Passionate about the need for education for all, he was already on Unitarian committees for charity schools, Sunday schools, Schools of Industry, and a sponsor for a 'schoolmistress for poor children'.[7] When he came back to Woodside in June 1797 he was the perfect unofficial tutor for the girls. Already deeply concerned about the education of women, he made careful notes on Maria Edgeworth's first collection of stories for children, *The Parent's Assistant*, and on Thomas Gisborne's arch-conservative *Enquiry into the Duties of the Female Sex*, balanced by Erasmus Darwin's progressive pamphlet *Plan for the Conduct of Female Education*. In late September, Sarah and Katharine joined him at Allonby, the popular resort on the Solway coast favoured by Carlisle families, with its inns and assembly room and Quaker library, its low dunes and pebbles and far-receding tides. James was staying here with his sister Margaret and the Spedding sisters. He took the girls to the beach and on boat trips, but he also spent part of every day teaching them, and reading aloud *Paul et Virginie*, Bernardin de Saint-Pierre's Rousseauian romance set in Mauritius, full of ideas about the corruption of the class system in the old world and the harmonious 'natural' life of the islanders.[8]

The seashore at the small resort of Allonby, where Carlisle's elite took the sea air on the Solway Firth.

The following year this close teaching relationship continued, although James was no longer the adored single uncle. At the end of January 1798, John, Margaret and Sarah travelled down to Aldingham, near Ulverston, in the south of the Lakes, to see James marry his long-time sweetheart, Cecilia Baldwin, the rector's daughter, on 2 February. Straight away, the couple set out for Bath, taking with them the twelve-year-old Sarah and James's sister Margaret, who was now thirty, and a lively personality. In Bath the previous year, Margaret Spedding had written, Margaret was their constant companion, 'and adds much by her merriment and good nature to the pleasure of our expeditions'.[9]

It is difficult to feel one's way back into the ethos of this extended family, where uncles and cousins played such a vital role, and where children moved between families, often leaving their parents for many months at a time. We have no girlish letters home from Sarah Losh, no chatter of excitement at new places, new books, new people. It must have been hard, yet exciting, for a girl from a Cumbrian valley to be confronted by the narrow streets and busy quays of Newcastle and the smoke and smell of the Walker works. And thrilling and strange to find herself in London, or in the elegant crescents of Bath, listening to the utopian ideas of her uncle James and his friends. She took it all in. And then she made her own judgements.

In Bath they lodged first in Pierrepont Street and then St James's Parade. Bath was still the height of fashion, caricatured that year by Rowlandson in his prints *The Comforts of Bath*, with their packed assemblies and bloated invalids. Jane Austen, eleven years Sarah's senior, had stayed here for the first time the year before, and this year wrote *Northanger Abbey*, with its shops and ballrooms, affectations and flirtations. Sarah went to exhibitions with James and Cecilia, had tea with the Southeys, went to the theatre and met all their friends, including the remarkable Sophia and Harriet, playwrights and authors, who ran an exclusive girls' school.

She helped her uncle work in the garden, and they went on walks together, often alone. 'Corrected Sarah's English translation', he wrote, or 'correcting S's exercises 3', or 'Sarah's lessons', the last curt note sharing the page with his views of Locke's theories of education.[10] They read aloud the poetry of Southey, Burns and Pope, and the yet unpublished poems of Coleridge and Wordsworth. They read Gilbert White's *Natural History of Selborne* aloud too, and Charlotte Smith's new novel, *The Young Philosopher*, Smollett's *Humphry Clinker*, Galland's *Arabian Nights*, and many books of travels. Reading aloud was a favourite pastime and one of the books they chose was Mary Wollstonecraft's dark and powerful collection of letters from her travels in Scandinavia. James saw much of her widower, Godwin, this year, and when he read

Wollstonecraft's 'Wrongs of Women', as he called it, he was moved: 'most excellent – a loss to the world it's not being finished'.[11] It was a wonderful, varied and advanced education for a young girl.

That summer Wordsworth pressed James to come and stay at Alfoxden in Somerset, where he, Dorothy and Coleridge were living and writing. He told James that he was at work on *The Recluse* – the first mention of this poem – and urged him to join them in living and studying in Germany: 'What say you to this? I know that Cecilia Baldwin has great activity and spirit, may I venture to whisper a wish to her that she would consent to join this little colony.'[12] But James was now a married man, with wife, sister and niece in tow, and a trip to Alfoxden, let alone Germany, seemed impossible. He was also worried about his health and his 'broken constitution', and now moved from Bath to Bristol to be near the new Pneumatic Institution, run by Dr Thomas Beddoes. Trained in Edinburgh, Beddoes was a chemist and geologist as well as an outspoken supporter of the French revolution. He had resigned his lectureship in chemistry at Oxford in 1793, and was currently attempting to prove his thesis that inhaling oxygen, hydrogen and other gases could help serious chest diseases, even consumption. On the advice of Erasmus Darwin he had moved to Hotwells near Bristol, where many wealthy patients sought cures, and there he met and married Anna, the daughter of Darwin's friend Richard Lovell Edgeworth. Here Sarah encountered another exhilarating group, including Anna's eccentric inventor father, and her older sister, Maria Edgeworth.

In May the small Losh household took a coach to Bristol and then walked to the village of Shirehampton, where they rented a house. Beddoes and the Edgeworths visited, and they walked in the woods and fields, and across to Hotwells. The new friends overlapped with the old: Southey and Coleridge came to Anna Edgeworth's salons, and that summer, Wordsworth and Dorothy, who were lodging in Bristol with the bookseller Joseph Cottle, often visited the Loshes and stayed for a few days. James had a copy of *Lyrical Ballads* hot off the press, heard the poets read their work aloud, and read the poems to his family. Sarah must have been one of the first girls to hear Wordsworth's 'Michael', or Coleridge's 'Ancient Mariner'.

Although Sarah and Margaret were away during the summer heat, they were back there in September, when James read 'Miss Lee's Canterbury tales' aloud with Sarah, and she read the Abbé Giovanni Mariti's *Travels through Cyprus, Syria and Palestine, with a General History of the Levant* aloud to him.[13] Mariti's book was full of descriptions of mosques and early Byzantine churches and accounts of ceremonies and beliefs, the kind of writing that intrigued her for the rest of her life. 'Every Greek and Latin church is surrounded by walls,' the Abbé taught her. 'The entrance is through a gate about three feet and a half in height; which is made so low, in order to prevent the Turks from introducing horses and other animals into the inclosure. The case is the same throughout all Syria.'[14] This was one of many books that introduced her to the Middle East. The following year her father's friend Joseph Carlyle set off with Lord Elgin to Constantinople, while James's friend John Tweddell was also heading east, writing detailed journals about his archaeological researches.

James Losh moved easily in these social, scholarly and radical circles, and enjoyed bringing people together, rousing intellectual excitement. Southey remembered how he had introduced him to Elizabeth Smith in Bath, and how he had borrowed from her, on Southey's behalf, a copy of Joseph Carlyle's translations of Arabic poetry. Elizabeth was the daughter of a rich banker whose business had folded at the outbreak of the war and who then joined the army. She was only twenty, but was already known as a prodigy, a poet and a scholar of oriental languages. She had learnt French and Italian from her governess but mostly she had taught herself from her father's extensive library, learning Arabic and Persian at eighteen from an oriental dictionary belonging to her brother. In 1796, in Bath, she began tackling Hebrew (she would eventually translate the Book of Job) and was studying music, mathematics, and astronomy, as well Spanish, German, Arabic, Persian, Greek, Latin, some Syriac, and Erse, an interest that had arisen when her father was stationed in Ireland.

In Bath and in Bristol, women like the Edgeworth sisters and Elizabeth Smith offered plenty of proof that one could be an independent woman and a scholar: you did not have to marry, lose your name and settle down to domestic life. Sarah was already an eager, studious child. She made great progress, according to Lonsdale, 'in Italian and French, Latin and Greek, music and mathematics, and trespassed rather closely upon the heels of her teachers, one of whom regarded her as a classic scholar of incomparable excellence for her age and sex'.[15]

Soon this Bath era ended, for Sarah at least. James paid his last visit to Beddoes that November, where he met 'a Mr Davy who is to be the Drs assistant in his pneumatic hospital, a very extraordinary young man of twenty profoundly acquainted with natural philosophy'. He just missed Humphry Davy's intoxicating experiments with laughing gas, which would make Robert Southey exclaim, 'I am sure the air in heaven must be this wonder-working gas of delight'.[16] By contrast, James was entering an era of sobriety, returning to Cecilia's family in Aldingham and then to Newcastle. James called at Wreay on his way to the Tyne, finding Isabella's sister Ann Bonner there too: some time later, helping John with his papers, he was busy executing a release from a trust 'to provide an annuity for Miss A. Bonner'.

He settled down to a lawyer's life in Newcastle, where William and George were already established with their new wives. Carlisle society was close and lively, especially in the winter when the country families like the Loshes, Speddings and Blamires moved into their town houses, and all the young people met at assemblies, balls, race meetings and parties. The dashing Losh brothers were much in demand, and George and William had scooped the prizes among the girls, two of the Wilkinson sisters, known as the 'Carlisle beauties', the daughters of a rich London merchant and his Carlisle-born wife. In November 1796 George had married Frances Wilkinson: 'They are to be married in less than a month,' Margaret Spedding told her brother William a couple of weeks before, with an almost audible gasp; 'I sincerely hope he will make a good husband'.[17] Theirs was a joint wedding with another sister, 'little Sally Wilkinson', who married Spencer Boyd, laird of a crumbling castle in Ayrshire. The following March William married Frances's equally stunning sister Alice. The girls brought large fortunes, and the weddings created a web of useful connections.[18] Their oldest sister, Elizabeth, was the wife of William Dacre of Kirklinton, from an old Cumbrian family, while their clergyman brother Joseph was an artist whose *Select Views* were later published with Wordsworth's introduction (the basis for Wordsworth's *Guide to the Lakes*). Even more important, Joseph's wife Mary was the niece of William Brownrigg, the famous Whitehaven doctor and scientist whose interests in minerals and salt, gases in mines and the growing iron industry, all overlapped with the Loshes' concerns.

In Newcastle, while William was developing his alkali works and iron foundry, George was embarking on many commercial ventures. He was manager of a firm of ship insurance brokers and head of Losh, Lubbren & Co., a corn-dealing firm on the quayside, in which William too was involved. George was also a partner in the Newcastle Fire Office and Water Company, and acted as Prussian vice-consul from 1794 to 1807 and Swedish vice-consul from 1801 to 1807. (This was a post established in many British ports, where foreign governments appointed local men to help with trade.)[19] George and Frances's first daughter, Mary Alice, was born in October 1797 and christened the following March.

When his fortunes were riding high, George Losh had this bookplate
engraved at the workshop of Thomas Bewick in Newcastle.

When James arrived, he stayed with George first and then with
his radical friend Thomas Bigge, publisher of a magazine, *The
Œconomist*, designed to provide cheap reading material for working people.[20] James contributed to this and also sent it to Wordsworth. But soon he left the Bigges, finding a house in airy Jesmond
on the outskirts of the town that would be his home for the rest
of his life.

The move to Newcastle, however, did not end James's education
of his nieces. In July 1799 John, Margaret and Sarah came to stay
in Jesmond, leaving Katharine with her mother. The weather was
hazy and warm: they breakfasted with James Thain, now superin-
tending the alkali works, and his small son William, who would
later figure largely in the life of the Loshes and of Wreay. When
Margaret returned to Woodside Sarah stayed on by herself. James
took her to see the new Iron Bridge at Sunderland, sponsored
by Rowland Burdon of Castle Eden, a prominent Durham landowner and MP. 'Burdon showed us his own bridge,' noted James,
'and seemed to take much pleasure in explaining it.'[21] The single-
arch bridge of over 240 feet, high enough to let sailing vessels pass

beneath it, had been made at Coalbrookdale, and was one of the wonders of the new industrial age. Newcastle was full of such sights. They went to more exhibitions – Captain Fisher's drawings and the new 'Panorama of London' – and had more family dinners with William and George. They read aloud together, especially the works of Maria Edgeworth and Hannah More, whom James dismissed as 'good but narrow-minded' with a 'faulty and affected' style.[22] (A few years later, Jane Christian Blamire's mother reported that 'we have been reading with great delight Miss Hannah More's Hints for Educating a Young Princess'.)[23]

Life seemed to achieve a settled rhythm. But then on 10 October, when Sarah was staying with William and Alice at Point Pleasant, harsh news arrived. Isabella, Sarah's mother, had died. She was only thirty-three. 'Heard by a letter from George,' wrote James, who was away at the Durham sessions,

of the death of my dear and excellent sister-in-law Mrs Losh of Woodside. Perhaps few people ever led a more innocent life, or died a more tranquil death – she was sensible, generous and humane in a very uncommon degree. When she erred in judgement, it generally arose from her ardent temper, which led her to think perhaps too highly of those whom she loved.[24]

Apart from the mention of her temper, the praise was conventional: best of wives, affectionate mother. But there was no doubt of James's distress at the loss of a 'sincere and tender friend'.

Ten days later John came to collect Sarah and on a day of pouring rain James travelled back with them as far as Hexham, where they stopped for a meeting at the brewery, in which the brothers and their uncle Joseph Liddell were partners. Sarah was soon back in Woodside, in a house marked by grief. Instead of their lively, spirited mother, or the theatre- and party-loving Cecilia, Sarah and Katharine were now in the charge of their aunt Margaret, a stronger, moodier character. She was remembered as a Regency beauty, elegant and dignified, but the calm hid a nervous energy that could sometimes slide into profound gloom. From the start of this motherless life, James kept an eye on Joseph and the girls, often visiting them when he was at Carlisle for the assizes. This Christmas he was at Woodside, and so were George and Frances and their children, but the loss of Isabella darkened the mood and the air of distraction was made worse by James determinedly helping John to 'sort out his papers' throughout the holiday. The chief problem now was how best to look after the ten-year-old Joseph, who was still extremely slow: two years later, James noted some slight improvement, but as time went on, this faded. In 1804 he wrote tenderly, 'Joe quite hopeless'.

In the warm, rainy September of 1800, after the assizes, James and Cecilia travelled south through the Lakes to visit her family in Lancashire. On the way they called on Coleridge in Keswick, and the Wordsworths at Dove Cottage in Grasmere. A year later, John Wordsworth told Mary Hutchinson, soon to be Wordsworth's wife, that Losh was not too convinced by Wordsworth's poetry: he was, he thought, 'a great favourite with my brother but that do not hit upon this point'.[25] It was true that James sometimes found Wordsworth's language inelegant but by 1801 he was convinced, as he told his diary, that 'he will, notwithstanding, some day, be a great Poet'.[26]

The Newcastle Loshes were doing well and Carlisle buzzed with their success. 'James and Cecilia are building a snug house and have a nice little girl, little Cecilia Isabella', reported the younger Spedding sister, Mary, in July 1802.

Mrs George Losh has got a fourth little Girl – they have taken a fine house in Newcastle and have a carriage – the latter is becoming a great luxury now a days – William and Alice are going into Poland on mercantile business – they have lately made a great deal of money in the Corn Trade.

Meanwhile James was beginning to make a name for himself in the local courts and the following spring, when he was in London for several weeks, improving his knowledge of chancery law, he found Margaret, Sarah and Katharine staying in John's London house in Beaumont Street, 'all well and apparently happy'.[27] In London, James fell back into his old circles and Sarah mixed once again with Southey, Coleridge, and Humphry Davy, who was now lecturing to enthusiastic audiences at the Royal Institution. 'I had much pleasant and interesting conversation at and after dinner' with Davy and Coleridge, wrote James, 'on Metaphysics chiefly'.[28] In March, William Frend was advising the girls on their reading; in April, James (who was reading 'Miss Hamilton on Education') was 'assisting Sarah in Latin'. At seventeen, Sarah was beginning to join her Newcastle uncles as a purchaser of books: her name appears beside theirs among the 350 subscribers to *The Works of Thomas Chatterton containing his Life*, by C. Gregory, with Southey's preface, in 1803.

The rich introduction that James gave her to radical politics, literature and poetry stayed with Sarah all her life. His links with this group gradually tailed off into sporadic meetings, but the lasting respect that these early friends had for him suggests the warmth beneath his upright manner. When John Tweddell died in Athens in 1799 – becoming such a well-known figure that even Byron visited his tomb – all his papers and drawings were allegedly sent home to James by Lord Elgin, via Joseph Carlyle (they never arrived, causing a considerable scandal, and suggestions that Elgin was keeping them for his own uses).[29] When Wordsworth's brother John went down with his ship *The Earl of Abergavenny* in 1805, it was to James that Wordsworth poured out his heart in a long and moving letter. When Southey spent a day with him in 1809 he reminded his brother Tom that he had always mentioned James 'as coming nearer to the ideal of a perfect man than any other person whom it has been my good fortune to know; so gentle, so pious, so zealous in all good things, so equal-minded'.[30]

7 Family Matters

Sarah was not altogether happy with the new regime under her aunt Margaret. In May 1801, eighteen months after her mother's death, James had to write a long letter to his niece, 'of a very serious nature', noting in his diary how hard it was to find the right words to help this determined fifteen-year-old.[1]

She went on educating herself, following the eclectic reading habits instilled by James, studying history, local and national, and learning from those around her, whether classicists or scientists.[2] She worked on foreign languages on her own, but for her Latin and Greek she turned for help to Parson Gaskin, whose definition of a good classical scholar was daunting:

You should be able to construe the Greek testament, anywhere, at sight, and to parse any verb. You should also be able to read any easy prose Greek author, as Xenophon, Lucian, Herodotus and also Homer . . . Then all the usual common Latin schoolbooks: you should be able to read at sight Virgil, Horace, Caesar's Commentaries, Tully's Oration. Lastly you should be able to write pretty correctly Latin prose – and a Greek play or two should be added.[3]

Gaskin was still a regular at John Losh's dinners, where naturalists mixed with poets, clerics with scientists and doctors such as John Heysham, founder of the city's dispensary, advocate of inoculation, and famous as a collector of data that enabled the first actuarial mortality tables. Heysham liked a good dinner, 'and its grateful accompaniments of good wine', wrote Lonsdale, 'and both were served most liberally to the visitors of Corby and Woodside'.[4] Another unconventional friend was John Leslie, the Scottish mathematician, chemist and physicist, whose work on heat was of vital interest to fledgling industrialists like the Loshes. He was a good friend of Isaac Milner, and when he later became professor of Mathematics in Edinburgh, he sent the Dean equipment for his experiments on heat, and, for fun, 'a splendid electrical machine of the newest and most approved construction, with [Leyden] jars of immense power. He was thus supplied with the means of gratifying his friends, and especially young persons, with the sight of many scientific wonders which he was always ready to explain.'[5] On his visits to Woodside Leslie astonished the locals with his curious clothes and collecting of snails and insects. He brought his finds indoors and was always ready to talk to the girls, impressing on everyone the importance of mathematics as part of a liberal education, with its need for patient reasoning and clear thinking, qualities Sarah was fast developing.

Short and stout, an eater of enormous meals, Leslie dressed carelessly (trying to pass as fashionable, he dyed his hair purple). Both clerics and scientists – and the roles were often combined – were forgiven for looking eccentric. If Leslie caught the eye with his hair, so did Dean Milner and Samuel Goodenough – the new Bishop of Carlisle and an expert botanist – who were the last of their ranks in Carlisle to wear wigs. The bishop's great-great-granddaughter remembered being told that his wigs were known in the family as 'Highty, Tighty and Scrub; the first for London and State occasions; the second for official appearances in Carlisle; and Scrub for home wear'.[6] But there was tragedy as well as comedy among the local scientists. One of John's protégés was a young Scottish engineer, Mr Chisholm, planning waterworks on the river Caldew. One day, after returning from Woodside,

Chisholm was suddenly taken ill, and though 'the best medical assistance was administered, and every attendance that friendship or humanity could dictate', the twenty-eight-year-old died, it was thought 'from a bursting of the artery of the heart'.[7] At every turn life seemed fragile.

In the years after Isabella's death John threw himself even more into county life, riding with the Inglewood Hunt, following the hounds of the Carlisle Harriers, which met at Wreay, dining with his old crony the Duke of Norfolk at Greystoke, betting at the races in Carlisle and Penrith. Cumbrian social life still had a tang of the high eighteenth century: a Twelfth Night ball in January 1802, with coach lamps lighting the way to the gate, and goose pie for dinner, saw the whole circle in fancy dress and masks: 'there were monks and nuns and the Devil, Punch and Harlequin, Pilgrims, old Men and Women, fruit & flower girls, Spaniards, Quacks etc etc . . . much dancing and running about, then supper and singing' and dancing until five in the morning before taking the long, cold road home.[8]

Such nights took no note of war abroad and persecution of liberals at home, but in Carlisle, John's Whig set met regularly in the Grey Goat Inn to lambast the government. Yet while John opposed the repression, he was no opponent of the war itself. Styled as lieutenant colonel, he joined Henry Howard's volunteer force at Corby and drilled with the Cumberland Rangers, an expensive venture as it meant kitting out yourself and your men in the force's chosen livery. The peace treaty of Amiens, signed in March 1802, brought a brief fourteen months of respite. But John kept his place in the volunteer troops and a few years later, as the wars grumbled on, he appeared as a major in the Loyal Cumberland Rangers.[9] In town he had many cronies, especially among the fellow members of John Heysham's informal club, who dined at each other's houses to while away the evenings in the gloomy winter months, sitting down at three and dining and drinking till ten, each consuming three bottles of port. 'On rare occasions,' wrote Lonsdale, 'such as a victory by Nelson or the dashing Cochrane, the fourth bottle to each man was held to be the right mode of rendering the fact historical.'[10]

James thought his brother's preference for Carlisle was 'largely from indolence'.[11] He raised his eyebrows at his way of life and sent firm letters of advice, which went unheeded. However much he played the country gentleman, John was still a businessman. His Carlisle bank was doing well, and the partners were noted for their generosity to the poor. But there were worries about forged notes, and around 1799 John's brother George asked the engraver Thomas Bewick to produce a note that could not be copied. John was also still the senior proprietor of the alkali works, and a guarantor of his brothers' projects. His role as guarantor brought problems when William and George formed a new company, the Leven Iron Works, in 1800, in response to an advertisement placed by the Earl of Leven, whose estate at Balgonie in Fife was in a bad financial way, for a company to set up a foundry and iron works to exploit his reserves of coal and ironstone. In 1801 the lease was signed: but there was not enough water in summer to power the mill, machinery was delivered late and bad roads delayed sales. The workers' wages and the earl's rent went unpaid.

Then in June 1803 a small handbill appeared on the streets of Carlisle announcing that the bank of Surtees and Burdon was suspended, and none of their notes could be honoured. The founder of the bank, Aubone Surtees, had died in 1800 and the crash was blamed on the speculation of the younger members of the Surtees family – including investments in different Losh enterprises. One of the worst sufferers was Rowland Burdon, promoter of the Sunderland Bridge that James and Sarah had so admired, who lost many thousands and saw his shares disposed of by lottery.

When the news broke John and William rushed to Carlisle and then back across to Newcastle. Their own family bank, Liddell,

Losh and Wilson, was forced to close a fortnight later.[12] On 6 July James wrote: 'At George's with John and his family. This was a day of great anxiety: everything looks hopeless.'[13] There was little they could do: three months later both George and William were declared bankrupt. At first it seemed a temporary setback. Their Carlisle bank paid off its creditors in full, with Joseph Liddell selling land at Moorhouse and John Losh his lands at Harraby. By February 1804 they had settled all the claims but it was the end of their banking days: with public trust lost, the bank was never reopened. James wrote wryly in his diary:

I have just heard of the sale of Moorhouse and Sandsfield by my uncle Liddell . . . this property ought, in the common cause of things, to have come to me or my children, and it has often been distinctly promised by my uncle . . . his unfortunate speculation (and, I may add, perverseness) has, however, fallen heavy on me as well as himself, but thank God I am content.[14]

In Newcastle George withdrew from his old quayside firm of Losh, Lubbren & Co. and announced he would now operate independently as a commission merchant and insurance broker. Meanwhile James wrote diplomatic letters about their Scottish investment, John guaranteed George's debts and soon the Balgonie company was up and running again. But George had lost almost everything, and had to give up his large house on Westgate Street in Newcastle and move into their uncle Joseph Liddell's house at Saltwellside, near Gateshead, 'a pleasant retired mansion in the fields'.[15]

The girls were well aware of these financial ups and downs. The four brothers, their father and uncles, close as they were, had become very distinct personalities: John, the big, expansive, energetic squire, James, the serious lawyer, George, the wayward businessman, impetuous and argumentative, and William, kindly and unassuming, completely absorbed in his experiments at the works. Throughout these times the sisters moved constantly between Woodside, Carlisle and Newcastle, visiting their uncles and aunts and a growing host of small cousins. They were not always together. In the autumn of 1802, for example, Sarah stayed in London while Katharine spent a few weeks with James and Cecilia in Jesmond, seeing the stately homes and castles of Northumberland and Durham – Alnwick, Castle Eden, Raby – and William Gaskin brought Joe to spend a week breathing the sea air of Tynemouth. Joe was certainly improved, James thought, 'but I much fear he will always be greatly deficient in understanding & a severe affliction to my brother'.[16]

If John was sadly disappointed in his son, whom he loved despite his disability, he was unashamedly proud of his daughters. Both the Losh sisters would soon have to take their place in Cumberland society. Sarah stepped out first, attending her first ball in Carlisle at the age of eighteen in August 1804, and in family recollections, she was hailed as the greatest beauty since Sara Blamire, sister of the poet Susanna, a generation before.[17] Carlisle was full of colour: the canons and clergy in their black robes, the militia in their uniforms, the men of the Carlisle Hunt and their partners, all in white and green. In the winter there were dances and assemblies; in summer the families decamped to Allonby. That September, the Losh sisters and Margaret, and their aunt Ann Bonner, who was now living nearby in Brisco, were all in Allonby. George was there too. There were domestic tensions as well as money problems in the Saltwellside family and George was often in Carlisle, while his wife and four little girls were equally often with James and Cecilia at Jesmond. Receiving a gloomy letter from Margaret, James noted laconically, 'Bad acct of John & not a good one of George'.[18] A hopeless businessman, George fell deeper and deeper in debt until in 1808 the Balgonie works had to be sold. He stayed on as manager, but within two years the company's debts had mounted to over £30,000 and it was put up for sale at the Royal Exchange in Edinburgh. No buyer appeared; the creditors accepted a low settlement of ten per cent, and George Losh was forced out altogether and effectively ruined.

There were dark undercurrents at Woodside too: at one point John declared angrily that he would let his farm and move to Edinburgh to sort out the Balgonie problems. He was often away from home, and though he remained one the Twelve Men of Wreay, his place as their head was taken by the farmer Joseph Bewley.[19] But the storms passed. The next few years saw the usual large family gatherings, and occasional long stays at Jesmond, where Cecilia shepherded the sisters to the theatre and to the balls. Among the people they saw regularly were James Thain, who was living near the works at Walker, and his son William, who stayed for several summers in Wreay, either with the Gaskins or with the Bewleys at Townhead Farm.

As Sarah grew older Margaret was more inclined to leave her in charge at Wreay, staying for months at a time in Newcastle. It was livelier there, a contrast to the Petteril valley, where after five or six weeks of continuous rain, it was impossible, wrote Jane Blamire, even to get to church in the carriage. The autumn skies were often tossed by storms and thunder, high winds and hail; in winter the snow could lie for weeks.[20] And on Tyneside the family houses were soon full of small children. To begin with there was sadness: James and Cecilia lost their first two sons as infants, at three months and nine months, and William and Alice lost a son before his first birthday. But in time George and Frances had six daughters and William and Alice two, while James and Cecilia had eight children – five sons and three daughters. Sarah and Katharine were very much the older cousins, almost aunts.

Soon Katharine, as well as Sarah, was 'out' in Carlisle society: at the assizes in August 1807, in James's view his nieces were '"the Belles of the Ball" in all respects'.[21] Not that these were always joyous occasions. In one of his despondent moods, James looked around the room at an Assize Ball and despaired: 'The men gave themselves airs and seemed to consider dancing as too much exertion, while the ladies sat like so many animals waiting for a purchaser, this is always to me a mortifying sight, and a strong mark of the barbarism of our manners.'[22] Boring or not, the sisters were supposed to enjoy such evenings and to follow the pursuits of well-bred young women: drawing and embroidery, mild charitable work, decorating bonnets and cultivating the garden. 'Let me warn you, beloved girl,' her mother advised Sarah's bookish friend Jane Blamire in 1806, 'not to sit too much in the house, for you will not only lose your looks, but your spirits – I long for you to walk with me in the Garden – the flower seeds are all come up & I have a great show of Blossom'.[23]

Sarah was a good gardener, especially keen on unusual shrubs and trees. But she was eager to learn and often stuck to her desk and her books. On their forays to London, she made a strong impression, as she always would. 'Indeed one of her London masters', according to Lonsdale, 'was so struck with her capacity that he offered her various subjects of study, and the higher he aimed the higher she soared. With powers to grapple with Euclid and algebra, she had but to give her attention to any subject to master it.'[24] She loved the classics, and would take a Latin book and read it casually in English with no hint of the effort of translation; when her current passion was Greek, she studied it for three hours a day, until she could translate virtually any Greek play 'almost on sight'. This was not a young woman who would be happy remaining a belle of the ball, spending her days in embroidery and making polite calls, dreaming of dandling babies. She anticipated women like George Eliot's Dorothea in *Middlemarch*, set in the 1830s, fired by a desire to learn. Like a real-life Dorothea, Sarah Losh might well have thought Casaubon, labouring on his key to all mythologies, a more desirable husband than an amiable, hard-drinking Cumbrian landowner or Newcastle merchant.

The balls were a local marriage market, and not all the marriages went well. There were dramas among their relations: Sarah's cousin Henry Warwick, at Warwick Hall, separated from his wife Mary, who wrote tearful letters to the great correspondent and linchpin of Cumbrian society, Kitty Senhouse:

> my affairs grow worse . . . Mr Warwick now has determined to take all my boys and to make me quit Warwick Hall – he has employed Mr James Losh to negociate matters and to draw a deed of separation . . . My situation is very uncomfortable and would indeed be almost insupportable were I not convinced that a gracious Providence orders everything for the best.[25]

James was the go-between but his negotiations did not end the misery: the four girls went with their mother and the boys stayed at Warwick Hall.

Marriage and family life did not appeal to the Losh sisters. Although they were acknowledged to be handsome, charming and rich they rejected all the proposals that came their way. They were happy in each other's company, holidaying by the sea at Allonby and enjoying their life as the accomplished daughters of John Losh. And while Sarah was more studious, Katharine was lively and open, enjoying her social life. She was as different from her older sister as George Eliot's Celia was from Dorothea: softer, 'fonder of geraniums, and seems more docile, though not so fine a figure'.[26] On her trips to Jesmond she became a favourite of James's wife Cecilia, who whisked her off to dinners and teas, parties and plays, sometimes fitting in a party and a ball on the same day. In January there was a week of such festivities, including young Willliam Thain in the party, and on some evenings James, who had to work, was left trailing in their wake. 'Dinner at home', he wrote briskly, 'John, Catherine, W. Thain – they all went to the play & I joined them at ½ price. Cold day.'[27] When she left them after a stay of several weeks, James decided that she was 'uncommonly amiable and unaffected, with a cheerful disposition, pleasing manners, and a good plain understanding.'[28] The 'good plain understanding' may have stood in marked contrast to Sarah's moody brilliance.

Over the past few years, the main news had always been the war, with its setbacks and victories, the most notable being the battle of Trafalgar in October 1805. Dr Heysham rode south to meet the stagecoach for news, galloping back to Carlisle in tears when he heard of Nelson's death, and the market cross at Wigton was burnt in a wayward mix of celebration and mourning. The following year the Carlisle mayor, Thomas Blamire, organised a collection 'for the relief of the unfortunate Widows and Orphans of the brave Men who fell, and of the wounded'.[29] Carlisle, like the rest of the nation, grieved for Nelson. A monument had been erected in Egypt to commemorate the battle of the Nile in 1798, and when this was blown up by Napoleonic troops, Captain Wood of Maryport had brought a fragment back and set it into the gable of his house in George Street, Carlisle. Now Nelson's name and date of death were added to the stone, while the new gardens at the end of the street were 'laid out to represent the deck of the Victory'.[30]

Until British troops landed in the Iberian peninsula in 1809 the war was mainly at sea. British warships sailed into the Dardanelles to help Russia, at war with Turkey, and the navy bombarded Copenhagen (a misguided tactic), to prevent the Danish fleet being taken by the French. In Newcastle, the press gang roamed the streets, pouncing first on experienced keelmen and then on any young man who might make a sailor. Employers often wrote letters begging for men to be released. In 1806 William was writing to officials at Tynemouth on behalf of a merchant ship's captain, requesting the release of Joseph Paul who was 'now on board the tender at Shields', and who had already been granted an exemption – adding that he had been requested to send the application 'by my brother George Losh, Swedish Vice Consul at this port'.[31] The appeals did not stop. Two years later he was sending an eloquent note on behalf of Robert Bland, who had worked in the foundry for five years, stressing that 'his being sent to Sea would be a great inconvenience to me as I should have another man to procure and instruct'.[32]

Despite the bank failures and the war and the threat of impressment, Carlisle was expanding rapidly. By 1807 there were calico and muslin and cotton printers, hat-makers, soap-boilers and tallow chandlers, tanners and skinners as well as three foundries and four breweries. The corporation was busy: new street lamps were erected, a 'School of Industry' was built in the slums of Botchergate, and a workhouse on Harraby Hill. Yet many visitors commented on the city's air of neglect, especially its ruined walls. In August 1803, Dorothy Wordsworth, who came with William and Coleridge to see the judge pass sentence on the forger John Hatfield, famed seducer of the Maid of Buttermere, had noted that they 'walked upon the city walls, which are broken down in places, and crumbling away, and most disgusting from filth'.[33] Over the next few years, Carlisle's medieval air faded as three gates and most of the old walls were demolished. To the north, Robert Smirke – whose father came from Wigton, and who had been working on the massive Gothic remodelling of Lowther Castle – designed a broad new bridge over the Eden. To the south, the corporation planned to remodel the old towers of the Citadel, erected by Henry VIII in the 1540s to defend against invasion through Scotland, to designs by Thomas Telford, later completed on a grander scale by Smirke. The new Citadel was the Court House, with the civil and criminal courts, and soon a grand-jury room and a prison.

The city the girls had known since they were small was changing fast and their family were key figures in its transformation. For a long time John had been a member of the Harmony Lodge

The western tower of Carlisle Citadel, decked out for an
agricultural fair in the mid-nineteenth century.

of Masons in Carlisle, joining at a time when the Masons were
associated less with mysterious handshakes and business deals than
with radicalism and support for change: many were suspected of
subversion during the years of the French revolution. The Harmony Lodge, however, was a sociable affair, which had returned
to its original base, the old coaching inn the Blue Bell in Scotch
Street, after a few years at the Black Bull.[34] In February 1801 John
was appointed provincial grand master for Cumberland.

When the great two-ton cornerstone of the Courts was laid on
6 June 1808, John proposed 'that this great design, which embraces
almost every object interesting to the feelings of humanity, should
be executed in Masonic form'.[35] This was agreed, and indeed it
was common practice for major buildings, like the new Covent
Garden Theatre, for which the prince regent, as grand master,
laid the stone in December 1809. The event proceeded with due
'solemnity and splendour'. At eleven in the morning, the men
of the Harmony and Union Lodges processed from the coffee-
house to the Courts, where they divided their ranks to make a
passage for John to approach the stone. As they gathered round,

he placed 'a bottle, chemically sealed, containing parchment and paper manuscripts' in a hole in the stone. These included the order for the building of the Court House, 'a copy of verses, by a young lady' (could this have been Sarah?), two recent newspapers, current coins and medals, a Carlisle banknote and Telford's original manuscript plan, and, 'according to ancient masonic practice, a phial, replete with corn, wine and oil'. John then 'applied the proper instruments' – the Masonic set-square and compasses – and implored the help of God to prosper the work. After the formal laying of the stone, his extempore speech was greeted with cheers and hullooing and 'the joyful acclamations of the workmen and the immense concourse of people'.

Sarah was always intrigued by processions and rituals, by the rosettes on the Masonic emblems that looked back to the rose of the Song of Solomon and the lotus, and the pinecone that topped the deacons' staff, an ancient symbol of regeneration, often seen in Masonic halls where it was etched into the walls, carved on posts or suspended from the ceiling. John Losh, however, was not a man of mysteries and symbols. He was clever, but he was a bluff, open, hard-living soul who felt that farming was 'the best and happiest' life. His Masonic role was social, a measure of his growing status in Carlisle. He was enjoying himself and doing well. Summing up the family's finances at midsummer 1809, James was sanguine about John and his other brothers, although falsely optimistic about George: 'George's affairs have been a thorn in my side, but even they promise to be more tolerable in future – William seems likely to do well in the end, and John is opulent enough to become fortunate and independent. I apprehend, after paying all his debts, that his property is worth more than £40,000.'[36] Two years later James helped John to write 'a short temporary Will leaving his whole property equally to his daughters. This has relieved me from some anxiety.'[37]

John's standing in the county was confirmed when he was

appointed high sheriff of Cumberland in 1811, and a hundred of the neighbouring gentry and yeomanry met in Woodside park and escorted him on horseback to the Carlisle assizes. The four or five days of celebration cost, it was said, £1,500 – more than Sarah's church would cost thirty years later – a wild extravagance, catering not only for the elite but 'the tipstaffs of the court, and a hungry and thirsty multitude out of doors'. His flamboyant gesture looked still more conspicuous the following year. A slump hit the Carlisle weavers: there were hunger riots and attacks on the mills, and 'sheep were stolen and slaughtered for food, potato clamps broken into, and doors and fences and the like broken down and burnt in the streets for warmth'.[38] The trouble spread to the edge of the Lakes and fells. 'Every day brings some new outrage committed by the rioters,' wrote the Blamires' aunt, Mary Simpson. 'Mr Hutchinson's house in Ullswater has been robbed when his servants were out, & much mischief done.'[39] Kitty Senhouse was equally aghast at the frequent robberies on market days in Carlisle and other towns, '& two Houses in this Neighbourhood, one near Dailmain & the other near Pooley each by four men in disguise were entered at an early hour in the Night, & took off what Money they could get, pieces of Cloths & other articles'.[40]

The Woodside family were not unduly rattled. They were more worried in early 1812 by John's sudden bad health. When John and the girls came to Jesmond that summer, James thought he looked 'old and ill tho better than I expected – with care I hope and trust he may overcome his present disorder'.[41] He was well enough, and rich enough, to pay fifteen guineas for a full set of new teeth. And back at Woodside the summer continued without alarms, with big parties at Corby Castle to see the new summerhouses, watching salmon being caught on the Eden and ending up at the inn at Wetheral. The weather was fine, the gooseberries excellent, the corn was cut early. When James took his young sons to stay at Woodside the following spring, he noted how prosperous it looked in the fine March weather. 'It is always pleasant to me to wander about this snug and well-wooded place, and to recollect the haunts and amusements of my childhood – Woodside is now a very comfortable and handsome place and the woods around it thriving and extensive.'[42]

But prosperous as his estates were, heavy drinking, overeating, managing his estates, and worry about the bank and George's affairs at Balgonie had taken their toll on John. In August 1813 he had an alarming fainting fit – though not a stroke – and a month later it was feared that he had had three epileptic fits. In October the Jesmond family paid another short, packed visit to Woodside, listening to Gaskin's sermon and admiring his two small sons, going for drives and walks and dining with local friends. In the distance there was already snow on the mountains, a hint of the bitter winter to come. When James got home after the long carriage ride across country, he scribbled in his diary:

I had a long conversation with my Brother, whom I found upon the whole better than I had expected. His faculties seem quite perfect and in no respect disturbed by his illness. His spirits were by no means bad and his looks and appetite give promise of a gradual recovery – His constitution is however I fear much shaken.[43]

After Christmas the snow fell deep, all across the north, lying in great drifts. The rivers were frozen and the ice was so thick on the Tyne that people put up tents and built bonfires. The frost endured for weeks, with constant storms and snow until the middle of March. That month, on 28 March 1814, John Losh died.

II

SISTER

8 Wanderings and Waterloo

For a clever woman, what was there to do? Sarah was twenty-eight and Katharine twenty-six, and neither sister seemed to want to marry, much to their family's frustration. Sarah was proud of her name, and wanted to keep the land under the name of Losh, as her own will would show. As a single woman, independent and well off, she need not fear the 'interference with her own wishes' that upset her as a girl. But although she and Katharine could run the estate with the help of the Bell family from Low Hurst, their home farm, they were no pioneering agriculturalists. Although Sarah was interested in politics, writing copious notes on current issues with a strong bent towards reform, she could not immerse herself in local politics as her father had done – indeed she could not even join the Twelve Men of Wreay, although she was the owner of the village's largest estate: instead, John's vacant place was taken by James. She and Katharine could not be industrialists or lawyers like their uncles. They could not be Masons, with their secret ceremonies. But perhaps they could be masons in a literal sense – builders in stone.

When the express arrived in Jesmond bearing the news of John's death, James noted the time in his diary, 11.30 at night, and summed his brother up curtly but affectionately as a 'good and amiable' man who never quite fulfilled his promise:

He had great talents, fine taste much improved by reading and observation – a very handsome person and pleasing manners. With these advantages and an independent fortune what is there that he might have been! But he was indolent and had suffered habits unfavourable to steady application to grow upon him. – Hence it was that he wasted many of the fair prospects before him: but still he was a most valuable man, kind to all around him, affectionate to his family, charitable and considerate to the poor and a most useful Magistrate. I can safely say that not only my Brother & I never had the slightest quarrel in our lives, but that I believe we never either of us felt a moment's ill humour to the other.[1]

James and William arrived from Newcastle to find the household 'tolerably well except Sarah who seems quite overwhelmed with sorrow'. Next day James wrote, 'Had a very affecting interview with my niece Sarah, who spoke to me with great candour. She seems to suffer from those doubts and anxieties which are too common to minds of sensibility. It shall be my constant and earnest endeavour to be the comfort and friend of this excellent young woman.'[2] If her doubts concerned her faith and the existence of God and the afterlife, these anxieties also contributed to the philosophical underpinning and imagery of her buildings, in which time and eternity press upon the living but the perpetual renewal of the natural world offers consolation.

On the last day of March, John was buried beside his wife Isabella in Wreay churchyard. His three brothers were all at the funeral, with the local landowners, farmers, neighbours and Carlisle friends, and 'every person seemed much affected'.[3] Later James dug out the temporary will John had made with him three years before, a single paragraph leaving his whole estate to Sarah and Katharine in equal parts, as independent individuals: 'tenants in common and not as joint tenants'. They were now heiresses, to the land, the alkali works and other interests. James was executor, along with William Gaskin. But it turned out that in October 1813, John had added an important codicil in his elegant, clear hand. In this he appointed Sarah as sole guardian of her older brother Joseph during his life, but he also provided for another Joseph, his illegitimate son by a young Carlisle woman, Mary James, news that may have startled the sisters. He left Mary an annuity and her Joseph a sum of money when he reached twenty-one. 'In the mean time,' the will continued,

I wish (and I know my wish will be attended to) that the said Joseph James should be brought up at some decent farm house with such allowance and no more as may be fitting for one intended for the oc-cupation of husbandry in my opinion the best and happiest and where he may have the opportunity of being taught reading writing and common arithmetic.

This very private codicil, with its wistful evocation of farming as the best and happiest life, was witnessed by his three old serv-ants, Jane Lorraine, Adam Pearson and Mary Johnston. He also left handsome sums to them, as he did to the three children of his friend William Gaskin.[4]

No more is heard of a farming life for little Joseph Losh James, who was five when John died. He lived nearby and became a bookseller near Durham; by 1840 he was bankrupt and had disap-peared to London and Kent, a world away from Wreay.[5] Mean-while his half-brother, the legitimate Joseph, now aged fifteen, left Woodside and went to live a mile away at the Wreay vicarage with the Gaskins. When Isabella Gaskin died in 1820, his uncle James had more long conversations with Sarah and Katharine and Wil-liam Gaskin, 'and we determined upon what I trust will do good'. 'Poor Joe', as James called him, never came home to Woodside. In later years he moved to the Loshes' other house, Ravenside, just up the hill, where he lived with devoted servants to care for him, under the supervision of Gaskin's second wife, Sarah.

In the weeks following John's death James continued to look after the sisters' affairs, taking his small sons over to stay while he checked all their documents: already Sarah and Katharine had visitors, he noted, and 'a little boy the son of Mr Elliott has been at Woodside 2 days to the great delight of my Robert & William'.[6] George came too, to help with the family papers, which John had left in some confusion. Sometimes too, the sisters clashed with their aunts, Margaret and Ann Bonner. In a sweltering late July James noted in his diary, 'I had a long & painful conversation with Miss A. Bonner as to the Woodside family. Fine day. Hot' – and then he sat down to write firmly to the other aunt, his sister Margaret.[7]

A month before, Joseph Bewley of Townhead Farm had also settled down to write a letter. This was to William Thain, the son of James Thain, the former soldier and friend of James Losh and supervisor at the alkali works. After going to school in Newcastle, William had been sent to finish his education with Mr Gaskin – perhaps with a view to studying for university – and had stayed with the Bewleys at Townhead. They kept his Latin grammar book, marked with his name: 'Wreay school. William Thain's book'.[8] But instead of following an academic path, at fifteen William joined his father as a volunteer in the Northumberland militia, and in 1813, when he was sixteen, he obtained a commission as an ensign in the Yorkshire West Riding Regiment, the 33rd. The regiment had been commanded by Arthur Wellesley, later the Duke of Wellington, since it was founded in 1793, and over the last few years it had fought in the West Indies, Holland, Mauritius and India, helping to defeat Tippoo Sultan, the 'Tiger of Mysore'. After sixteen years abroad, the 33rd had returned to England and when William joined it the regiment was based at Hull, about to head abroad again.

With hundreds of other raw recruits, William was sent out almost immediately on the ill-fated expedition to support the Dutch rebels against Napoleon, and took part in the attack on the impregnable fortress of Bergen op Zoom. When they were forced to surrender, hundreds of British soldiers were taken prisoner. It was a national humiliation, but William was safe, and when peace was signed with France and Napoleon exiled to Elba, he was made town adjutant in Antwerp, then full of allied troops. He was only seventeen and found his new post, he told his old Newcastle schoolmaster John Bruce, 'a very arduous employment which requires all my attention'.⁹

Bewley was replying to a letter that William had sent in April from Vielsalm in Belgium. At that point William thought he would be heading for Cork, before his regiment was posted to America, where the war was still continuing (in August this year a British raiding party would set fire to the White House). Bewley gave him all the local news, including the birth of Gaskin's son John and a series of deaths: old Henry Gill, his own sister Miss Bewley, Mrs Robley, a servant at Woodside, and 'your much respected friend, Mr John Losh'. John's loss would be much felt in this neighbourhood, he said, but 'the two Miss Loshes continue at Woodside with little alteration in the family, except that Joseph is come to Mr Gaskin's with a person appointed to look after him'.¹⁰ The big moves were all from the Bell family at Low Hurst, cementing the links between Wreay and Newcastle. The Bells' daughter Grace had married Michael Sewell, the potter from the village of St Anthony, next to William's works at Walker; her brother John had gone to Walker as clerk to his older brother Thomas, who was already one of William's partners in the iron works, and his sister Jane had gone too, to keep house for him. The old farm was almost swept clean of Bell children: 'What a sudden alteration in that family!' But the pub, Bewley reported comfortingly, was still the same. 'Old David keeps the corner chair, and old Betty the landlady is as rough as ever.'

Sudden alterations, however sad, could bring unexpected benefits, as Sarah found. A certain freedom came from being an independent young woman of considerable means, rather than a daughter on an allowance. Sarah made the best of her position: she was tall with long brown hair, a clear complexion that set off her blue-grey eyes and a mobile face that showed her emotions, and at this stage in her life she made a point of being well turned out, almost flashy, 'dressed gaily and expensively'.[11]

She was now a moneyed woman, free to travel, and like so many others, after the peace treaty of Paris and Napoleon's departure she headed for Europe, with Katharine and Margaret. In early August 1814, after spending a day by the sea at Cullercoats and Tynemouth while George Losh made enquiries about a ship, the trio sailed from Newcastle to Holland. For the next two months they toured the Low Countries and France, returning in early October full of praise for the Dutch and disdain for the French, according to James, who noted only their political opinions, which were shrewd if not original:

They say the people of Holland and Brabant are very hostile to each other and equally averse to a union. The latter wish much to be under the protection of the English. The French they think are still very far from being settled and tranquil, and they consider the return of Napoleon to power as by no means improbable.[12]

Their return prompted a family reunion. On 9 October James and Cecilia threw a dinner party at Jesmond where nearly all the Big Black Squire's descendants were present – twenty-three of them: Margaret, Sarah and Katharine (but not 'poor Joe'); Frances with her six daughters, William and Alice with their two daughters; and James and Cecilia with six out of their eight children. Like many family parties, all was not calm: 'a very foolish quarrel took place in which William and his Wife were to blame'. The row, it seems, was largely between the two Wilkinson sisters, Frances and Alice, and Frances, thought James, was very hard done by: 'Cecilia & I in truth had nothing to do with the quarrel'.[13] Frances was there alone while George was still in Edinburgh, but the tension of dealing with George's affairs told on everyone, and Margaret, Sarah and Katharine were also swept up in the arguments and allegiances. Frances and her troop of girls now went north to live with George, and soon the Woodside women joined them for a long visit, taking James's eldest daughter Cecilia to spend a few months in Edinburgh, where she could find good teachers in dancing, French and drawing. (The following year, writing about her own girls, one friend declared that Edinburgh was absolutely the place to be, adding that their dancing master there 'has been to Paris of course, and has brought a number of French steps & dances. Anne & Isabella are learning a beautiful French Waltze, quite new in this part of the world'.[14])

In the year after John's death, his daughters were hardly at Woodside at all, staying away for months at a time. But their aunt Margaret's visit to Edinburgh was not solely for pleasure: she had been unwell all year and cancer was briefly suspected. And then when they came home at Christmas, to find the temperature plummeting below freezing and gales toppling the Woodside trees, Sarah too fell ill. She rallied, but suffered repeated collapses for the next few months. The strain of the past two years was telling. She found it hard to eat and lost weight and energy. When James visited in late March he found Margaret better, 'tho' I fear far from well – Sarah is dreadfully thin and emaciated, and I cannot help (in spite of what the medical men say) thinking her in great danger'.[15] The danger passed, but she was nervous and restless. As late as May James heard from Dr Ramsay 'bad accounts of the health of my dear & excellent Niece Sarah'.[16] But by the end of that month Sarah was on the mend, to the relief of her uncle. The illness of his sister and niece brought out all James's fondness for them, expressed in his anxious, buttoned-up way. After they visited Jesmond that August, he wrote of his pleasure in the visit, 'tho' I cannot help thinking the health of both Margaret & Sarah very precarious. My nieces are most amiable & excellent women & every way most deserving of the ample fortune which they possess.'[17]

Sarah and Katharine's ample fortune still came largely from the Tyne. Since 1809 William had been extending his iron trade, setting up the Walker Iron Works, with his clerks Thomas Wilson and Thomas Bell, the eldest son of the Low Hurst family, as partners. Soon Losh, Wilson & Bell was rivalling Boulton and Watt as producers of steam engines for the mills and collieries, and William was working with the local engineer George Stephenson, whom he invited to spend two days at the iron works, offering him a salary of £100 a year. Together they developed stronger rails to carry the coal down to the river where the ships were waiting, and in 1814 began building 'locomotive engines' for nearby collieries. A year later William patented new designs for 'working engines, and for other uses in manufactories', and then jointly with Stephenson in 1817 for 'A method of or methods of facilitating the conveyance of carriages, goods and materials, along railways and tramways, by certain inventions and improvements in the construction of the machine, carriage and carriage wheels, railways and tramways, for that purpose'.[18] (The new engines were too heavy for the wooden rails, and the early cast-iron rails were too brittle: their new design was stronger, preventing breakage.) All the Losh brothers supported Stephenson's experiments. In December 1815, when Stephenson's safety lamp was exhibited at the Newcastle Literary and Philosophical Society, James was on the committee of colliery owners who presented him with a silver plaque. This provoked a furious letter from Humphry Davy, who also claimed to have invented the lamp, written, James thought, 'with much ill humour and little discretion', denouncing James and all who opposed him as enemies.[19] In a crushing reply, James defended his right to acclaim Stephenson, concluding that despite Davy's achievements, 'I consider myself at perfect liberty to testify my esteem for the genius and merits of any other person, in whatever way I may think best'.

While William's works prospered, his older brother George's affairs were on the slide. He had never really recovered from the Balgonie disaster and often talked about taking his whole family to France, where they could live more cheaply. Although his plans were delayed by Napoleon's return from exile, he and his family eventually sailed in October 1815, settling near Rouen. James wrote wearily,

My brother George and his six children all arrived this day at Jesmond Grove, being about to remove into France: my heart bleeds for their misfortunes, but after all they must be attributed in great measure to indolence, and the want of that degree of regularity which is necessary to success in every pursuit of life.[20]

The family always stayed close. George reported back on French iron-working and alkalis, and his daughters Fanny and Alicia stayed for months at a time at Jesmond, while James's daughter Cecilia lived with George's family in Rouen for a year to improve her French.

Carlisle shared in the outpouring of emotion at the victory at Waterloo, with bonfires and street processions. But as the beacon flared on the summit of Skiddaw, the city mourned its dead, including a thirteen-year-old ensign, Charles Graham, and celebrated its heroes too, like Captain Hew Ross, who had served with Wellington in the Royal Horse Guards throughout the Peninsular War and commanded his famous Chestnut Troop at Waterloo (they had ridden chestnut horses since they were formed in 1793). Covered with glory, and later knighted, Ross married a Graham heiress and settled at the grand Hayton House, near Brampton, just east of Carlisle.[21]

Soon news came to Wreay of the exploits at Waterloo of their own adopted hero, the eighteen-year-old William Thain. During the winter William had become adjutant to the 33rd, moving with the regiment to Paris. But by March 1815 they were back in Belgium, with Wellington as their commander, and three months later they fought at Quatre Bras and Waterloo. William wrote to his father from Brussels the next day, 'after one of the hardest fought and bloodiest battles that has yet been recorded'. The 33rd had held the centre of the ridge all day, beating back Napoleon's Imperial Guard until the evening, when 'fortunes appeared to change against us':

It was about that hour that the squares were ordered to advance against the enemy's artillery, the 33rd forming half of the front and the whole of the left face, that I received a musket ball through the left arm a little below the shoulder, but as the bone is not fractured I hope to be soon well again. We all thought from the strength of the enemy and the manner in which their artillery mowed us down in the evening that we had lost the day, but I am happy to inform you that the French are retiring in all directions . . . Feats of personal courage were shown by every individual and the British have placed the ball at the feet of the northern allies who will find no difficulty in kicking it on to Paris. French Imperial eagles have been paraded through the streets by a party of our dragoons and columns of prisoners are marching through continually for Antwerp to be embarked for England. Never was a more glorious day for our dear country.[22]

Almost half the regiment were killed, and William knew that he was lucky to survive, receiving the Waterloo medal and a year's pay. Back in Newcastle, when he called on John Bruce, his old teacher, Bruce's son remembered feeling 'rather astonished and not a little disappointed that he did not talk all dinner time about that glorious victory'.[23]

After Waterloo, no one was sure what to expect. In July, a month after the battle, Napoleon was packed off to his final exile, walking the decks of HMS *Bellerophon* when it anchored off the Devon coast before sailing to St Helena and showing himself theatrically to the massive crowds on shore and in a flotilla of small boats. The euphoria in Britain was short-lived. The country emerged from the wars with a crushing national debt and high taxes. A sixth

A popular image of blood and heroism at Waterloo, where William Thain
fought and was wounded, showing the death of General Picton.

of Britain's adult men had served in the army or navy, and now
the roads were full of wandering ex-soldiers and the ports with
returning sailors. In Newcastle there was trouble between ship
owners and keelmen, and in Lancashire and Yorkshire factories
closed when contracts for uniforms and guns suddenly ended. On
the land, farmers faced new taxes on everything from hops and
barley to horses and sheepdogs. The price of wheat crashed; the
gentry found loans and mortgages hard to repay; bankers pressed
for money; landowners pressed for rents; shopkeepers pressed for
payment. To aid the farmers the first of the Corn Laws was passed
in 1815, banning the import of corn until home-grown wheat
reached eighty shillings a quarter; as a result, the price of bread
rocketed, and the poor starved.

The weather did not help. 1816 was known as 'the year without
a summer', after the largest volcanic eruption for over a thousand

years, from Mount Tambora in Indonesia, swept volumes of ash into the upper atmosphere and caused a prolonged winter across the northern hemisphere. There were floods in the spring and frosts in July. In the autumn, fields lay unharvested, the potato crop failed and sheep died in their thousands. The winter that followed was exceptionally cruel and there were food riots in many towns.

Carlisle was still a poor city, despite the growth of its industry, and in these dark days tensions rose. The conservative, evangelical Isaac Milner, still Dean of Carlisle, unnerved by the spread of the 'democratic spirit', helped to found a new weekly paper, *The Patriot or the Carlisle and Cumberland Advertiser* (always known as the *Patriot*) as a competitor to the Whig *Carlisle Journal*. He also joined the Carlisle Pitt Club, a body of men who met annually to honour Pitt's memory, and who aimed, they said, 'to stem the torrent of Revolutionary Principles which threatened to overwhelm the venerable fabric of our Constitution, and to shake the very foundation of the Social Edifice: who braved the sneers of the envious: the calumnies of the disaffected: and the threats of the common enemy'.[24]

The Loshes, however, would never agree that the common enemy was now on their own shores. In the depression that was about to descend they stood consistently on the side of the poor, arguing for the rights of the people.

9 Italy

Once the Continent was open again Sarah and Katharine were off across the Channel, like many well-to-do British travellers escaping the misery at home. At the end of 1816, Sarah was thirty and Katharine twenty-eight. They travelled independently, although for much of the time they were with their uncle William, who was keen to catch up on trading developments and scientific advances in France and Italy. Like other readers of antiquarian works Sarah made copious notes on places, buildings and customs, and although she later destroyed most of her writings, she did keep the journal of this trip, in 'seven manuscript copy-books'. In the 1870s her heir, James Arlosh, lent these to Henry Lonsdale, after which they disappeared from view. Luckily, however, Lonsdale outlined their journey in his chapter on Sarah in the *Worthies of Cumberland*, and included a few extracts from Savoy, Rome and Pompeii, all places that struck her strongly.

The sisters had been to France before and had many connections there, but then they ventured into new territory, taking a long trip of several months, wandering south through Savoy towards Switzerland, the Alps and Italy. In the Haute-Savoie Sarah was tart about the peasants, 'who begged with great vociferation. Some of the women had goitres, which did not, however, induce them to lay aside their gold necklaces.' The children, she noted, were the most persevering beggars of all, following them for miles, long after their money was exhausted, 'with a clamour which one felt almost heartless to listen to'. But the day after these encounters, 11 May 1817, the tone of her diary was very different.[1] It was Rogation Sunday, the fifth Sunday after Easter, a day of prayer for the crops, across Catholic Europe as well as Anglican England, and often for beating of the parish bounds. Sleeping in their inn, high in the mountains, the sisters were woken before dawn by the sound of psalms. They thought at first that these were announcing a funeral, until their elderly hostess told them it was the Rogation Day procession and announced 'with some satisfaction' that her husband marched at the head of the men and her daughter of the women. Sarah was moved by the psalms' simplicity and the beauty of the setting, prompting some 'picturesque' epithets:

the mists still rested on the hills, and the dew spread its pearly fretwork on the valley; all was still and solemn, not a breeze disturbed the blossoms, nor was a human creature to be seen stirring, except where, turning the point of a jutting crag, a long line of villagers, clothed simply in white, moved slowly forward.

She noted the line of people, walking and chanting, or kneeling to appeal for a blessing on their fields and their work. The poorest walked in front with a banner, and lanterns. Then came rows of veiled women in white, then the men, followed by the curé, carrying a crucifix covered with a black scarf, flanked by two more lantern-bearers. Reflecting on this, Sarah moved from consideration of ancient mysteries to the psychology of participation in such processions, and their function as mutual support:

Though the primary object of these ceremonies is to obtain the fructification of the earth, yet those who partake in them become also linked in a sort of association to one another and contract or cement the obligation to reciprocal offices of kindness and charity. A remnant of such observances may still be traced in England among the gardeners, who on a particular day of the year go in regular order to church and hear a sermon. The grand and gloomy scenery of Savoy seems well calculated to heighten religious feelings . . .

She was serious, but could never be entirely solemn. The link between scenery and religious feelings reminded her, she said, of stories about the monastery of the Grande Chartreuse, where the monks lived in an isolation very different from these communal villages. They spent twelve hours out of twenty-four in church, never ate together, 'live always on potatoes, and, except on Thursdays, are never permitted in interchange a single word. Whether or no such life might fit one for death, it would have the effect of reconciling one to it.'

Sarah veered often between amusement and reflection. On the one hand she respected the ceremonies that bore witness to the long memory of a place and a community and to deep, even pre-Christian, beliefs; on the other hand, coming from a family of freethinkers, she was committed to enlightenment and education, the casting aside of superstition and fear. In Chambéry she met a bookseller's wife who complained of a new tax on paper, citing Rousseau's proof of the 'preference of the inhabitants for eating to reading, that for one bookseller's there were twenty restaurants'. Here too she saw the house of Rousseau's benefactor Madame de Warens, noting the inscription in memory of the 'eloquent, indignant and querulous enthusiast', and copying the final verse:

> *A la gloire, à la vérité*
> *Il osa consacrer sa vie*
> *Et fut toujours persecuté*
> *Par lui-même ou par l'envie.*[2]

Then they were off, like true Romantic travellers, crossing the Alps, a realm of avalanches and torrents and hurtling crags, and journeying slowly down through green valleys to the cypresses and red-tiled roofs of Italy.

The writer and art critic Anna Jameson, making the same journey a few years later, admitted that the landscape of Switzerland was grander and more majestic, but infinitely less 'poetical': 'Switzerland is not Italy; it is not the enchanting south. This soft balmy air, these myrtles, these orange-groves, palm trees; these cloudless skies, this bright blue sea, and sunny hills, all breathe of an enchanted land, "a land of Faery".'[3] Italy overwhelmed Sarah, as it did so many of the artists and poets who flocked there in these years, including Byron and Shelley and Keats. 1816 was the year that the Shelleys and Claire Clairmont stayed at Byron's villa on Lake Geneva, driven inside by the incessant rain of that dark summer, telling their ghost stories in the lashing storm, the cradle of *Frankenstein*. Two years later the same trio set off again to Italy, this time taking Allegra, Byron's daughter with Claire Clairmont, to her errant father. They travelled the same roads as the Losh sisters, and took lodgings in the same cities, including Naples and Florence. Their fellow lodgers in Florence, Sophia Stacey and her older travelling companion, were like Sarah and Katharine – British women travelling abroad on their own, confident and easy, absorbing everything they saw.

Italy was still in a ferment of political strife as the patchwork of different states and cities, their boundaries redrawn in their former pattern by the Congress of Vienna in 1815, tried to reclaim their identity in the aftermath of Napoleonic rule, resisting and resenting the new, creeping influence of Austria and the Habsburgs. Already there was talk of unification, an idea strongly opposed by the Pope, who feared the Papal States would lose their power. Sarah, always alert to political tensions, could not really escape them, even on this magical tour. But she concentrated instead on the life of the people, the architecture and the art. As they travelled across northern Italy, she saw the Lombardic churches of Pavia, Parma and Ancona, and the Byzantine basilicas of Ravenna, the mosaics and alabaster windows. Then they ventured inland, stopping at Spoleto in the foothills of the Apennines, a place that Shelley thought 'the most romantic city I ever saw', with its aqueduct between two mountains and its castle on the precipice overhanging the red roofs of the town.[4]

Rome, when they reached it, was a city full of bustle and building, dusty narrow streets opening on to grand vistas, shops where the sisters, like all eager tourists, bought prints, gold necklaces and mosaics to make into brooches. The streets here offered Sarah plenty of processions. Some were exuberant, colourful and rich with pageantry. Others were grim, like the execution of three robbers that Byron saw this May, 1817, watching determinedly through his opera glasses, finding it far more impressive than the 'ungentlemanly' English way, with 'the masqued priests; the half-naked executioners; the bandaged criminals; the black Christ and his banner; the scaffold; the soldiery; the slow procession, and the quick rattle and heavy fall of the axe; the splash of the blood, and the ghastliness of the exposed heads'.[5] Death, as well as beauty, marched the streets. And the processions were matched by the panoply of symbols, on ancient columns and new buildings, in temples and market squares. Among these were plenty of pinecones: the Pope carried a carved cone on his staff; a pinecone fountain stood outside the old church of St Marco, and the largest cone in the world, flanked by two peacocks, was found at the Vatican. This was the only original Roman fountain remaining in Rome, the Fontana della Pigna, dating from the first century AD, which had once stood next to the Temple of Isis in the Forum, spouting water from the top.

The classical city itself was in chaos, with great excavations ripping the smothering creepers and the dust of centuries from the ruins of the Forum and the Colosseum, and workmen tearing down the hovels and stalls that had grown up between the ruins. Artists crowded among the columns with their easels, but there were still sprawling allotments between the arches on the Palatine hill and market traders and fishmongers under the Roman porticoes. Visiting the artists' studios, Sarah was dismayed to see how the taste for picturesque topographical prints was banishing myth and mystery from their paintings. Landscapes and genre scenes were nudging aside 'loftier and severer' paintings of action and character: 'Saints are contemned, angels disbelieved, and devils no longer wondered at. The ancient Greeks and Romans cause ennui, the Saracens are nearly forgotten, and modern heroes are most unbecomingly dressed.'

She was equally irreverent about acclaimed works of the past. In the Sistine Chapel, she found Michelangelo's *Last Judgement* gloomy and horrible, 'so ludicrous that one fancies Buonarotti insensible himself to the deep feelings he intended to excite, sporting with the fears and credulity of the people till his art has the malice of the demons he exhibits', and she shocked their Italian guide by saying that 'the devils had the most satisfactory part in it'. Her condemnation was less of the style than the imagery, the cruelty of the idea of hell and damnation, and the use of art to instil fear in a credulous public. The *Last Judgement* showed, she felt, the inadequacy of the human mind to imagine a future existence. While Correggio had invented fit forms for messengers of paradise – 'bright, beneficent, and blissful' – Michelangelo merely 'evoked fiends and conjured hell to appal mankind to aspire to heaven'.

This anger, so resonantly Protestant, found in so many later writers, like George Eliot and Henry James, also chimed with Shelley's response at almost exactly the same time. Pressed by Leigh Hunt to see the Sistine Chapel, Shelley was horrified by the *Last Judgement*, finding it 'deficient in beauty & majesty both in conception & the execution . . . & it is a dull & wicked emblem of a dull & wicked thing'. Michelangelo, he fumed, had 'no sense of moral dignity and loveliness; and the energy for which he has been so much praised appears to me to be a certain rude, external, mechanical quality'.[6] Both responses are a mix of aesthetic and moral, but they are different, of course, in that Sarah fumed less against the idea of an ultimate despot than against the whole idea of cowing people into submission by the threat of an immortality of pain.

Although she admired the simplicities of pre-Renaissance art and architecture and disliked the extravagant convolutions of Mannerism, Sarah Losh was not a pre-Raphaelite ahead of her time, as her approval of Correggio and Guido Reni shows. Full of sentiment and feeling, Guido was the most admired painter of the day and Sarah was following fashion: here too she was in line with Shelley, who felt, as he looked at a Guido *Madonna* in Bologna, as if 'the spirit of a love almost unsupportable from its intensity were brooding and weighing down upon the soul, or whatever it is without which the material frame is inanimate and inexpressive'.[7] When Sarah saw Guido's fresco of Aurora in the Casino of the Borghese Palazzo Rospigliosi on the Quirinal hill she was moved by the energy and lightness of the goddess of dawn, rising against a landscape pared to essentials, where 'the contrast of earth and air is as strong as possible, yet their harmony is that of nature itself'. Her attention was riveted, she said, by 'the simple energy of the composition and the luminous tone'.

Guido Reni's Aurora fresco in Rome, which Sarah greatly admired.

She decided that Guido's skill lay in not attempting to represent the sublime, an impossible task, but in trying to find an image 'which creates in the mind analogous sensations'. She too aimed at simplicity and harmony, and her church would banish sacrifice and judgement and try instead to evoke 'analogous sensations' of awe at the harmony of nature and the dream of rebirth, like dawn following night. She may also have remembered the way the classical facade of the Casino itself incorporated slabs from Roman sarcophagi, retelling myths of love and death and immortal souls.

As they travelled south, Sarah's mood could shift abruptly from dry amusement to lyrical immersion in place. At the port of Terracina, where the Volscian hills meet the sea, they endured a supper 'of rice swimming in water, peas swimming in oil, and fish swimming in goat's milk, with cheese apples and fennel root' washed down with wine 'literally impregnated' by flies. But afterwards, in their rooms, she and Katharine opened the window:

and so mild was the air that we sat long listening to the sounds of the waves which, shining like silver in the moonbeams, dashed with violence against the rocky shore. It was such a night as that which Virgil assigns to Aeneas when he sailed from this very shore where Caieta still gives her name to Gaita.

'*Aspirant aurae in noctem: nec candida cursum*
Luna negat: splendet tremulo sub lumine pontus.'

Aeneas sails on after burying Caieta, his old nurse: 'the winds breathe fair in the night, nor does the silver moon oppose his voyage: under her trembling light the ocean shines'.[8] And the sisters moved on too, further south, to Naples.

To the British, Naples was a place of legend: mystery mixed with squalor, faith with scepticism, glamour with grime. It was the great city of the Greek colonies, the Roman port, the modern city where shops crammed with goods nudged against churches and palaces, medieval, Renaissance, Baroque. For five hundred years the city had ruled its own realm, the kingdom of Naples:

now, in 1816, that kingdom was united with Sicily and Naples was capital of the Two Sicilies. After the wars it was full of artists eager to paint the *lazzaroni*, the Neapolitan peasants, and with sculptors keen to learn the neoclassical style.

William had business here and in Sicily, which was a key source of sulphur for the alkali works, and the sisters were free to roam the noisy streets, like Anna Jameson, who admitted, reluctantly, that Naples had no parallel on earth:

Viewed from the sea it appears like an amphitheatre of palaces, temples and castles, raised one above another, by the wand of a necromancer: viewed within, Naples gives me the idea of a vast Bartholomew fair. No street in London is ever so crowded as I have seen the streets of Naples.

The crowds never ceased, day or night, and all daily life was carried on in the open:

all those minute details of domestic life, which, in England, are confined within the sacred precincts of *home*, are here displayed to public view. Here people buy and sell, and work, wash, wring, brew, bake, fry, dress, eat, drink, sleep, &c. &c. all in the open streets. We see every hour, such comical, indescribable, appalling sights; such strange figures, such wild physiognomies, picturesque dresses, attitudes and groups.[9]

If Rome is the heart of Italy, it has been said, Naples is its soul. We do not know what Sarah saw there, but almost every week brought a new festival, a new procession: every September huge crowds flocked to see the Miracle of St Januarius, their patron saint, whose dried blood turned liquid in the presence of holy relics. Even a recently built church could seem laden with codes. In the chapel of Sansevero the famous statue of the veiled Christ seemed to breathe from within the white marble, and the allegorical groups of the prince's family were strikingly suggestive: 'Modesty', with the curiously immodest veiled mother; 'Disillusion', with the repentant profligate father shrugging off a net, which could be read as man escaping sin or, in Masonic terms, as 'Liberty and Man of the Enlightenment fighting against obscurantism'.¹⁰ The chapel's creator, the Prince of Sansevero, Raimondo di Sangro, was an inventor, a naturalist, a scientist, and a leading Mason, Grand Master of the Rite of Memphis and Misraim. His baroque extravaganza rose, literally, above bodily mortality. In the crypt were two unnerving anatomical models, made of beeswax, silk and wire, but long thought to be the corpses of his servants. This was another side of Naples, beneath whose streets ran hundreds of tunnels, Greek and Roman sewers and aqueducts, and catacombs packed with bones.

Sarah was always moved by the world beneath, by fossils from the mines or by Roman stones found beneath the fields. But nothing she had seen, not in Naples or Rome, or Terracina, compared to Pompeii. Pompeii stunned her, took her by surprise. The site had been excavated slowly for a century or more, but under the Napoleonic rule, when Joseph Bonaparte and then Murat were successive kings of Naples, teams of archaeologists had uncovered areas not shown in the prints published in Britain: the house of Salliusto, the house of the Faun, the forum and the basilica. Murat's wife Caroline, Napoleon's sister, poured her money into the project, commissioned a survey, corresponded with experts across Europe and commissioned guide books, complete with maps. Under her patronage the architect Charles François Mazois compiled his great work, *Les ruines de Pompeii*, whose volumes with their wonderful engravings appeared slowly over twenty-five years.

Visitors came loaded with new books and maps, and eager guides took them on romantic walks through the tombs and monuments, or put on grisly shows, mixing skeletons with the charred remains. As Sarah walked through the villa of Diomedes and the temple of Jupiter above the forum, the site was a revelation. Pompeii was a domestic city, with its houses, kitchens, shops and streets, its walls painted with ferns and, yes, pinecones, lotuses

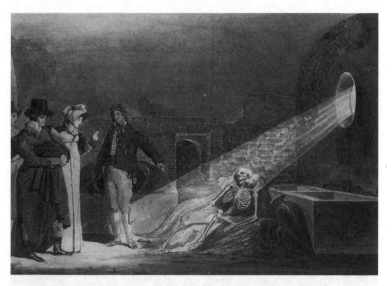

Guides entertained visitors to Pompeii with specially staged scenes
of grisly death.

and water lilies, and its household altars carved with eggs, dates,
figs and nuts.[11] But beyond the house and temples, when she
climbed to a point where she could see the ancient site laid out
before her, with the bay of Naples beyond and Vesuvius behind,
Sarah was overwhelmed. 'The view from the upper ranges of the
amphitheatre', she wrote, 'exceeded in beauty, grandeur and fascination all that we had ever seen or could have imagined.' As
she basked in the sun, gazing at the circle of mountains, sea and
islands, she could feel the buried city beneath her feet and wondered how its citizens could reject this natural sublimity for the
brutal, man-made amphitheatre and 'the writhings of agonised
conflict'. Further south at Paestum, with its great temples in the
plain beside the sea, she imagined a race long gone, whose history
had perished so entirely that

Lizards crawl unheeded over the symbol of the Syren which is still
seen on the solitary gateway . . . It seems as if Fate had spared a casual

trophy of human art and of human glory to remind succeeding ages that the feebler works they produce will still more entirely and more speedily decay.

Pompeii, the view across the plain in 1817

Sarah was a stylist who relished balance, enjoyed the rhythm of her sentences, and meant to make an impact. When James Losh read her journals some five years later, noting her 'indefatigable' attention to art and architecture, he felt that if they were published they would be 'one of the most amusing and instructive works on Italy' of recent years.[12] But if they were 'amusing' – marked by her inability to tolerate fools – they were also profoundly romantic. Everything she saw in Pompeii or Paestum spoke to her of transience, of the wiping out of great ambitions and achievements of the past, as in Shelley's 'Ozymandias', published a year after their Italian trip. Memories of Naples, where the British stayed in villas with cool loggias and shady gardens looking across the blue bay with its white-sailed ships to the volcano beyond, and where Katharine read on the shore while Sarah sketched her, would stay with her always.

10 Mullioned Windows

Back home in Wreay, the Losh sisters settled into a routine of reading, drawing, gardening, paying visits to relations and friends. They had one particularly good friend nearby, Jane Christian Blamire, who was now living a couple of miles away at Thackwood. She had moved here in 1814 to live with her brother William, standing by him when he decided to become a farmer rather than choose a professional career, although their joint decision did not please their mother: 'perhaps I think it is rather a pity', she wrote, that 'your mutual talents should be buried in such an obscure place'.[1] But the retirement was not for ever: fifteen years later William re-emerged to become high sheriff of Cumberland, an influential MP and the first Tithe Commissioner. Jane was a cheery soul, clever and warm-hearted. 'She was rather short', a relative remembered, with 'dark hair, quick bright eyes of dark bluish colour, with a rosy complexion – a cheerful, bright manner & step – an expressive face, which when sad showed strongly the change of feeling. She was very clever, with decided, quick judgment.'[2] William, the writer insisted, was the love of Jane's life, a closeness mirroring that of Sarah and Katharine.

Such sibling bonds were common in their day, a pattern seen with Jane Austen and her sister Cassandra. The closeness could vary from Dorothy Wordsworth's fierce dependency on William to the easy-going devotion of Jane and William Blamire, or the hard-working partnership of the astronomers William and Caroline Herschel. With Sarah and Katharine the bond was one of lifelong companionship: they did everything together, Sarah cleverer but more reserved, Katharine easy and outgoing. Through the gulf of time and in the absence of letters Katharine becomes Sarah's shadow, absorbed into her older sister's story, but in her lifetime she was much loved by her uncles and aunts and cousins for her sweet temper and adaptability. The sisters did not, of course, always get on perfectly and every now and then there were tensions and rows, something their father recognised when he made his will, leaving the property to them in equal, independent shares and saying that if they quarrelled about its disposal they should each choose a valuer, and a neutral umpire should be appointed. But no such thing was needed, and they ran the estate in the old way, sharing the tasks.

At Christmas 1817, their uncle James visited Woodside, where he found 'a pleasing young lady of the name of Inge was staying there'. On Christmas Eve he and the sisters went to Carlisle to pay Christmas calls: 'Carlyles, Paleys, Dacres, Clarkes, Lodges, Briscoes, Andersons etc'. James came over regularly to the Carlisle assizes, and there were frequent family visits, back and forth between Wreay and Newcastle. The stagecoaches left Carlisle market-place at six in the morning, swinging along the turnpike road, stopping in Brampton and then climbing slowly up to Haltwhistle, over the moors, before heading down the valley of the Tyne to Haydon Bridge and Hexham, where the horses were changed. The coach then rattled on to Corbridge and along the hills above the river until the windmills and market gardens on the outskirts of Newcastle came into sight.

The Losh families often made this journey, with James's boys spending occasional holidays in Wreay and the older Woodside girls staying for a month or more at a time in Newcastle. Sometimes the sisters were away for longer stays with friends in Bristol and the south. It was a trouble-free time, apart from worry over Margaret's health. In 1818 she stayed for some months with James and Cecilia in Jesmond, feeling frail and ill, and the following January at Woodside James noted how worn down she looked: 'She never had a strong constitution, though she has the appearance of good health. She now looks thin and old and seems willing to retire from the world and sink into the habits of an elderly person.'[3] For the next three years there were alarms about her health, but they need not have worried; she would live to a fine old age.

One of the first things Sarah and Katharine did when they returned from the Continent in 1817 was to draft an application to divert the footpath that led across the park in front of their northern lawn and down through the fields to Newbiggin Hall. Instead, they suggested, this could be moved half a mile nearer to Wreay – thus helping the villagers – out of sight behind the trees to the south. Their view was then clear across the ha-ha and the park with its clumps of trees, towards Carlisle and the Scottish hills beyond.

That done, they set about making their home their own and 'improving' it, as each generation had done. In her twenties Sarah combined her love of poetry, of Scott's novels and the ballads and tales of her homeland, and the churches and castles she knew, with a more precise interest in architecture. She had grown up at a time when there was an increasing vogue for books of topographical prints, beginning with John Britton's *Beauties of England and Wales*, published in weekly numbers from 1801 and bought by the gentry in their thousands. Britton went on to produce the *Architectural Antiquities of Great Britain*, which appeared in five lavishly illustrated volumes between 1807 and 1826.[4] In the first volumes he presented, he said, a motley selection of 'picturesque' scenes and details, but as time went on he found that 'men of science' had 'expressed a wish to possess a more systematic display of the rise, progress and characteristics of the ancient Architecture of England'.⁵ The later volumes placed his plans, elevations and views in chronological order, 'covering all aspects of the building'.

Sarah and Katharine had no desire to turn their house into a stately home, but they were interested in the efforts of contemporary architects to turn buildings back in time, making them resemble something from a previous era. The Scottish expert John Claudius Loudon, who began by publishing books on gardening and agriculture (his *Encyclopedia of Gardening* appeared in 1822, and he started the *Gardener's Magazine* four years later), had now moved on to buildings, for country as well as town: cottages, farms and villas. Like Loudon, the Losh sisters started with their garden, making a 'Pompeian court' on the eastern slopes and building a thatched cottage, or hermitage, under the spreading trees. The hermitage was now a little unfashionable but it was a refuge to read in and enjoy the view. Everywhere they planted shrubs and decorative trees. The road along the edge of their land was like a green tunnel, with hedges of hawthorn and holly. Behind them one could glimpse laurels, yews and laburnums, rambling roses and honeysuckle, silver firs and unusual pines, as well as the oaks John Losh had planted.

Behind this barrier of green, Sarah and Katharine worked on the house, enlarging it and adding rooms, creating space and light. They found plenty of history as they worked. In the basement were massive walls of cobblestones and clay, remnants of the first house, with 'dungeon like chambers' where stolen cattle could be hidden, and steep stone steps 'leading to some upper place of refuge or espial, and a stout oaken bar, sliding back into the wall's thickness' to pull across the gate.⁶ Round this core, you could see how the house had grown. First came the yeoman's kitchen, with its great Tudor arch over the fire; then the broad Jacobean staircase with its dark, heavy balustrade; then the formal Georgian entrance hall, with a straight passage ahead and parlours on each side, and the marble fireplaces and stucco work added by a

The marble reliefs of Sarah's parents, John and Isabella Losh, were sculpted by David Dunbar for the mausoleum. The portrait of Sarah was drawn by the Carlisle apothecary T. H. Carrick, later a professional artist.

Carlisle from without and within. The romantic view of the walled city and castle, seen from the road to Scotland across the Eden bridge, and the busy market-place, with the cross and town hall, and cathedral beyond.

Cottages at Wreay, on the lane down to the river Petteril, and the steep lane at Brisco, leading down to St Ninian's well, which Sarah restored. Her own home, Woodside, lay between the two villages.

The mortuary chapel, based on the church in the dunes at Perranzabuloe, Cornwall, and the male and female heads at each side of the door, sculpted by young Thomas Hindson.

Excursions into the past: the winged-turtle gargoyle and the alabaster cut-out windows based on fossils found in Cumbrian and Northumbrian coal-mines.

The west facade of St Mary's Church Wreay,
and the eastern end with the apse.

The door and windows in the west facade, rich with carving of lotus flowers, pinecones, fossils, insects and birds.

A kaleidoscope of colour in the large windows, made by William Wailes of Newcastle, and a waterlily and poppy shining among the fragments in the small windows above.

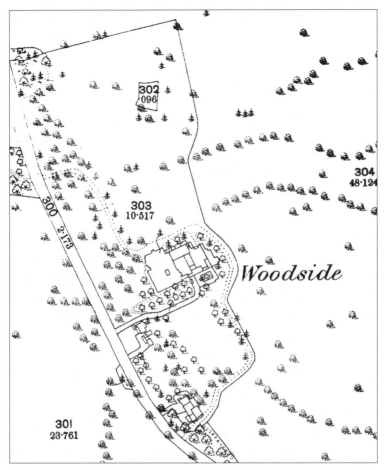

The Woodside grounds near the house, showing the gardens that Sarah and Katharine planned and cherished.

young squire, perhaps Sarah's grandfather, on his return from a Grand Tour.

The sisters' most dramatic change was the remodelling of the south front. This was an age where domestic architects often turned to the past, in the spirit of the 'Merrie England' that had become so popular during the war, fostered by the novels of Scott, who gave Gothic architecture a central role in *The Monastery* and *Kenilworth*, in 1820 and 1821. Aristocrats and *nouveaux riches* merchants were turning their houses into Gothic piles, often being richly mocked in the process. In 1821, when Cobbett arrived at Mr Montague's park at Burghclere in Hampshire, he wrote:

Of all the ridiculous things I ever saw in my life this place is the most ridiculous . . . I wonder how long this sickly, this childish taste is to remain? I do not know who the gentleman is. I suppose he is some honest person from the 'Change . . . and that these *gothic arches* are to denote *the antiquity of his origin.*[7]

The Losh sisters had no need to worry about the antiquity of their origin, but they did share the desire to conjure up the family house of the past. Woodside's Georgian facade was reworked in light stone from Shawk Foot (also called Chalk) quarry near Dalston, and given mullioned windows with Gothic inner frames, so that it evoked the Tudor house of the time of the Catholic martyr, 'the Blessed Christopher Robinson'. In this they were absolutely in tune with the times, if not ahead, as several influential books appeared in the 1820s and 30s recommending the Tudor style.[8] A stone frieze, modelled with rosettes, topped the Woodside facade. Seventy years later, the magazine *Building News* was full of admiration. 'The sunny front', its article read, 'is entirely of Ashlar, a creamy white freestone from the nearby quarry of Chalk – and was added to the then existing mansion before the year 1835, and is, therefore a most remarkable revival of Domestic Gothic architecture designed and carried out under the personal superintendence of a most accomplished lady, an artist and her own architect.'[9]

Certainly, the facade was handsome, but Sarah could never reproduce a past style without modifying it, adding a personal signature. At each end of the frieze of rosettes, as if to place the sisters' mark, two wise stone owls took up their posts. The carving of the owls, heavy yet full of character, is very like that of the

Woodside in the 1880s, with further additions to Sarah and Katharine's Tudor-style facade. The carved owls are circled on each end of the frieze below the roof.

gargoyles later carved for the church. These were proud decorations, the birds of Minerva, goddess of wisdom.

Inside, Sarah and Katharine added three large halls and rooms in different styles, a panoply of romantic themes. The North Hall had a gallery added, running round it, and a wrought-iron lantern hung from the ceiling, like a manorial hall from a historical novel. On the walls were hung pictures, some of which may have come from their trips abroad, like the *Entombment* by the seventeenth-century Carlo Maratta, or the landscape attributed to Salvator Rosa, and some that might well have belonged to their father, like the print from Joseph Farington's *Views of the Lakes of Cumberland*, of 1785.[10]

The Middle Hall was an even wilder extravaganza. It too had a new gallery, but, as recorded in the catalogue for a sale at the turn of the century, all the walls were covered with weapons: an Indian sword, two scimitars, two dress swords, two fencing foils, an old crossbow and a flintlock gun, as well as daggers, duelling pistols and powder flasks. It is strange to imagine the sisters hanging up these bloody trophies, and perhaps Sarah's heirs were to blame. But it was the fashion in the 1820s, when the sisters were decorating their house, to have armour and weapons on show, and the motley array suggests that these were brought back by Losh relatives over the years, or by friends, for instance the sons of the Senhouse, Spedding and Hudleston families, who served in India and the Far East. The effect was similar to that which Walter Scott himself created at Abbotsford, in his attempt to make his own home look like 'an old English hall such as a squire of yore dwelt in'.[II] In the gallery above stood the bronze bust of Napoleon, surrounded in later years by a circle of family portraits: the beautiful sisters, Frances and Alice Wilkinson; the Losh men, John, James, George and William; Robert and Margaret, painted by Romney. Elsewhere there were portraits of friends, political allies and national heroes: Henry Howard of Corby, Henry Brougham and Charles Grey, and the Duke of Wellington.

And so it went on, a house packed with treasures from home and abroad: a Roman brass lamp, a 'Bacchante' by Poussin, an Elizabethan inlaid chest, Dutch and Turkish carpets, Dresden china and Louis Quatorze clocks. Amid the baronial grandeur there were comfortable spaces, including a drawing room with Chippendale furniture, a morning room and a small boudoir. Looking back to his childhood, Sarah's eventual heir, James Arlosh, remembered it as a warm house, every room different, and especially loved the library, 'with its rich ceiling of carven beams and rafters, and its coloured shadows flung now and again by the shifting sunbeams through the upper lights of coloured glass'. Sarah remained a voracious reader, and there were good booksellers in Carlisle, favourites being Charles Thurnam, who opened his shop in 1816 in English Street, and Samuel Jefferson in Scotch Street, who was also a prolific publisher of works on local history and antiquities.

An image of a galleried hall, strongly influenced by Walter Scott's novels, that the Victorians associated with 'olden times'.

By contrast to the library and the other downstairs rooms, the bedrooms were plain, and so were the servants' quarters. The house was large and despite the fires in every room draughts whistled down the long corridors. Ten years after they began their alterations, perhaps thinking about the winter ahead, the two sisters turned up unexpectedly when James was taking tea at William's house in Newcastle: 'Their object seems to be to consult their Uncle William as to the best mode of warming their house.'[12]

There is no mention of an architect or designer in connection with this work: the sisters made their own plans. It was with her house, the domestic space, that Sarah first expressed a practical, hands-on interest in building and in the crafts of stonework, glass and carving. She learnt from the local mason, the experienced William Hindson. But she also, at some point, taught herself to work in wood and stone, a new mark of independence and difference from her peers. On her visits to the Continent, she would have seen work by women *sculpteuses* that was just beginning to find a place in public: busts and reliefs, usually against the wall or in niches rather than taking up prominent space.[13] Women, who were supposed to spend their time on embroidery and watercolours and pressing flowers, could also, it seemed, learn the 'harder' crafts. In terms of modelling, there was a long tradition of women working in wax, but Sarah now learned to model in clay, which was far more unusual – and messy – for a well-brought-up woman. She was rich enough to fit up an outhouse as a studio and to employ a teacher, a local artist or sculptor, perhaps from the Carlisle Academy, and she also knew skilled craftsmen in the villages around who could teach her to work in wood. In a sale after her death, one of the small items on the auction list was a set of woodworker's tools.

In their improvements, Sarah and Katharine were keeping up with their friends and neighbours, like Henry Howard and his son Philip, whom James found dining at Woodside in August 1822. He was proud of what his nieces had done. After a visit to Hutton John he wrote disdainfully of 'the curious old house which had been most tastelessly modernised. Some part of the ancient windows etc remain and resemble very much what my niece Sara has effected with so much taste and pains at Woodside.'[14] Woodside compared well, too, with the new mansions on the other side of the city in 'the *Dukery*', the houses of cotton magnates, 'some of the nouveaux riches at Carlisle'. Even the new Edmond Castle, which the architect Robert Smirke had designed at Hayton, near Brampton, for the Graham family, was 'something in the *Collegiate* style, with, in my opinion, somewhat too much of Gothic ornaments'.[15]

Despite all the upheavals and comings and goings of builders and decorators, life at Woodside was little changed from John's time; the old servants still carried out their duties, though rather more slowly, and with more grumbling, as they grew older. Some had gone now. 'I miss poor Adam, the old butler (who died some weeks ago) very much,' wrote James in May 1821: 'he was a very valuable servant, honest, intelligent and sincerely attached to the family.'[16] Others still went on stoutly into old age, like Bella, who stayed with them nearly thirty years, and Nanny Blaylock, whom James visited every year. She was living with her brother Bill, who had also been a Woodside servant, and James was pleased to find that in her mid-eighties Nanny was alert and happy, could walk five miles or more without tiring, and had not a single white hair on her head.

The Woodside women managed well, with their income from the alkali works balancing the decline in rents and farm profits, but it was a dark time for many landowners across the country. Robert Keen, an agent writing to his Cumbrian employer at Candlemas, February 1820, about her London property, explained how hard it was to collect the rents: 'This Winter has put on a Gloomy aspect – the intense frost has been very destructive to the Vegetable World (as was never before remembered), the Turnips Cabbage Plants and Brocoli are Dearly Destroyed – it has also been fatal to many People.'[17] In January the fields around Wreay were frozen hard. From Hutton-in-the-Forest, further up the valley, the squire's wife Elizabeth Hudleston wrote to their son Andrew, who had just landed in Calcutta, saying that they could not recall such weather. The land had been covered with snow for six weeks and they were desperate to sell their timber at Hesket, determined to have it cut down and new planted.[18]

The late spring brought fine weather; the farmers settled in their crops, the peas and beans were planted, and all hands worked to repair fences after the ravages of the winter. The summer too was kind, and in July, when the hay was cut, the crops looked promising. But the good harvests hardly helped. Farming, trade and manufacturing were in the doldrums, not improved by another terrible winter, in which the mails and the goods wagons were constantly delayed by snow and the ruts frozen hard in the roads. At Candlemas the following year, Robert Keen found his task even harder. He was faced with evicting two families, which he was 'very reluctant in Doing if possible if it could be avoided', since one of these families had ten children.

The Loshes escaped the worst: if anything, they prospered. At last, on the death of his uncle Joseph Liddell, James had his own land in Cumberland, inheriting Moorpark near Burgh-by-Sands, along with shares in Hexham Brewery and Tynemain coal mine, which finally relieved him of financial anxiety. In Newcastle the alkali and iron works were thriving, especially after the Loshes' Cumbrian ally, John Christian Curwen, persuaded the government to abandon the salt tax in 1822. Curwen's concern was to get rid of a tax that hit the poor, but its removal was a huge boost to the alkali makers. The only brother still suffering from money problems was George. In the spring of 1820, when James was in Carlisle on business connected with the local elections, he drove over to see his new property at Moorpark, taking Margaret with him, and used all his persuasion on her. She 'readily agreed', he said, 'to my proposal to give up to George's family what was left to her by Mr Liddell, reserving only £100 a year for herself'.[19]

James enjoyed being a landowner, even in difficult conditions. That summer he saw his Cumberland land agent, went over his plantations, marking trees for sale, and sold off some detached farms and fields. The farm sale took place in the evening, began slowly, and before it 'strong punch was supplied to the whole party in great abundance': no bids at all came to start with until 'the liquor beginning to warm the persons intending to buy, they went on very briskly indeed'.[20] Most of the buyers were 'statesmen', the fiercely independent yeomen of the area with small landed estates. Although James was initially patronising, noticing the farmers' uncouthness and canny dealings, he grew to understand them better, as Sarah did. At a dinner for the cattle show a couple of years later, he enjoyed himself among them: 'They seemed as far as I could judge, to be shrewd, intelligent and active men, with more book-learning, as to farming, the corn trade etc. than I expected to find among them.'[21]

When he toured the Lakes in the late summer of 1821, James wrote rapturously about the beauty spots of Lodore and Borrowdale, and carefully noted all the fine properties and 'improvements'. He also visited Wordsworth, and although they steered clear of any political discussion, James then wrote to him amicably about their differences and received a long reply, in which Wordsworth explained bravely and honestly why he had modified his ideas about France and the war, why he approved of severe restrictions on the liberty of the press and of holding back from concessions to Catholics, and had doubts about parliamentary reform. This rare personal statement from Wordsworth, who refused to reply to criticism in the press, was a measure of his respect for his old friend.[22]

In the early 1820s, despite his new Cumbrian interests, James seemed to be on every committee in Newcastle: the Literary and Philosophical Society, the Antiquarian Society and the newly founded Horticultural Society, passing on news, garden tips and details of lectures. He even uncovered and attempted to preserve the ruined Norman chapel of St Mary's on land he had bought in Jesmond.[23] At the same time he was campaigning for the emancipation of slaves in the West Indies and United States and, in Britain, for schooling for the poor. He was not entirely convinced by Robert Owen's report on his model community and schools, but he pored over Henry Brougham's plans for education and became a keen supporter of his Society for the Diffusion of Useful Knowledge. The brilliant, erratic and charming Brougham, one of the founders of the *Edinburgh Review,* became a lifelong friend. Another radical lawyer and anti-slavery campaigner (and eventually Lord Chancellor), he was also a small landowner near Penrith.

Horrified by the Peterloo massacre in 1819, James lobbied hard for reform in the hard-fought elections of 1820, his antigovernment stance intensified by disgust at George IV's treatment of his wife, Caroline of Brunswick, who was eloquently defended at her trial by Brougham.[24] James campaigned actively in Newcastle and in Carlisle, where the election brought 'trifling riots' but ended in triumph, with the independent candidate William James, who lived at Barrock Lodge across the valley from Woodside, trouncing the Lowther interest. Carlisle workers stuck up portraits of 'Billy James the Radical', and other heroes such as Brougham and Harry 'Orator' Hunt, over alehouse doors. The news was not so good from Westmorland, where the Lowthers were still riding high, defeating Brougham and winning both county seats. Elizabeth Hudleston reported from Hutton: 'it is said though with what truth I cannot tell, that Lord Lonsdale made all his Stabel Boys freemen & others who were all kept in reserve, to come up, when Mr Brougham's other voters were at a distance'.[25] The margin was narrow, only sixty-four votes, and when the celebratory chairing of the new MPs took place the *Carlisle Journal* reported that 'it was more like a funeral than a chairing of members of Parliament, without the usual joy expressed on such occasions'.[26]

The following year brought a new regime. In July the former prince regent was crowned as George IV in a lavish ceremony, a staggering display when half the country was starving. The foolish pageant, thought James, 'may add to the deep feeling which pervades the country, that some great changes are necessary'.[27] In Carlisle, there were milder excitements, including a new Society for the Encouragement of Fine Arts and the arrival at Paul Nixon's new marble works of the young Scot David Dunbar, a pupil of the celebrated sculptor Sir Francis Chantrey. Dunbar, the *Patriot* told its readers, 'has in hand several models for Sculpture, which have attracted a great many visitors and are universally admired' and were bound to 'command the liberal patronage of our nobility and gentry'.[28] In 1822, with the painter Matthew Nutter, Dunbar was one of the secretaries to the new Academy of Arts, of which Philip

Howard was president. His work was known for its calm dignity. When Elizabeth Stevenson – Elizabeth Gaskell after her marriage – was staying in Newcastle with the Rev. William Turner, Dunbar sculpted a bust of her, resulting in much teasing. 'Mr Losh told my cousins in town that he thought my bust so very like Napoleon – do you?' she wrote to her friend Harriet Carr.[29] Some years later, when Dunbar had his studio refitted, the local paper noted that 'among those who have been sculptured by him' were: 'The Honourable Lady Ravensworth; the Honourable Georgina Liddell . . . Miss Losh, Woodside★; Miss C. Losh★; Miss Fanny Brandling; and many other darlings, at home and abroad.'[30] The asterisk denoted 'those sculptured in the purest marble from the caves of Carrara'.

Sarah and Katharine dutifully took their place among the gentry darlings and attended the assizes balls although they were now in

Carlisle Academy in Finkle Street, where David Dunbar worked and local artists exhibited.

their thirties, comfortably out of the marriage market. At their dinner parties they notably included single women among their guests, counter to normal practice. To Woodside for dinner, noted James in October 1820, 'The Dean of Carlisle and his wife, Miss Hodson, Mr James, Miss Dand, Miss E. Carlyle, Mr Irwin and Mr Gaskin. We had a pleasant cheerful day, the dean being a good humoured, unaffected man, and all the party apparently satisfied with each other.'[31]

The sisters were satisfied, too, with their income, although every now and then there was a lurch in their affairs. In February 1822 the north was ravaged by floods, which caused great damage in Carlisle, and three months later, briefly, they thought they faced ruin when the East Lothian Bank stopped trading. This was a small country bank, founded twelve years before, and most of its investors were local farmers. The crisis was caused when their chief cashier, Borthwick, aged only twenty-two, absconded with all the funds: to add colour to the drama, it was discovered that he had planned to kidnap the directors, imprison them in 'well-ventilated wine-puncheons' and pack them off on a trade ship to Danzig. Although this wild plan went unfulfilled, he did manage to escape to America, and his escapade spurred a rush of local verses:

> A sad confusion has happened here,
> By William Borthwick our cashier,
> He's run away with a' our gear –
> A roguish turn.
> Which many ane, I am apt to fear,
> Have cause to mourn.[32]

Although the partners rapidly put together a rescue package, losing their own fortunes in the process, they still owed over £60,000. A particular problem in Carlisle was that two-thirds of the city's trade was done in Scottish notes, and the collapse caused the stoppage of the Carlisle Bank of Elliot and Forster, who had circulated the East Lothian notes: this was where the sisters had placed much of their money. 'I know that my nieces *may be* liable to a large amount for Mr Elliot', wrote James glumly.[33] On 19 April, John Elliot placed a notice in the *Carlisle Journal* suspending payment to creditors and customers. Once again, James stepped in, employing a Mr Norman to act as agent for the sisters at £40 a year, and opening an account at Forster's bank. This was a decade of bank scares: in June 1825, seventy banks suspended payments in panic. Although most of them slowly repaid their customers over the next four years, this led to an examination of the banking system in England in 1826. Credit was tight, and the main source of loans within the Losh family was William's increasingly profitable firm of Losh, Wilson & Bell.

Although money was scarcer, the sisters still travelled to London, Bristol and possibly to France. News also came from abroad. In 1822, William Thain's regiment had sailed for the West Indies, a notorious deathtrap for British soldiers: during their years there, the 33rd lost over five hundred men from malaria, yellow fever and dysentery. But William said nothing of this. Instead he wrote home of the flying fish he saw on his crossing from Jamaica to Antigua, of the forests and the mountains, and the rain. Like so many men of his time, he too had now become a naturalist, keeping a rain gauge and a record of the temperature, which he sent back to James Losh. He made notes on the pepper plants in his garden, collected and sent home shells, and was determined to get to grips with Phillips and Conybeare's books on geology. 'I have a very nice collection of silicons & agatized fossils, for which the island is remarkably distinguished,' he told his father, 'and specimens of petrified woods of tropical kinds, principally of the Palm tribe.'[34] If polished, he thought, they might make beautiful ornaments. Just the kind of thing to add to the collection that now filled Woodside, with its book-filled rooms, its paintings and vases, and new mullioned windows.

11 The Misses Losh

As the years passed, the dynamic of the large Losh family altered. The younger generation left home and a bewildering array of relationships evolved. The first to move on was George's eldest daughter Mary, who married an Irishman, James Kemmis, in Paris in 1817. To make things more complicated marriages were often family affairs. On a July morning in 1820 St Andrew's church in Newcastle saw a double wedding, of James's daughter Cecilia to her cousin William Gale and of George's daughter Fanny (who had been living with James and Cecilia at Jesmond) to Francis Hutchinson of Newcastle. Two years later, in March 1822, William's daughter Margaret married her cousin Spencer Boyd, the laird of Penkill, son of the third of the beautiful Wilkinson sisters, and that August her sister Alice married James Anderson, from a well-known Newcastle family of Baltic traders. Margaret, Sarah and Katharine usually followed these courtships with a benign interest – Cecilia and Fanny had stayed for a month at Woodside, with friends including Cecilia's fiancé, the year before they married – but their cousin James's marriage was particularly important to them because they planned to make him their heir, and in 1827 they took a decided, unexplained dislike to poor Maria Bigge, whom he hoped to marry. Maria died during the engagement, but their uncle James was hurt for a while over their apparent coolness towards him and the Jesmond family.[1]

While their cousins grew up and married, Sarah and Katharine, having rejected all suitors, were inseparable. In 1825, James wrote admiringly of Sarah's 'great powers of mind' but worried about her single status, and felt at the same time that her brilliance could have shone more brightly. The problem, he thought, was that 'a languid constitution and an over delicacy of feeling have prevented her from taking that rank in society to which she is, in all respects, justly entitled'.[2]

In his own family, his eldest son, the quiet, bereaved James, struggled at Trinity College, Cambridge, before heading for Lincoln's Inn to follow his father into the law. The younger ones posed more problems. Baldwin had always been lively and wayward: an advertisement in the Newcastle papers when he was eight, describing him as wearing his 'blue Jacket, Nankeen Pantaloons, and a white Hat' and last seen in Jesmond Fields with an umbrella in his hand, offered a reward for anyone who brought him home.[3] Now he was about to join the army, the start of a far from glorious career. Meanwhile John was facing rustication from Cambridge for failing his exams, but ironically, unlike Baldwin, he would have a fine career in the Indian army, eventually becoming military auditor of Madras. The younger sons, Robert and William Septimus, left Durham School together in 1824. James planned to send them to George's family at Rouen and then to Germany, to learn languages and 'acquire a competent knowledge of mathematics, chemistry and general literary, before they begin the practical part of a merchant's occupation'.[4] Both went to Germany for nearly two years, from 1826 to 1828, and then, at different times, returned to France.

While the family shook itself into new patterns, in the country at large there were faint signs of recovery. Slowly, the price of agricultural products rose, interest rates fell and manufacturing started up again, while legislative changes allowed trade unions to develop more freely. Even the perennially worried James was more sanguine, hoping – although it proved a false hope – that at last the government had begun to employ the 'sensible and liberal methods' that the opposition had been suggesting for so long. 'The public attention seems now awakened and governments every where are compelled to try to improve the condition of their subjects, tho' *as yet*, obstinately refuse to grant them any extension of political rights.'[5]

Sarah was as radical in her political views as her father and her uncles, and as ecumenical, disregarding differences of belief or dogma. Henry Lonsdale, who knew her in later years, noted that he saw at her table 'Unitarians and Episcopalians, Catholics and Christians unattached'.[6] But the culture around her was less tolerant. When the first bill for Catholic emancipation was being debated 'No popery' handbills were posted on Newcastle trees. In Carlisle, the prejudice was racist as well as religious. By the 1820s Scottish and Irish immigrants made up nearly half of the city's population, prompting a typical outburst in the *Carlisle Journal* in 1826: 'Never in the memory of man were crimes so abundant in the North of England as they are now in the neighbourhood of Carlisle. The current talk is of robbery, robbery . . . We are now, indeed, becoming like the inhabitants of ANOTHER IRELAND!'[7]

The robberies were born of renewed poverty, intensified by another terrible winter in 1826. In good times work at the cotton-spinning factories and calico printers' went on day and night, employing men, women and children.[8] William Farish, who worked at the Loshes' calico printers in Denton Holme, began on the bobbin at the age of eight, moving to the loom two years later. Hard as it was, the families needed the money. Now, however, out-of-work weavers were paid a few pence a day to build a walk along the north of the city, from the castle to the Eden Bridges, still called 'the Weavers' Bank'. Resentment was fierce and during turbulent elections that year, a mob captured the Tory candidate, Sir Philip Musgrave, forced him to weave at a loom, and ducked his supporters and corporation members in the mill dam. When troops intervened and fired over the heads of the crowd, a woman and child were killed.[9] Two years later the town had a small police force, but for years it was too dangerous for them to serve arrest warrants in the weaving districts.

A primitive painting of the canal basin around 1825, with the city of Carlisle behind.

Yet paradoxically, at the same time, the town was becoming more prosperous. One boost was the opening in March 1823 of the canal, which ran from the city to a hamlet east of Bowness on the Solway, now proudly renamed Port Carlisle. In the eleven miles of its length the canal was lowered sixty feet by eight locks, a great and costly feat of engineering. And there was a new venture on the horizon, in which the Loshes were involved from the start: the railway. In the 1790s a Carlisle man, Ralph Dodd, had put forward the idea of a canal linking the Tyne and the Solway, the North and the Irish seas. It was wildly impracticable and was soon set aside, but after the short Carlisle–Solway canal was opened the idea was proposed again. James Losh was a keen supporter until 1824, when he discovered that a railway would cost only a third as much as a canal. Almost immediately he began organising meetings about a railway line from Carlisle to Newcastle, now an international port, handling over two hundred thousand tons of merchant shipping a year. At this stage, the idea was to have horses pulling the engines, as in the coalfields. A company was formed, James was elected chairman and William a director, and about £20,000 was immediately subscribed, James putting his own name down for £2,000, at £10 per share.[10]

The balloon was going up, in more than one sense. In 1825 the balloonist Charles Green made ascents from Kendal and York and came on to Carlisle in September, inflating his balloon in the castle grounds with gas fed along specially laid pipes from the Carlisle Gas and Coke Company, founded in 1819.[11] The band played as hundreds of spectators crowded into stands inside the castle, and a thousand gathered on the river banks below. The scarlet-and-gold balloon shot into the air, sailing off to land at Beattock Bridge, over twenty miles to the north. There was a second display a few days later, and several of Sarah and Katharine's friends, including Philip Howard and his wife, dined with the aeronaut. But the wind drove the balloons north and east, far away from Wreay.

In the summer of 1826 James Losh, recovering from exhaustion and nervous collapse, came to stay at Woodside for several weeks. In a hot and thundery July, he and James junior toured southern Scotland before heading back across the border 'to pass some time with my Nieces, who had kindly pressed me to do so for the recovery of my health by quiet, regular exercise, and my native air'.[12] The weather was stifling, over eighty degrees in the shade and seventy at night, but the house was cool and they appreciated the shady walks and the countryside around. The wheat, barley and oats were already cut, 'strawberries, raspberries and currants quite over, and gooseberries nearly so – tho', as the crop has been most abundant, there still remained sufficient for us'. The temperature stayed high: by mid–August the harvest was nearly all in, and one night, with rain threatening, they saw a 'lunar rainbow' and a spectacular display of northern lights.[13] As the summer wore on they went on excursions, driving across to Nunnery or Rose Castle or up Ullswater to Patterdale. Mostly, however, James recorded, 'we lived with the greatest regularity. Breakfast at ½ past 9, dinner 3, and tea and Coffee (as a kind of meal) at 7 – I drove out in the Gig generally, rode on my pony, walked or worked in the garden.'[14] In the evenings they played whist.

This portrait of James Losh, by an unknown artist, captures his quiet intelligence and kindliness.

They made trips to town to pay calls and go shopping and to see the exhibition at the Carlisle Academy of Art, which was judged not quite as good as the previous year. (It was probably around this time that Sarah was sketched by the young Thomas Heathfield Carrick, a local – and unsuccessful – apothecary, who would soon leave his trade to become a respected miniaturist, exhibiting at the Carlisle Academy, in Newcastle and later at the Royal Academy.[15]) As well as these diversions, the Woodside visitors toured the cotton-spinning mill at Warwick Bridge, and Sarah and Katharine, squired by their cousins James and Robert, set off for the race-week ball. James saw their lawyer, Mr Mounsey, about his own and his nieces' business and sorted out problems on the estate, such as a farmhouse badly in need of repair. The hedgerows were heavy with blackberries and the Woodside orchards were laden – they picked greengages and plums and morello cherries, and ate apples baked or boiled every day for three weeks. It was not until late October that James finally 'left our affectionate and excellent friends' and went back to Newcastle, to his family and his busy life in court.[16]

One day in September, during James's visit, they called on the Gaskins and then went on to see Mr Parker's celebrated orchard, where fruit was trained on every wall. Sitting in the sun talking to Parker's daughter, 'Sarah mentioned a singular Family which lives in the Neighbourhood (at or near Warwick Bridge)'. It consisted, she said,

of an elderly Lady with an unmarried son and daughter, and a married daughter and her Husband. They have all the manners of very genteel persons, and when at Church are dressed like Ladies and gentlemen. The two gentlemen manage the garden, go to market, clean the shoes, wait at table, lay the Cloth, etc – the Ladies make the Beds, Wash, Cook etc – they keep one woman servant only, who clears the Rooms, makes the fires etc . . . it seems understood that they were formerly people of fortune, who have been reduced by circumstances to a state of poverty, and that they have adopted their plan, for the purpose of maintaining their independence, and avoiding the necessity of separating from each other.[17]

Without such a strict need for economy, Sarah and Katharine also lived a simple life and dreaded separation. In Wreay they gardened, sketched, and read – the poetry of Byron and the novels of Scott, as well as books on history, architecture, customs and religion, science and geology. They knew all the farmers and tradespeople: the carpenters William Nicholson and Joseph Strong, the blacksmiths David Robinson at Wreay and Joseph Graham at Beckhouse, William Weightman the shoemaker, Thomas Atkinson the miller at Petteril Crooks and Thomas Pickering the stonemason. They gave money to the distressed Carlisle weavers and to their local poor. There were hard times at Wreay; five children under eleven died in the hard winter of 1823, and even more in 1830. These were several single mothers in the village – the baptism register records a series of illegitimate births, especially to servants – and they too needed help. Some labourers and their families were permanently in need, like Henry and Jane Gill and their many children, whose names appeared in the minute book of the Twelve Men against small handouts for year after year until the matriarch, Jane, finally died at the age of ninety-three.[18] Every week the sisters handed out money, and in years like 1831 when the snow lay deep for weeks, 'at Christmas they caused a quantity of coals to be divided amongst such of the poor cottars as could not afford to purchase a sufficient quantity of fuel to protect themselves from the inclemency of the winter.'[19]

The Misses Losh owned virtually the whole village. Sarah had bought land from John Robinson and Thomas Slack, so that their fields and woods stretched wide, from High Moss to Chapel Hill, from Old Ravenside Wood to Low Hurst, and they owned farms from Brisco to Mellguards.[20] Their father's plantations were maturing, and the timber was sold; their sheep and cattle were sent to market in Carlisle, and although the estate as a whole was looked after for them by their agent and by John Bell of Low Hurst Farm, Sarah kept a close eye on the accounts. Within the village, almost everyone was a Losh tenant: they owned seven cottages in Wreay, as well as the Plough Inn with its cottage and outbuildings, two cottages at Brisco and the blacksmiths' shops in both villages. They even owned the village shop, where you could buy almost anything from brooms to gingerbread, calico aprons to butter and cheese, bread and onions, and sometimes even luxuries like tea.

The sisters knew everyone, from the farmers and squires at Scalesceugh, Barrockside and Newbiggin, to Margaret and Jane Harrington, who came in to do the washing, and labourers like Josiah Blaylock, who earned three shillings a day for casual work, while his wife Jane earned one and sixpence gathering stones.[21] They knew the children at the school and the elderly characters like John Scott 'who at the age of 94 seems to have his senses and his faculties as persons usually have at 70. He writes what he calls *poetry*, which tho' not very poetical, shews considerable shrewdness and observation', and old Mr Parker, who still went out greyhound coursing at four in the morning, breakfasted on hasty pudding and cold bacon and drank 'any kind of bad spirits which he might happen to meet with, getting drunk also regularly one market day at the least every week'.[22] 'Mr P' sounds like a former Cumbrian wrestler, 'a tall man, of great breadth of chest and uncommon bodily strength, warm tempered but cheerful and kind to his family'.

Sarah and Katharine took their local responsibilities to heart and emptied their pockets. During these years, there was much talk about the bad condition of the bridge across the Petteril to Little Barrock and when this was finally repaired, the Misses Losh were prominent on the list of subscribers, contributing £50 (outdoing the Dean and Chapter of Carlisle by £20), with an extra £5 from Margaret and £1 from their aunt Ann Bonner. When the funds came in short Sarah subscribed an additional £20. In the parish book the costs were carefully listed, from the price of advertising in the Carlisle paper to the overseer's fees, the quarrying and walling by William Hindson, and the planting of a new thorn hedge.[23] All the local names were on the list, John Bell from Low Hurst, John Robinson from Scalescleugh, the Carricks, Slacks and Fletchers, the Lowthians from Newbiggin and the Aglionbys from Armathwaite, and William Gaskin – almost his last public duty for the village before his death the following year, in November 1832, at the age of eighty-one.

The sisters were also engaged in another, even more substantial building project for the village. Sixty years before, John Brown (their great-grandmother's brother), who farmed at Mellguards, a cluster of old stone houses a few miles up the valley, had bequeathed money to the church and schools at Hesket and Wreay. As Brown's heir, their grandfather had used this to buy land next to both schools, and had put up a monument in Hesket church:

Mr. John Brown
of Mellguards in the parish of Hesket,
By an almost constant residence in that parish
from the time of his birth,
Became not only a true patron to it in his life-time,
But willing to extend his regard to its welfare
Even after death,
Gave by his will
To the church of Hesket — 200/.
To the school of Hesket — 200/.
To the school of Wreay — 200/.
To the chapel of Armathwaite — 100/.
He died on the 15th day of July 1763,
Aged 69 years,
And had this justice done to his memory
By John Losh esquire his nephew and heir,
A. D. 1765.[24]

The remaining money, about £60, had never been spent and had come to Sarah and Katharine as part of their inheritance. In 1818, the author of a vehement description of endowed schools noted that the sisters 'generously intend to legalize Mr Brown's Will, which was invalidated by the Mortmain Act'. This should be a lesson to others: '*Let those who*, under similar circumstances', raged the correspondent, had '*seized upon*' an estate left to a school, 'BLUSH *at their improper conduct*'.[25]

Having proved their goodwill, Sarah and Katharine began to look at the school in their own village with critical eyes. So far there was nothing in Wreay for girls and in the late 1820s they put this right by building a new 'Dame Infant's School' on the road up the hill from the village, with a Mrs Little in charge. Then they turned their attention to the main school. The Free School had been established by the Twelve Men in the seventeenth century, but lessons were held in the church until around 1750, when a rough schoolhouse was built. By 1830, according to Sarah, this was already falling down. It was their first chance to build, with the full approval of the Twelve Men, then led by John Robinson and Thomas Slack of Intack.

It was quite common for the women of landowning families to fund and supervise the building of schools on their estates. It was another thing altogether for them to design the buildings, to work as architect and site manager. Yet this is what Sarah and Katharine, determinedly independent, chose to do. 'The old schoolhouse having become ruinous, my sister and I erected a new one, which was completed in 1830,' explained Sarah.

The tything men had made over to us the old one that we might employ the materials in the work. We left the walls standing to serve for a court, and made use of the other materials on the spot, with the exception of some broken tables that were sold for 19 shillings by Mr. Robinson and Mr. Slack, who had obligingly consented to become trustees of the School.[26]

Before the grand opening the whole village turned out to mow the green, which the children would use as a playground for almost a century to come. It was thirsty work, and Robinson and Slack, noted Sarah, spent the money from the sale of the tables 'to refresh their neighbours, who very kindly made a boon day to smooth the green: a greater number having come than could have been expected, our supply of ale was exhausted, and we were sending for more when they anticipated'.

When James Losh was in Carlisle in September 1830, watching the work begin on the railway, he drove out to Wreay to see the new schoolhouse, deciding that 'it is built with great taste and is well calculated for the purpose both in appearance and reality'.²⁷ The school was a village and family affair: aunt Margaret contributed £100, a stove and an oak chair for the schoolmaster, 'which is curious, as being copied from one which had belonged to Glastonbury Abbey'.²⁸ (The old chair was still there in 1930, but has since vanished.) The chair was fitting, as the little two-room school had distinct pretensions, with an elaborate chimney and the same style of mullioned windows and door surrounds as Woodside, on a simpler scale. The *Carlisle Journal*, in between notices of art exhibitions, thefts of sheep and meetings of the subscription library, published a notice of the opening:

The Misses Losh, of Woodside, near this city, whose many kindnesses have been so often experienced by the poor of the neighbourhood in which they reside, have recently erected a new school-house at Wreay, in order to enable the indigent families of that village to have their children educated free of expense.

In some ways, shortly before he died, this was a present to William Gaskin, who had been so devoted to their family, and had been the vicar here for over fifty years.

Money was needed, too, to keep the school running. Although the poorer children were taken in free, most families paid three

Wreay school in July 1836.

shillings a quarter for their children to go there, and those from beyond the parish bounds paid more, but this was far from sufficient to pay a teacher. Most of John Brown's original bequest had been spent on land, which was rented out to pay the master's stipend, and another five acres were added after the 1778 Enclosure Act, assigned to 'William Gaskin and his successors, schoolmasters of Wreay for ever'.[29] It was hard for outsiders to make sense of the school's finances and when the Charity Commissions visited in 1831 they reported that 'the affairs of the school . . . had got into some confusion'. It transpired that at some point Gaskin had found it hard to let the school land, and had asked John Losh to do this for him: the result was that the Losh family were paying the schoolmaster, in quarterly instalments, from income made up by the rental of the land, the interest on John Brown's legacy, the original school stock, and a £50 gift dating from 1786. It had virtually become 'their' school.

The commissioners were suspicious, suspecting that the payments were too low, but Sarah was furious at the implied slur on her father and a heated correspondence began. The commissioners, she declared, could not have understood the arrangements, 'nor have *fully conned*, I think, the papers in question'.[30] In past centuries, she explained, the chapel had been more of a school than a church, since the Dean and Chapter of Carlisle only arranged for a monthly service by the Hesket curate, whereas it had been a schoolroom 'time out of mind'. Since the village needed a resident curate, the Twelve Men had appointed a schoolmaster, and then petitioned the bishop 'to confer Holy orders upon him'. This tradition continued until John Brown's bequest allowed for a separate schoolmaster's salary, and the land purchases followed: the Losh family were benefactors, not defrauders.

Sarah's brisk, detailed description of the complex history showed a clear understanding of the legal and financial implications, including the legal expenses of each transaction. She had clearly kept every receipt and document (apart from one which was buried among family papers in James Losh's study in Newcastle) and she knew every detail of the history. Having obtained the commissioners' approval for the remainder of Brown's legacy to be invested in land, providing the Gaskins and the Loshes appointed two trustees to manage it, Sarah set out, with the help of a surveyor, Mr Bowman, and the schoolmaster, Mr Noble, to allot some land that she had bought to the north of the church. The school took the large field running down to the church, and the Losh sisters kept the rest, 'altho' not so good'. They were anxious, she explained, that the school money be properly spent, and indeed it had purchased 'more land than it was entitled to', but since rents from land rarely equalled the interest on money they built a house for the new schoolmaster which could be let at £5 a year, in order to make up the deficiency. Any money left over was invested in the new Newcastle and Carlisle Railway, now well under construction.[31]

The schoolmaster's cottage stood in one corner of the school field, just down the lane, and was built in the style of one the sisters had seen, and doubtless sketched, in Pompeii. No one seemed to find the idea of a Pompeiian cottage eccentric — or at least no one said so, as the local people felt great affection for the two Miss Loshes. Sarah always continued her involvement with the school, taking care of the deeds, drawing up conditions of lease for the schoolmaster's cottage, worrying about the heating and the children themselves: 'I am so glad you have got little Blaylock admitted as a scholar,' she wrote years later.[32]

12 'The Antient and Present State'

The school was built in the yellow sandstone local to Wreay, whose cottages and barns have quite a different air from the dark red freestone of the Eden valley and Carlisle. There were two local quarries, one by Upper Wreay Bridge and the other near Newbiggin, where the sandstone was in bands of both yellow and red, but for special stone Sarah looked to Shawk Foot, about ten miles west of the village at Cumdivock beyond Dalston, where a beck ran down through rocky banks to reeds and marshes. The quarry had a long history, for the Romans had taken its stone for their fort at Carlisle and later masons had used it for the cathedral and medieval walls. It was unusual, because three different kinds of stone were found here, as a gazetteer of 1847 explained:

free stone, of an open grit; another of *very white free stone*, of a close body; and a seam of *limestone* . . . There is, on a protuberant cliff, seven or eight yards above the rivulet, the following Roman inscription – *Legionis Secundae Augustae milites Posuerunt Cohors tertia Cohors quarta*. The fact of this rock retaining an inscription since the Romans were in Britain, proves the durability of the fine free stone of these quarries.[1]

Shawk Foot had its own tales of violence and war, and felons escaping the police: 'The cliff formerly rose several yards above the inscription, and was called *Tom Smith's Leap*, from a person of that name having thrown himself over the awful precipice to avoid being taken prisoner, and was killed on the rocks beneath.'

More stones carved with Roman names turned up in old workings in the next parish. Nearby were ancient barrows like Toddle Hill, and although this nicely named lump had been entirely flattened by the late 1840s as its stones were used to mend roads or build houses, Mannix and Whellan's gazetteer described how men digging here had uncovered 'several urns, containing ashes, skulls, bones'. The banks of Shawk Foot itself were full of fossils, including many shells. New buildings were literally constructed from the bones of the past.

Sarah knew the history of her area well, displaying the antiquarian interest typical of her day. In February 1809 Jane Blamire, the mother of Sarah's great friend Jane Christian Blamire, had written to Kitty Senhouse, in the middle of a letter about shopping commissions and red scarlet cloth from India, about the uncovering of one ancient fort:

Tell Mr Senhouse Petriana the Roman station is just opened by the owner, who wants the stones for a fence to a new enclosure, he has got so far on the outside to see the form which is circular, or rather oval, with stones nicely wrought & the foundation on large flags, the enterence is visible & they have found several coins very perfect, & a small lamp in the form of a bird of a metal perfectly bright, I am sorry I cannot give any account of the coins which are found – but we have a Farm directly opposite, & my son is often there I will endeavour to learn more of the matter if it would interest my good friend – & we hope more will be found when the middle of the building is cleared . . .²

And so it went on. James Losh made drawings in 1812 of the discoveries at Old Penrith fort, and Sir Walter Scott was fascinated by the excavations there, which he called Petreia. Discoveries were all around: there was a Roman fort just to the north-east of Wreay and a hoard of Roman coins were found in the Petteril. The Cumbrian women exchanged news of recent finds, like Jane Matthews who sent a friend a drawing of a stone in April 1816, which, she was sure, was from the time of Marcus Aurelius, dug up at Old Carlisle near Wigton, with the inscription *Pro Salute Imperatoris Domine*.[3] Women could not be members of the antiquarian societies, but they copied papers, made translations, corresponded with each other and made their own investigations in the field.[4] Sarah was thus not unusual in her interest – but she was unique in the serious way she pursued it and applied what she learned.

In their long years together the Losh sisters took trips within their own region – into the fells, or along the Solway. In the village of Bridekirk near Cockermouth the old church of St Bridget held a twelfth-century font, an object of fascination that James Losh discussed eagerly with other members of the Newcastle Antiquarian Society.[5] It was carved by Richard of Durham, who showed himself on one side with his huge hammer and long chisel, and the inscription, *Rickard he me iwrocht, and this merthr gernr me brokte*, 'Richard me wrought and to this beauty brought'.[6] The carving, with its Nordic style and runes, mixed scenes of the

An engraving of one side of Bridekirk font (1816)

expulsion from Eden and the baptism of Christ with transforma-
tions and monsters: a cross growing into a vine; a bird with two
snaking necks biting a tail that bursts into flower.

There were other wonders. Sometimes they went north
through the small market town of Brampton, and on to the medieval Naworth Castle, the home of the Earl of Carlisle and the
place that William Morris would call 'certainly the most poetical
in England'.[7] Edward Burne-Jones's *The Last Sleep of Arthur* would
be commissioned for this castle, and a sense of antiquity and
legend hangs over the whole area. Across the river Irthing, Lanercost priory slept in its meadows. As at Holm Cultram, the nave of
the Augustan abbey had been saved as a parish church, but the high
ruined arches of the crossing, with the solid Dacre tombs beneath
them, stood open to the skies.

Following the lane up to the ridge, Sarah and Katharine crossed
Hadrian's Wall, where the antiquaries were busy, and from there
they took the lonely road over the moors, where the shadows of

The arches of the crossing and the Dacre tombs at Lanercost priory.

clouds scudded over the bending grass. The dusty track wound upwards past the fortified farm known as Askerton Castle before dipping down over Gallows Hill into a lonely valley. On the ridge opposite was the hamlet of Bewcastle, and here by the church they saw the old Bewcastle cross. Their father's friend Henry Howard had written of both Bridekirk and Bewcastle when they were girls, in a letter published in the journal *Archaeologia*, accompanied by careful drawings of the inscriptions.[8] At Bridekirk the vicar had cleaned the moss off the font for him with soap and water, and in true antiquarian fashion, Howard made rubbings, concluding that the font had been made to celebrate the conversion of the Viking warrior Eric, who ruled over the Northumberland Danes. At Bewcastle he had made rubbings again, but had given up in the effort to interpret the runes, although some scholars read them as dedication to the king of a part of Northumbria, Alchfrith of Deira, who had died here and whose mother was a local princess from the northern kingdom of Rheged.

The cross was carved in the late seventh or early eighth century like its fellow at Ruthwell, on the Solway plains in Dumfriesshire, thirty miles to the west. Ruthwell, inscribed with lines from the Anglo-Saxon poem *The Dream of the Rood*, had its own legend – that the cross was brought by sea, shipwrecked and 'removed as the result of a dream to a place where it could by heaven's decree pass no further'.[9] Bewcastle too was the site of stories. This low sandstone hill was an ancient settlement with many Stone Age and Bronze Age sites nearby. It had been the setting for a Roman fort as well as a later castle, and was known to be a Roman cult site, dedicated to the Celtic god Cicidius, a deity of war and water woodlands. Ever since it was mentioned by the historian William Camden in 1607, this obelisk – for no cross topped the pillar then – standing in its 'wilde and solitarie country' had always seemed profoundly mysterious.[10] There was much discussion about its runes, figures and beasts, knots and interlacing, and the carvings of a falconer with his bird, Christ standing on the heads of lions, and John the Baptist holding the Lamb of God – a figure that antiquaries like George Smith in 1742 had firmly declared was a Virgin and child, a female offering.[11]

Sarah and Katharine never forgot the Bewcastle cross, rooted in a land of moors and bogs and rolling skies.[12] They planned, some day, to erect their own copy as a memorial to their parents. Although the idea was unusual the Losh sisters were typical of their day in the desire to link themselves, their parents and family with the distant past of their region, church and nation. During the Napoleonic wars, the desire for some connection with a lost past became exaggerated into a quest for the roots of nationhood. The hugely popular works of Walter Scott delved back into a mythic medieval land, from his two-volume *Minstrelsy of the Scottish Border* in 1802–3 (so closely connected with Liddesdale, just over the hill from Bewcastle) and his long introductory essay to *The Border Antiquities of England and Scotland* (1814–17), to his later Waverley novels which contain several stories of the reivers riding that way, and settings in the border country of Carlisle and Solway. To nineteenth-century readers, the joy of Scott's novels, whether it be a Jacobite tale like *Rob Roy*, or *Ivanhoe* set in the twelfth century (but also a contribution to the current campaign for emancipation of the Jews), lay in the detail. The vividly described clothes and food and furniture gave them the sense that they were gleaning accurate information about what it was actually like to live in those hidden ages. In *The Antiquary*, published in 1816, Scott also provided an abiding image of the antiquarian in the character of Jonathan Oldbuck, a gentleman historian and fervent, if misguided, collector and archaeologist, the accidental centre of a Gothic novel full of secrets, romance and mysterious illegitimate sons.

The public thirst for information about the past, particularly the romantic Middle Ages, became almost an obsession, running

A woodcut of George Smith's drawing of the Bewcastle obelisk in 1742, identifying the top figure as the Virgin.

alongside an equally intense preoccupation with the new, especially discoveries in science. Increasingly, however, writers like Carlyle, Cobbett and Mill looked back to the Middle Ages as an alluring contrast to their own degenerate, materialist age.

Sarah represented both worlds. She identified herself as a 'soda maker', a woman of a modern, scientific, commercial world, and she read eagerly about the latest discoveries and scientific theories, but she also filled her travel notebooks with studies of architectural styles and meditations on past cultures and time-hallowed rituals. She and Katharine subscribed jointly to the *Family Topographer*, covering 'the Antient and Present State of the Counties of England', by the antiquarian Samuel Tymms, which appeared in seven volumes between 1832 and 1843, and to his edition of Camden's *Britannia*, 'epitomised and continued'. She was fascinated by architectural history, 'not only as a study *per se*, illustrating the curiosities of ancient and medieval structures', remembered Lonsdale, but as 'realising to modern eyes the life of the past'.[13]

This connection between architectural and social history – a kind of early anthropology – had intrigued travellers and antiquarians for the past half century. In Athens in 1798, James Losh's friend John Tweddell had made sketches, with help from a French artist named Preaux, of 'every temple, and every archway . . . every stone, and every inscription . . . with the most scrupulous fidelity', but he also made detailed notes on the '*ceremonies*, and *usages*, and *dresses* of the people' of Greece.[14] James shared this double interest: thirty years later, when Joseph Woods lectured in Newcastle on 'Architecture as illustrating history and the state of society in different nations', James prevailed on him to stay for four days.[15] Woods himself embodied typical sets of overlapping interests: founder and first president of the London Architectural Society, and editor of the final volume of Stuart and Revett's famous *Antiquities of Athens*, he was also a geologist and botanist, making field trips across Europe and Britain, and discovering several new species of plant.[16]

The two ways of thinking inherent in the disciplines of history and natural philosophy flowed into a common search for origins as explaining present forms, whether of natural phenomena or human societies. When Joseph Priestley began writing on natural philosophy in the 1760s, he called his first book *The History and Present State of Electricity*. Antiquarian and scientific clubs often had the same members: in Newcastle James Losh was on the committee of both the Society of Antiquaries and the Natural History Society.[17] At the Newcastle Lit and Phil, lectures on 'The Minerals of Cumberland' or 'The Mechanical Properties of Air' sat beside papers on 'The Runic Inscriptions of Great Britain'. Most important of all, the interest in classification that had marked the advances in botany, mineralogy and chemistry – even the nomenclature of clouds – was now being applied to historical styles, objects and buildings. When Sarah wrote that the shape of the door arch of the old church at Wreay indicated that it had been built in the reign of Edward II, she was writing in this new, 'scientific' mode – using a specific feature to identify a class, as an ornithologist used the shape of the beak.

As far as architectural styles were concerned, over the past fifty years Gothic architecture had been increasingly admired at the expense of the earlier round-arched Norman style. Scholars became fascinated by the mystery of the pointed arch and its derivation, coming up with some novel theories: James Murphy held that medieval pinnacles derived from Egyptian obelisks; James Hall (a distinguished chemist and geologist) opted for willow poles and arches; Rowland Lascelles decided that the mother of all Gothic arches was the keel of Noah's Ark.

Setting aside arguments about the derivation of Gothic, which he simply called 'English', the Quaker antiquarian and architect Thomas Rickman published the first edition of *An Attempt to Discriminate the Styles of Architecture in England* in 1817, when Sarah was thirty and still captivated by her Continental trip. Rickman's terminology is that which we still use – Norman, Early English Gothic, Decorated and Perpendicular Gothic – so familiar to us now that it is hard to realise how new it was in Sarah's day.[18] Rickman was a doctor and an apothecary, then a clerk, before he began his great 'attempt'. He based his classification and chronology not on historical records, but on careful examination and diagnosis of building materials, stylistic details and ornaments, 'steeples, naves, transepts, windows, arches, fonts and monuments', noting how buildings evolved over time, with contributions from different centuries. His drawings were clear and elegant and his lively writing was designed to inspire the 'rising generation' and, he hoped, to provoke the clergy into realising what treasures they had and looking after them better.[19]

After Waterloo, there was a rash of building in London, including the grand, celebratory schemes for Waterloo Bridge and Regent Street. In towns and cities across Britain there were plans for new squares and streets and for churches, to control, it was hoped, the swelling urban population. In 1818 the Church Commission was established, with the vast sum of a million pounds at its disposal, a sum increased again in 1824. This meant that it was no longer necessary to pass an act for building each new church. Robert Smirke, who had designed Carlisle's new gateways and courthouses at the Citadel, joined the architects Soane and Nash to write general guidelines for church builders and in the rush to begin, Rickman submitted a neo-Gothic design to the commission. He went on to become one of the leading church builders.

When Hugh Percy became Bishop of Carlisle in 1827 and was keen to make a splash in his new diocese, he summoned Rickman to build two new churches in the workers' districts, Christ Church in Botchergate and Holy Trinity in Caldewgate (both now demolished). Rickman also worked on the bishop's residence, Rose Castle, repairing old civil-war damage and return-

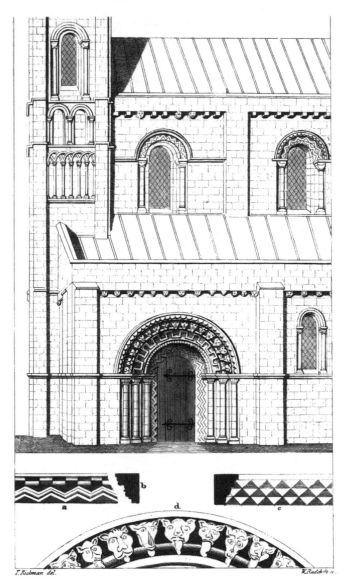

Thomas Rickman's clear illustration of 'The Norman Order' in his influential *Attempt to Discriminate the Styles of Architecture in England*, 1817.

ing it to its Tudor style, and he built a Gothic villa, Brunstock, for George Saul, chapter clerk to the cathedral, and a relative of the Loshes' old lawyer, Silas Saul. He was moving in circles well known to Sarah. She might visit ancient churches and crosses but in Carlisle there was plenty of new building, in the style of the old, for her to look at and judge.

13 Broken Glass

Sarah was forty-one in 1827 when Rickman came to Carlisle, and Katharine was thirty-nine. They had made a place for themselves in the village and the county, and their life could have continued smoothly and inconspicuously in this way for many years. There were sadnesses: this year William's son-in-law Spencer Boyd died in Newcastle, aged only twenty-eight, leaving Margaret a young widow with two small children, and in 1828 George's wife Frances, who had put up with so much, died in Paris after a sudden heart attack. James Losh was horrified, writing to James Thain lamenting the death of his sister-in-law, so amiable and affectionate with her 'fondness for poetry, and her tranquil temper'.[1]

The sisters' cousins were all beginning to make their own way. In January 1830 James's youngest son, William Septimus, set out for Paris to study French and 'attend lectures on chemistry, mechanics etc.' It proved an eventful year. In three days in late July, known to many as *les trois glorieuses*, the citizens took to the streets to overthrow the elderly Bourbon monarch, Charles X. In his six years' rule Charles had almost wilfully courted unpopularity, imposing strict penalties for disrespect to the Catholic church and heavy indemnities for property confiscated during the revolution and Napoleon's reign. In heated elections, the voters overthrew the government: in response Charles passed new censorship laws. Factories closed, banks refused to lend, workers were turned out on the streets. The crisis came when Charles disbanded the National Guard. Barricades were thrown up, shots fired and civilians killed, but the people took the Tuileries, the Louvre and the Hôtel de Ville. It was clear even to the stubborn king that his reign was over. As he fled to Britain, the Duc d'Orléans was proclaimed the 'citizen king', Louis Philippe.

George Losh, who now hobnobbed with Parisian aristocrats, feared fresh convulsions unless the new government was firm, but William Septimus was straightforwardly thrilled by the 'glorious struggle', as his father told Brougham:

He is an active young man of 19 and of course saw a good deal of the fighting. He speaks in the highest terms of the courage and discretion of the Patriots and says that their victory was wonderful, considering how imperfectly they were armed – very few indeed having muskets. He lives in the house of a Professor of Chemistry, who is, I suspect, an ultra patriot but even he, William says, is satisfied with the new King.[2]

William was also a good antiquarian and magpie like his cousin Sarah, and in the chaos of the streets he picked up some stained glass from the old archbishop's palace, the fifteenth-century Hôtel de Sens in the Marais. This had been caught in the crossfire, and its wall still shows the mark of a cannonball, with the words *28 Juillet 1830* carved beneath it. William brought his glass home, storing it away for ten years or more until it found its place in Sarah's new church at Wreay, the work of medieval craftsmen given new life in a Cumbrian village.

The following year at the British Embassy Chapel in Paris William married his cousin Sarah, George's petite, strong-willed daughter. When they came back to Newcastle Elizabeth Stevenson (later Mrs Gaskell), who knew the Loshes well, reported that the doctor's wife, Mrs Ramsay, 'has been to call on the little French bride, Mrs Wm Losh; and that she is the very least little person there ever was . . . I would be a giantess beside her.'[3] William returned to work as a clerk for his uncle William at Walker, a job he had begun in 1828 before his trip to France: soon he was in charge of the alkali works and was making his own applications for patents.

The affairs of William senior now stretched in many directions. He was Swedish and Prussian Consul for Newcastle, as well as running the alkali works and iron foundry. After the war the demand for alkali had grown rapidly and William built his own lead-chamber to make sulphuric acid to speed up the process. Four years later he was making over four hundred tons of alkali per year, and by 1830 this had reached 986 tons, a third of the entire Tyneside output. Three years after that William set off to Italy again. He travelled south as he had done with Sarah and Katharine fifteen years before, talking to chemists and manufacturers and intending to spend the winter in Sicily – the principal source of sulphur for his acid.[4] As for the iron works, in 1827 the partners built new, larger works at Walker, with new processes and plants. Unpretentious and easy-going, William was still a technological wizard, at the forefront of all new developments. Although George Stephenson had turned his back on the Walker works, preferring wrought-iron rails to their cast iron, the Loshes followed his progress with keen interest. William was present at the vital Rainhill speed trials in 1829, where Stephenson's *Rocket* was the only engine to finish successfully, and went on to patent his own improvements in carriage wheels. Like James, he was also energetically involved in the new railway to Carlisle.

Although prospects looked good for the iron-masters and railway entrepreneurs, the start of the new decade was turbulent. The revolution in Paris fired uprisings in Belgium, Italy, Germany and Poland. In Britain, the death of George IV and accession of his brother, William IV, prompted a general election and while Wellington hung on as prime minister, the Tory majority was slashed and the pressure for reform began to swell. Young Henry Aglionby, speaking on the hustings at a by-election in Carlisle in

Walker in the late nineteenth century, with smoke rising and
ships waiting.

terms designed to appeal to radicals like the Loshes as well as the
working people, declared himself 'the enemy of monopolies, a
friend to improvement in the representation of the people, inimi-
cal to all sorts of exclusions for religious belief, and as disposed to
eradicate the whole system of the game laws, root and branch'.[5]

When the months passed and the reform movement seemed
stalled, there were outbreaks of rick-burning in the southern
counties, led by the elusive 'Captain Swing', and growing unrest
among industrial workers in the north. In September, Carlisle
radicals held huge meetings on Carlisle Sands to press for reform,
and a group of middle-class merchants, lawyers and gentry joined
with a delegation from the weavers to form a pressure group. In
November Wellington outraged many by claiming that he considered the present legislature was perfectly adequate and felt it
his duty to resist reform. London was overwhelmed by rioting,
and Carlisle saw a week of huge torch-lit processions: up to six
thousand people marched from Caldewgate and circled the market cross three times; on the first night an effigy of Wellington
was burned, on the second, one of the home secretary, Sir Robert
Peel. One hundred and fifty special constables were sworn in,

mostly local shopkeepers, who were heckled by working women on every street.

In the uproar Wellington resigned, prompting a jubilant repeat of the Carlisle procession. Unsurprisingly, when wheat and haystacks were burned near Carlisle later that month and the local gentry received threatening letters signed 'Swing', people assumed that the workers were turning violent. The truth turned out to be the opposite. During the trial in March 1831 witnesses revealed that the fires were started by petty criminals hired by the Tory corporation and the city's chief constable, 'to look after' the 'Radical Concern', in order to justify a fiercer clampdown.[6] The *Carlisle Journal* expressed the outrage felt by many citizens and the radical workers were vindicated.

Sarah's biographer Henry Lonsdale reported that Sarah made notes on this, as she did on all political events, but later destroyed them. Nothing seemed to have gone quite as planned since the end of the wars: the peace had brought confusion rather than harmony and progress. The 1830s saw a flurry of religious sects, all aiming to purify and regenerate the world. A widespread fear that the very fabric of society was crumbling spawned a series of books, of which Thomas Carlyle's *Signs of the Times*, which first appeared as articles in the *Edinburgh Review* in 1829, was the forerunner. Responding to the heated public debates after the 1828 repeal of the Test Acts – the seventeenth-century penal laws that had barred dissenters and Roman Catholics from holding civic office – and the subsequent Catholic Relief Act, Carlyle set up an opposition between two approaches to life. He mocked 'the rage for prophecy' that had overwhelmed the nation, but explained it as panic caused by the seeming frailty of the old-established institutions, especially the church: 'The repeal of the Test Acts, and then of the Catholic disabilities, has struck many of their admirers with an indescribable astonishment. Those things seemed fixed and immovable; deep as the foundations of the world; and lo, in a moment they have vanished, and their place knows them no more!'⁷

They were living, wrote Carlyle, in a 'Mechanical' age, in which 'nothing follows its spontaneous course, nothing is left to be accomplished by old natural methods'. There were engines for everything, from mincing cabbages to planning schools: but if progress had brought material improvements it had wiped out some aspects of 'Dynamics', the profounder science 'which treats of, and practically addresses, the primary, unmodified forces and energies of man, the mysterious springs of Love, and Fear, and Wonder, of Enthusiasm, Poetry, Religion, all which have a truly vital and *infinite* character'. 'If we look deeper', he went on:

we shall find that this faith in Mechanism has now struck its roots down into man's most intimate, primary sources of conviction; and is thence sending up, over his whole life and activity, innumerable stems, – fruit-bearing and poison-bearing. The truth is, men have lost their belief in the Invisible, and believe, and hope, and work only in the Visible; or, to speak it in other words: This is not a Religious age. Only the material, the immediately practical, not the divine and spiritual, is important to us. The infinite, absolute character of Virtue has passed into a finite, conditional one; it is no longer a worship of the Beautiful and Good; but a calculation of the Profitable.⁸

Sarah Losh, with her money from alkali and iron, and soon from the railways, spent plenty of time on calculating the Profitable. She was, in many ways, a material person, concerned with the practical. But her buildings were an answer to Carlyle's plea, bricks and mortar imbued with spiritual energy.

Wellington's resignation in November 1830 opened the way for a Whig administration led by Lord Grey, the old friend of James Losh, who had been campaigning for reform now for nearly forty years. In the following March Lord John Russell introduced the first Reform Bill, correcting abuses, removing rotten and pocket boroughs, and extending the franchise to many more middle-class voters. This was steered through the Commons but defeated in committee, and the tensions in the House were such that Grey called for a dissolution. In the subsequent elections the Whigs trounced the Tories. In Cumberland William Blamire reluctantly left his beloved farm, like Cincinnatus, and stepped forward with James Graham to oppose the Lowthers. His sister Jane, Sarah's friend, 'walked and drove, directed and canvassed' with irresistible force.[9] Their victory was hailed as a triumph.

When the new government met, Russell brought in the second Reform Bill. Once again the Lords rejected it (the bishops' vote was crucial), but not before a dramatic intervention by Henry Brougham, now Lord Chancellor, who flung himself on his knees with his arms open wide, exhorting his fellow Lords: 'By all you hold most dear – by all the ties that bind every one of us to our common order and our common country, I solemnly adjure you – I warn you – I implore you – yea, on my bended knees, I supplicate you – reject not this Bill.'[10] More riots followed the rejection. In Carlisle, weavers desperate for news clubbed together to buy the London newspapers, waiting anxiously for the mail coaches that brought them. Their favourites were the *Weekly Dispatch*, with its accounts of the rick-burnings and reform meetings, and the *Evening Mail* issued three times a week by *The Times*, which summarised the previous two days' news. William Farish remembered how the weavers gathered round the fire in his father's workshop about nine o'clock in the evening to hear him read the news, going over the debates until long after midnight.[11] As Brougham wrote to James Losh, 'The Reform feeling is not dead, but sleeps', and its opponents would see it becoming 'far more universal and ungovernable'.[12] He was right: in December 1831 the third Reform Bill was introduced.

Much of James's time was taken up with meetings and his own pamphlet on reform was published this year. He was seen as the leader of the Whig party in Newcastle and was exhausting himself addressing huge public meetings of seven or eight thousand people, as well as engaging in constant correspondence and meetings with Brougham and Grey, both of whom he had known for many years, and both of whom relied on his local knowledge and general advice. The Bill passed the Commons on 23 March the following year.

A month before, a new terror had reached London, cholera, spreading across the Continent and moving slowly north. In a strange return to pre-Enlightenment ways, the government declared a 'National Day of Fasting and Humiliation', as if to ward off the dread disease by prayer. In Carlisle the weavers held a furious gathering on the Sands, carrying placards that blamed food shortages rather than the wrath of God for the disease. During the epidemic the distress committee in Caldewgate 'did not find half a dozen serviceable blankets among fifty families; whole families of five, six and seven people were huddled in one small bed, covered by a few rags'. Many had 'no beds but merely a little straw with an old wrapper thrown upon it'.[13] Every day, until the cold weather came and the disease abated, the number of new cases and deaths was posted at the market cross.

Meanwhile, with parliament in turmoil, the Reform Bill moved inexorably towards its passing. In April, when Grey resigned after a deadlock in the Lords and Wellington failed to form a government, many observers worried that the country was on the brink of revolution. Some protesters swore to withhold taxes and called for a run on the banks. But in May William IV accepted Grey's suggestion that he should create new peers to force the Bill through the Lords, and the Great Reform Act finally became law on 7 June 1832.

The Act was a turning point for James Losh. At first he was enthusiastic about his work in implementing the new provisions, and working as a revising barrister. But by March 1833 he had had enough. Henceforth, he wrote in his diary, he would stick to his profession. 'The Whig gentry', he wrote exasperatedly, 'with a few exceptions, are, in Northumberland, a set of very shabby fellows, and the inhabitants of that county, *generally* speaking, a cold-hearted, selfish race. I have exerted myself zealously in this business, but have found little support and I am sick, very sick, of Northumberland politics.'[14] Instead, he turned back to his plans for the railway and education. Work on the Newcastle–Carlisle line had gone slowly, mainly due to the pressure on the banks after the crisis of 1826, which made borrowing difficult, but finally – after a spate of arguments in the Commons – the necessary Act was obtained in 1829, and the building began.

In May 1831, when the navvies were digging their way past Corby Castle, James had gone to see them with Henry Howard and his son Philip, now a Carlisle MP. 'They seem to be stupendous works', James wrote, 'and at present exhibit appearances of much confusion and difficulty, but no doubt order and usefulness will be the result.'[15] The difficulties were the need for a deep cutting or tunnel between Brampton and Carlisle, and a high bridge over the Eden at Wetheral. Sarah suggested boldly that they erect a bridge 'similar to the Pont du Gard, a few miles from Nimes, as calculated to harmonise well with the lofty banks of the river and the exquisitely wooded scenery of Corby Castle'.[16] She sent drawings of her proposed plan, and Henry Howard approved them, but, not surprisingly, they went no further. The directors were already worried about the cost. In the spring of 1833, James set out to London to obtain an Exchequer loan of £100,000.[17] He obtained the loan and found his trip stimulating, but met trouble nearer home: at a railway meeting at Haydon Bridge a great row was on the verge of breaking out between the Carlisle and Newcastle directors. Disaster was averted, as so often, by James's diplomacy 'and after a great many toasts, and pushing the bottle somewhat briskly about, I got the whole party into great glee and good humour and we parted the best friends in the world'.[18]

The railway bridge over the River Eden at Wetheral, which Sarah hoped
would be built as a copy of the Roman Pont du Gard at Nimes.

There were, he thought, reasons for optimism. He was pushing on with his drive for education, working with the Bishop
of Durham to establish the university and campaigning with
David Dunbar for a new exhibition room in Carlisle where the
Mechanics Institute could join forces with the flagging Academy
of Fine Arts. He worried about his sons: about James, who was so
silent and grave; about Baldwin, prone to foolish flirtations and
facing court martial for cheating at cards (an absurd accusation,
thought James, wrongly); about William Septimus at Walker, and
John, away in India, settled in Madras in his house, Wolf's Crag,
filled with animals and birds. In his eight years there, John had
proved a brilliant student of Indian dialect, passing examinations
in several Indian languages and becoming 'the best linguist in the
Madras Army'.[19] In October 1832, as a young lieutenant, he was in
Bangalore on leave from studies in Madras when the Indian government took charge of Mysore and ended the rajah's rule. There
was broken glass and blood in the streets of Bangalore, as there
had been in the cities of Europe. John wrote home vividly of the
riots and of his own part in uncovering a conspiracy, when sepoys

from Bangalore joined forces with Muslims to mutiny and attack the British regiments. The reprisals were brutal, ending in violent executions with six conspirators tied to the mouths of cannon. The ghastly death took a long time, 'and the excessive heat of the day, the might of the arms, and the sight of the mangled bodies covered by hordes of vultures and kites rendered the transaction anything but pleasant to the spectators'.

John's news was horrifying, but he was alive. James was proud of him, and of all his family, including his Woodside nieces. In Newcastle his reward came when he was awarded the freedom of the city in 1830, the year after the restrictions against Dissenters holding public office had been removed. Then in early 1833 he was unanimously elected Recorder of Newcastle, 'despite being a Reformer and avowed *Unitarian* all my life'.²⁰ He ploughed on tirelessly with the railway and the Coal Committee and the Mechanics Institute, and with new campaigns for relief for factory children and for the repeal of the Corn Laws. In early August, he noted:

My old friend Wordsworth, the Poet, dined with us at Woodside. He is now an old and somewhat infirm man, but he retains all his activity and energy of mind, having at the same time got quit of much of his pompous and declamatory manner of conversing. I avoided politics & all subjects likely to cause irritation on either side, and we passed a very pleasant and tranquil evening. His sister & son accompanied the Bard.²¹

In fact his wife Mary was with him, not his sister Dorothy, an interesting slip: the year before, Wordsworth had found a job for his son Willy in Carlisle as 'a sub-distributor of Stamps'.²²

James felt well during July and August 1833 and at that dinner he clearly felt himself to be young, although he was now seventy, a good seven years older than his 'old and infirm' friend. He seemed calm and peaceful, able at last to stand back from events. But on 23 September, returning from Durham, he collapsed with a stroke. His son James and Fanny's husband Francis Hutchinson – now a qualified doctor – rushed to fetch him but he never recovered. He died at Greta Bridge and was buried four days later at Gosforth, not far from his home in Jesmond. His funeral in Newcastle was followed by a procession of mourners over a quarter of a mile long.[23] Nearly the whole of the town's legal profession came first, 'walking two by two' behind the family, then the members of the Lit and Phil, the Anti-Slavery Society, the Schoolmasters' Association, the Hanover Square congregation and the Mechanics Institute, and after them the mayor and aldermen and corporation, and lines of carriages of the local gentry.

After a packed meeting at the Assembly Rooms, nearly £700 was subscribed towards a memorial. Newcastle's leading figures spoke, among them William Turner, now aged ninety-one, who declared that:

Mr Losh was emphatically the friend of the poor, and he had no doubt that many persons present had been indebted to him for their education, which had placed them in a respectable walk of life. He therefore hoped that those of the humblest station of life would testify their gratitude to him, by contributing their mite, however small it might be . . . for he was sure, that what might be given, would come from a grateful heart.[24]

In the summer of 1834 David Dunbar's bust, made from life, was sent to the sculptor James Lough, then working in Rome. In Lough's marble statue, the nervous, hard-working, family-loving and idealistic James was transformed into a stoical, toga-clad dignitary. He still stands thus, a solemn upholder of liberty and learning, on the stairs of the Newcastle Lit and Phil.

14 A Thousand Ages

Sarah and Katharine missed James's visits to Woodside. As they had done when he stayed with them all the long summer a few years ago, they tended their garden with fervour, revelled in their orchards and fruit and protected the birds in their grounds. But the life of birds, flowers and people is short, and James's death was a sharp reminder of the transience of all things mortal. 'Oh God, our help in ages past/Our hope for years to come,' wrote Isaac Watts in the hymn that Sarah's forebears and her own generation knew so well,

> Our shelter from the stormy blast,
> And our eternal home.
>
> The busy tribes of flesh and blood,
> With all their lives and cares,
> Are carried downwards by the flood,
> And lost in following years.
>
> Time, like an ever rolling stream,
> Bears all its sons away;
> They fly, forgotten, as a dream
> Dies at the opening day.

Watts's images, of life as a dream lost in the blink of an eye and of nations withering like flowers beneath the scythe, were tropes that had long become platitudes. But they were given new force in this period by the findings of geology, which stretched time back to unknown beginnings. God, Watts sang, held sway 'Before the hills in order stood,/Or earth received her frame', but the new studies of the ordering of hills and the formation of the earth conjured an eternity that was not transcendent. It was of the earth, earthy.

The further you looked beneath the earth, the stranger and longer its history seemed. Sarah had known this since her childhood, when it had been fashionable for natural philosophers like her father to build up collections of minerals. The Lake District and the Pennines were rich hunting grounds, particularly the areas Sarah was most aware of – Caldbeck, Carrock Fell, Alston Moor and Cross Fell – almost the hills that marked the horizon round Wreay. In the Caldbeck Fells, for example, copper, lead and baryte mines produced crystals with wonderful names: mimetite, pyromorphite, hemimorphite, plumbogummite. John Losh collected fossils as well as minerals, joining a craze that swept Britain in the late eighteenth century. Fossils were used as evidence in the debates about the formation of the world, whether they showed continuous development or, as Georges Cuvier suggested in Paris, a chain of geological periods ended by catastrophes in which whole species were rendered extinct, followed by new starts.

Sarah had grown up with the works of William Paley, who taught a generation to look at the natural world for evidence of the existence of its creator. The argument from design had been used since classical times, and had been taken up by Newton and others as an argument against atheism. Hume had argued devastatingly against it, pointing out that the perfect designer must himself have been designed, and so on ad infinitum, but Paley's accessible and clever *Natural Theology* made the theory popular again. Yet however much naturalists struggled to reconcile their findings with the Bible, they had long ago abandoned the creation myth and rejected Archbishop Ussher's confident assertion in the seventeenth century that the date of creation was exactly 22 October 4004 BC (a fact quoted in the margins of the King James Bible for two hundred years). In France, the Comte de Buffon estimated that the earth had acquired its solid crust seventy-five thousand years ago. The time-span kept lengthening: in 1833, Herschel suggested that it had taken six hundred thousand years for the earth to achieve its current orbit. Human history diminished almost to vanishing point. As the geologist Charles Lyell put it, 'All discoveries which extend indefinitely the bounds of time must cause the generations of man to shrink into insignificance and to appear, even when all combined, as ephemeral in duration as the insects which live but from the rising to the setting of the sun.'[1]

The discoveries Lyell mentioned came from the depths below: from minerals, strata, fossils and bones. Even by Paley's time, geology was already a battlefield. The Neptunists, followers of the German professor of mining Abraham Werner, argued that rocks were formed by minerals crystallised beneath the oceans: all things had developed slowly from one single act of creation, heading towards a single, absolute end. By contrast, the Plutonists, led in Britain by the Scot James Hutton, proposed that the earth, and the entire universe, was shaped continually by slow-moving forces which one could still see working today. Rocks formed by volcanic activity were eroded and covered by the sea then lifted up again by new convulsions. The history of earth was cyclical and indeterminate, with 'no vestige of a beginning, no prospect of an end'.[2]

The arguments were thrashed out in popular textbooks, like William Phillips's *Outline of Geology*, 1818, and the expanded version by William Conybeare published in 1822, which young William Thain settled down to study in the West Indies. A few years earlier, in 1815, William Smith had published his geological map of England and Wales and part of Scotland, the first nationwide map, and the result of a lifetime's work, based largely on identifying strata according to the fossils they contained. By the mid-1820s geology had became the most exciting and controversial area of science and the Bridgewater Treatises, funded by a bequest to the Royal Society from Francis Egerton, Earl of Bridgewater, for publications on the 'Power, Wisdom and Goodness of God, as manifested in the Creation', roused tremendous debates.

Gradually interest shifted from minerals and rock formation to the secondary formation of valleys and seas and mountain ranges. One school of thought was that over time the sea and land had changed places as great floods swept the globe. Cuvier defined a series of geological periods, each ended by a cataclysmic flood, which could explain why some boulders had apparently wandered hundreds of miles from the strata they belonged to, and how fossils of sea creatures turned up on mountain tops. Then in 1821 workmen in a limestone quarry at Kirkdale in Yorkshire stumbled upon a cave full of bones, which they used to fill potholes in a nearby road. When a local naturalist spotted them, he realised they were fossil bones, including those of mammals never found before in England – elephant and hippopotamus, bison and rhinoceros. William Buckland, the first professor of geology at Oxford, took the coach north to investigate, and the following year gave a paper to the Royal Society declaring this to be the den of hyenas, who had dragged their prey into the cave. Speculating on the existence of a large lake nearby, he tried to relate his findings to the biblical deluge. Buckland was a clergyman as well as a geologist, and if the Creation story was dubious, could he at least uphold Noah's flood?

In 1823 Buckland published his *Reliquiae Diluvianae*, 'or, Observations on the organic remains contained in caves, fissures, and diluvial gravel, and on other geological phenomena, attesting the action of a universal deluge'. Geology seeped into literature, to battle with theology. 'We, we shall view the deep's salt sources poured', wrote Byron in *Heaven and Earth* in 1823, the year of the *Reliquiae*:

> Until one element shall do the work
> Of all in chaos: until they
> The creatures proud of their poor clay,

Shall perish, and their bleached bones shall lurk
In caves, in dens, in clefts of mountains, where
The deep shall follow to their latest lair . . .

Byron spoke to the masses, but Buckland too was a vivid and
eccentric communicator, illustrating his lectures with displays of
fossils and minerals, enlivening them with jokes and even 'imper-
sonations of the gait of extinct animals'.[3] He lectured in quarries and hills, sometimes from horseback. At dinners in his Christ
Church rooms, packed with specimens and strange pets, guests
were served with 'toasted field mice, crocodile steaks, hedge-
hog, puppy, ostrich, and snail', and he aimed, he said, to eat his
way through the animal kingdom. For a time, Buckland's views
gripped public attention, although he slowly came to accept that
not *all* strata could have been created by a single flood, and agreed
that they showed the signs of many inundations long before there
was any evidence of man. The realisation that creatures had lived
and died long before humans posed yet another challenge to
Genesis, with its story of the eating of the fruit, in Milton's words,

Of that forbidden tree, whose mortal taste
Brought death into the world, and all our woe . . .

Death was there already, and so, perhaps was sin.

People liked the idea of cataclysm, of fire and floods and ice,
of nature sweeping man aside: a decade later, crowds would flock
to see John Martin's vast apocalyptic canvases such as *The Deluge*.
(Martin came from Bardon Mill, near Hadrian's Wall, and many
people find his vast panoramas are reminiscent of the North
Pennines.) But a broader approach arrived when Charles Lyell
published his *Principles of Geology* from 1830 to 1833, which revived
his fellow-countryman Hutton's argument of a single beginning
and constant change through minute, gradual processes, a theory
that William Whewell, president of the Geological Society, named
'uniformitarianism'. When the young Charles Darwin, setting out

on the *Beagle* in 1831, was given Lyell's first volume, he was utterly entranced and said that it influenced his view of every rock and island he saw on the voyage.

Lyell's book caused a new flurry of interest. Across Britain, collectors hunted for minerals and fossils and argued over competing theories. Geology was acceptable small talk at dinners, and although women could not be members of the Geological Society of London, they were welcomed as enthusiasts in the informal world of field work. Buckland's wife Mary was a noted researcher before her marriage, contributing drawings to the works of the geologist Conybeare and others, and she continued to go on field trips, collect specimens and make drawings and models of fossils, as well as bringing up nine children.[4] Mary Anning, the famous fossil hunter and dealer in Lyme Regis, discovered the first ichthyosaur and plesiosaur skeletons, and her friends, the 'lady geologist' Philpott sisters, contributed their specimens to museums; Etheldred Benett, ten years younger than Sarah, was recognised for her work on strata and fossil sponges. In 1834 Charles Hennell, a close friend of Marian Evans – the future George Eliot – wrote to his sister Cara, 'When Aunt comes to town we will talk in the first place on Geology, after that, Geology, and lastly a little more Geology.'[5]

Buckland's treatise, *Geology and Mineralogy Considered with Relation to Natural Theology*, also put forward the gradual, progressive theory, but unlike Lyell in his *Principles*, Buckland tried to relate this to design (as Paley had done) by suggesting that fossils showed a sequence of 'divine' creations, preparing the earth for human life. Both books were something that every intellectual young woman had to read, however caught up they were by household duties. 'Bye the bye,' Marian Evans wrote to her friend Martha Jackson in March 1841, 'I have read Buckland's Treatise on Geology with much pleasure, and I believe Lyell's is good, though it differs in Theory, but alas the superficies of the earth are monopolising my attention. I can neither delve nor soar.'[6]

Sarah was a sceptic when faced with extreme theories. But she was fascinated by fossils. Books on these appeared regularly, describing new findings of arthropods and trilobites, molluscs and ammonites and the minuscule forms that make up the limestone rocks. At the other end of the scale some discoveries were large and dramatic. In the 1820s four bizarre early reptiles were found: the aquatic ichthyosaur, the plesiosaur with its curving, dragon-like neck and crocodile teeth, and the land-based megalosaur and iguanadon. In 1829 a flying reptile was added to the list, the ptero-dactyl, which Buckland described as looking a bit like 'our modern bats and vampyres', with an elongated beak and reptile teeth:

in short, a monster resembling nothing that has ever been seen or heard-of upon earth, excepting the dragons of romance and heraldry . . . With flocks of such-like creatures flying in the air, and shoals of no less monstrous Ichthyosauri and Plesiosauri swaming the primeval lakes and rivers, – air, sea, and land must have been strangely tenanted in these early periods of our infant world.[7]

The drama of the great dinosaurs: Henry de la Beche's vision of 'A more ancient Dorset', in 1830.

One way that Buckland identified these was by their tracks, often found in sandstone, like that of the Solway regions. In 1827, when he was asked to identify fossilised impressions on slabs of New Red Sandstone from a quarry near Dumfries, he became convinced that these were the marks of a tortoise, walking lightly on the sand. To test this, Mary covered their kitchen table with paste, while Buckland grabbed their pet tortoise and made it walk. The marks were identical. 'The whole geological world', reported the *London Magazine*, 'has been in raptures.'[8] The idea of such tracks had a haunting resonance, expressed years later by Ida in Tennyson's 'The Princess', when she compares the tiny span of an individual life to the 'deep time' of geology, thinking how the tracks left by her own generation might tell their story to women of the future:

> Would, indeed, we had been
> In lieu of many mortal flies, a race
> Of giants living, each, a thousand years,
> That we might see our own work out, and watch
> The sandy footprint harden into stone.[9]

If many contemporaries linked the large dinosaurs to the creatures of legend, they were equally enchanted by revelations about the smallest fossils. Striving to demonstrate a perfection of organisation that implied design, Buckland wrote of the trilobites, particularly of their compound eyes, made up of tiny crystals, 'nearly four hundred microscopic lenses set side by side', similar to those in contemporary crustaceans and insects.[10]

It was generally agreed that large dinosaur fossils dated from times when the earth was calm, not rocked by eruptions or swamped by floods. In such periods trees grew tall, ferns waved and plants flowered, fruited and seeded again. Fossil trees were found, calamites and cycads, primitive palm-like trees that had grown when the cold northern moors were a tropical forest. Cycads grow slowly and live long, some as long as a thousand years. Their leaves grow directly from the trunk, and whether male or female, they have cones, standing proud in the rosette of leaves. Their bracts overlap, with arcs and spirals veering clockwise and anticlockwise, in groups of three and five, eight and thirteen, twenty-one and thirty-four: like the pinecone and the shell of the nautilus, they display the perfect mathematical ratio of the Fibonacci sequence, one that has no end, like the Huttonian universe itself.

Neuropteris Acuminata, a fossil found in Felling colliery and described in Lindley and Hutton's *Fossil Flora*, 1833, one of several that Sarah copied for her cut-out alabaster windows.

The Losh family were familiar with fossilised trees and plants since so many were found in the coal-measures of Cumberland and Northumberland. In many mines, shale beds full of fossils overlay the coal seams and when a roof-fall took place, wrote one geologist, 'it is a curious sight to see the roof of the mine covered with these vegetable forms, some of them of great beauty and delicacy'.[11] The Newcastle Lit and Phil had specimens illustrating the strata of the coal and lead districts, 'and of curious fossil phenomena and other interesting mineral substances', and so did the Natural History Society of Northumberland. From its foundation in 1829 local people gave the society their personal collections of insects, crustaceans, shells, corals, minerals and fossils. The society's *Transactions* for 1832 carried an article on 'Fossil Stems of Trees at Killingworth Colliery', where George Stephenson had built his first locomotive in 1814, with William Losh's help. When Lindley and Hutton's three-volume *Fossil Flora of the British Isles* was published (with William as one of its first subscribers), it was full of descriptions of fossils from the mines.[12] The beautiful plates showed the markings on trunks and stems, the complex patterns of cones, the coral-like fronds of ferns. These were copied into notebooks and sketchbooks – evidence both of transience and endurance, a defiance of death in stone, a work of natural theology.

III

MAKER

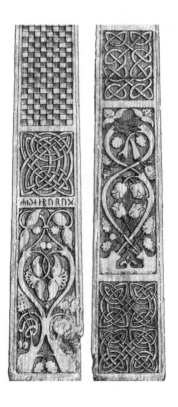

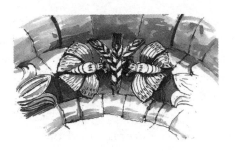

15 Mourning

When James Losh died in 1833, Sarah and Katharine lost a lifelong ally and friend. Worse was to come. In late 1834 Katharine fell ill, and it was clear that despite the doctors' efforts she would not live. Henry Lonsdale wrote, years later, 'Katharine Isabella Losh died in February 1835, to the almost inconsolable grief of her sister, who to the end of her days brooded over this sad bereavement.'[1] Sarah was left alone.

Katharine's death 'after a severe illness' was announced in a brief notice in the local paper, which added that 'her loss will be deeply felt and regretted in the neighbourhood – especially by the poor, who have never met with a kinder and more benevolent friend'.[2] She was buried in the family plot in Wreay churchyard, near her mother and father. The spring was stormy and wild, with gales and blinding rain.[3] As Sarah grieved her family and friends were all around her, but no one could replace the sister whom she had looked after and lived with since she was small. They had been so close that it was almost unthinkable that she should be alone, that she, the older sister, had not died first. When Jane Austen died in 1817 – the year that the Losh sisters were travelling together across Europe – her older sister Cassandra wrote, 'I have lost a treasure, such a sister, such a friend as never can have been surpassed, – she was the sun of my life, the gilder of every pleasure, the soother of every sorrow. I had not a thought concealed from her, & it is as if I had lost a part of myself.'⁴ This is what Sarah felt too, with a panic like that in ghost stories where a person loses their shadow, or looks in the mirror and sees no reflection. To survivors, the world can seem strange, disorienting. The house that was once full of easy, sisterly talk seemed dense with silences.

When her time of deep mourning passed, the grief remained, but Sarah burst into years of creativity as if trying to save something she had lost. She changed. Before she had been proudly fashionable, but now her clothes were sombre, like those of a widow, black, and then grey and mauve. In fact she never quite moved out of mourning. She stopped her work on the Woodside facade, facing the sun, that she and Katharine had planned together.⁵ But she was stoical and tough-minded. She was needed by her elderly aunts, Margaret at Woodside and Ann and Sarah Bonner at Brisco, however much she may have resented them living on while Katharine was gone. She was needed by Joe at Ravenside. She was still expected to give house-room to her cousins and their families, to oversee the estate, to take care of her business interests. She woke up, and began to build.

It helped that there were new lives in the family: William Septimus and his wife Sarah had a baby, James, in 1834, who would spend much of his childhood at Wreay, playing in the garden at Woodside. There were changes in Wreay itself, too. The villagers and the Twelve Men were expressing concern about the future of their church and school. William Gaskin's successor as curate, Mr Barnes, had accepted another benefice and moved away and everyone was waiting for a replacement. In October that year, squeezed between accounts of Henry Brougham's health, the grounding of the Solway steamer on rocks on its passage from Liverpool to Dundalk, and an inquest on a drunk carter, the *Carlisle Journal* ran a sharp, unsigned letter, headed 'Chapelry of Wreay', complaining that 'there is at present no resident curate':

The late Curate resigned his office in May last, and in August the parishioners petitioned the Bishop to have a resident minister appointed. But his lordship has since been much engaged in taking care of the Irish Church – so anxiously aiding his brethren of the lawn sleeves to impose upon Paddy parsons he does not want, that he has had no time to listen to the bleating of his own flock, who are in want of a shepherd. Divine worship is performed by accident in the afternoons, when an unemployed stray parson can be caught for the purpose. Does this not offer a proof of the necessity of relieving the Bishops from the toils of Parliamentary duty?[6]

It was true that Bishop Percy had spent much time in the Lords, and hardly any in Carlisle. Peel's government was set on reform in Ireland, where the church's large landholdings, heavy tithe demands and great numbers of clergy had been bitterly resented for years by the Catholic peasants who had to pay for them. Twenty years before, in 1813, John Christian Curwen had been appalled by the low living standards of the Irish poor, burdened with tithes imposed by the church.[7] Now Irish radicals, led by Daniel O'Connell, demanded change and, in response, in 1833 nearly half the bishoprics were removed and surplus clergy reduced. But Percy was stung by the accusation that he had neglected his own diocese. A week later the *Journal* carried a strong response to this 'unfounded attack', signed by 'a layman', again squeezed between important local news items like the finding of 'large potatoes', the Brampton cattle show and a robbery at Cockermouth. The letter pointed out that half the delay was due to counter-petitions from Wreay, one suggesting that a local minister might take on the role in addition to his own parish, the other asking for a resident minister. Now, an editorial note stated, a minister had indeed been appointed. This was young Richard Jackson of Ainstable, 'and a more worthy appointment, we will venture to say, was never made by that body'.[8]

The son of an old gentry family, Richard Jackson had followed a typical Cumbrian path, graduating from Queen's College, Oxford, and then acting as curate and priest in Borrowdale, deep in the fells. In 1832 he became curate at Ainstable across the Eden valley, from where he often rode over to read the service at Wreay. He was much liked in the neighbourhood. His nephew remembered him 'as a very kind, enormously stout gentleman ... he was a great lover of flowers & I well remember that he grew the beautiful old rose called "Safranao". He planted ones to climb on the palings at Wreay station.' But he was only thirty when he was appointed to St Mary's, on 4 November 1835, long before the railway and his rose-growing days. Signs in the sky augured dramatic things. 'Everything else in the Neighbourhood is in the usual quiet way', Francis Aglionby of Nunnery wrote jokingly when he described Jackson's move in an affectionate letter to his daughter Jane:

but last night there was a most beautiful Aurora borealis for more than two Hours, which quite illuminated the atmosphere and would doubtless alarm the superstitious fears of old Ann and all the other good old Women who interpreted this Phenomenon, *streamers* always being considered the forerunner of some awful Event; perhaps the River Eden may in consequence back its course . . .[9]

No such marvels took place, but Richard Jackson was instrumental in helping Sarah Losh to build her church. His arrival proved a spur. Less than a year after he came, Jackson signed the parish resolution allowing Sarah to divert the road to the west of the chapel yard. By then she had already started building, at the top of the hill above the school field.

In the summer of 1835, at the hamlet of Perranzabuloe, just south of Perranporth on the north-west coast of Cornwall, a local antiquarian, John Michell, was working in the sands of the great dunes. That September, the journal *The West Briton* carried this letter:

Sir, I have just removed the sand from the oldest church in this parish, which appears to have been overwhelmed by it, according to tradition, supported faintly by records, 500 or 600 years ago. This church is probably one of the most ancient ever laid open, and wants nothing to render it as complete as when first erected, except its roof and doors.[10]

There was a legend that St Piran, the patron saint of Cornwall, had landed on this beach from Ireland and built a small oratory of wattle and daub; when he died, his sorrowing followers built a small stone church over his grave. (According to the seventeenth-century antiquarian Nicholas Carew, St Piran lived over two hundred years 'in perfect health'.) As pilgrims flocked to venerate the saint the little church became so rich that a monastery was built nearby, but the gales blew the sands up and overwhelmed it and in the tenth century the oratory was abandoned. Trusting that the shifting sands would stop when they met a stream, the people moved their church a few hundred yards to the opposite side of the brook, until tin-mining in the late eighteenth century dried the stream up, when this building too was engulfed in sand and a new parish church was built.

Michell had uncovered St Piran's oratory, a simple building thirty feet long and about twelve wide. Inside, stone benches ran around three walls, and a stone altar stood at the eastern end. The

The church in the sands; the evocative frontispiece to the Rev. Collins, *Perranzabuloe, the Lost Church Found*, 1836.

door was richly carved, and the projecting keystone of the arch was ornamented with a 'tyger's head', while on the columns on either side were 'the head of a man and a woman, rudely sculpted in stone – of very remote antiquity'.[11] The masonry was crude but 'solid and compact'. There were no windows, except a small opening high in the south wall, making one imagine services held in the light of flickering tapers. It was a place of worship and a place of death: under the altar the skeletons of two men and a woman were found, with their toes pointing to the east, and the skulls of all three between the woman's feet.[12] Around the building, wrote Michell, lay thousands of human bones uncovered by the wind, bleaching in the Cornish light. 'If this description should appear of sufficient interest to obtain a place in your columns, it is at your service for that purpose,' he ended modestly.

His letter was of more than sufficient interest. It caused a sensation among antiquaries, theologians, and the curious public who rushed to see the site before it disappeared again under the dunes. When Michell's findings were reported in the *Gentleman's Magazine*, the writer suggested, in view of the scattered bones, that the chapel may also have been a mortuary.[13] It was a haunting place: 'how wild and cheerless is that long, bleak, barren belt of sand that girds the shore of Perran's Bay', wrote the Rev. Charles Trelawney Collins in 1836.[14] There were no trees, and even the gorse and heather of the moors had been left behind: 'All nature here is in a garment of sadness.' What Collins described was the landscape of Sarah's heart. Moreover Perranzabuloe was a place that had been entombed by time and by the forces of nature, brought back to the light after centuries, like Pompeii which had moved her so much. Collins himself made this connection, likening the shifting sands, seeping into every crack, to the volcano's smothering ash: 'Vesuvius has not more effectually thrown its sable mantle of volcanic dust over the city and gardens of Pompeii.'[15] Within a year the sand was making its inroads again, and soon the chapel would vanish, leaving nothing but a mound among the dunes.

In his book *Perranzabuloe, the Lost Church Found*, Collins cited

A reconstruction of the doorway at Perranzabuloe.

the simplicity of the building, and the fact that no crucifixes or ornaments were found nearby, to argue vehemently that this represented the early British church as following a 'Protestant' style of worship. In his view the Reformation had inadvertently restored a tradition of simplicity that was of far greater antiquity in Britain than that of the Church of Rome.[16] Other writers noted that the building seemed strikingly similar 'to the structures of the early Christians, especially in the East – at Byzantium and Antioch'.[17] (Once again, Sarah's interest in this style of building was in advance of others: for a while in the 1850s Early Christian churches like this were considered good prototypes by Anglo-Catholics such as John Henry Newman, because they were adaptable to modern liturgy, and were used as the model, for example, for the University church in Dublin.[18])

★

In her role as village benefactor, Sarah was concerned about the old, and the dying, as well as the young. One problem in Wreay was the threat of overcrowding in the graveyard. This was a common anxiety. Churchyards in the growing industrial towns and cities were becoming so full that decaying corpses were dug up to make way for new ones: visitors were appalled to see open graves, with bones scattered around. There were worries about crowded graves polluting the water supply and causing epidemics, and in 1832 an Act was passed to encourage public cemeteries. At that point Sarah and Katharine had approached the dean and chapter and the corporation and offered a field near Carlisle for a public cemetery. Rebuffed, they gave an acre of their land, beyond the school field, to be used as a cemetery for their own village, 'available to all denominations of persons – a free gift to the public'.[19] This was walled around and planted with ivy and shrubs, yew trees and thujas, the cedar-like tree often called *arbor vitae*, the tree of life.

Sarah now began to think of some way to integrate the new graveyard into the village, and of the need to build a small mortuary chapel. It was the custom in Victorian funerals, at least in towns with the new public cemeteries, for the body to be set down to rest in a chapel in the graveyard, with the mourners standing round in silence, before the final burial. St Piran provided her with the perfect model, laden with poetry, legend, history. She obtained precise drawings and measurements, and set about building what she called 'an exact replica', although, as with everything she did, she modified it to her own design. She built her chapel of the local yellow freestone and roofed it in Lazonby sandstone slabs, with a curving lath and plaster ceiling inside. Within she placed a stone altar, and a low stone seat around the walls.

She intended it, she wrote, as a chapel of ease, a place to lay the coffin before burial in the nearby graveyard. Its ancient form gave a sense of continuity across the centuries, the burials of those newly dead merging in imagination with the scattered bones of Saxon men and women on the Cornish shore. It was also an act of rescue, another form of resurrection or retrieval of things long buried under the earth, like the fossils and the Roman stones in the quarries. St Piran's was a work of human endeavour and belief, that had been hidden, uncovered, and would soon be covered again. Her copy might endure on its hillside as a reminder in centuries to come. It looked back and forward at once.

Sarah's mortuary chapel on the hillside.

Standing on the crest of the hill, on the short track from the road to the land designated for the new graveyard, the chapel was twenty-nine feet by sixteen, slightly wider than St Piran's, with two doors instead of one, on the east and south. The doors were made of studded oak planks, and the arches had roll-mouldings and carvings of a lion's head and two human heads, adapting the Cornish model. At Wreay the heads are both male, and both bearded. These strong, sombre carvings – finer on the east than the south door – were the work of young William Hindson, the mason's oldest son, who also carved a palm tree that stood inside the chapel.

The Hindsons had been tenants of the Loshes since the mid seventeenth century; in the will of Margaret Losh in 1667, David Hindson of Aiketgate was one of many men listed as owing her money. One branch of the family lived at Mellguards, where Sarah's forebear John Brown had lived, and where she had inherited Mellguards Farm, a large holding of 189 acres.[20] Now in his early fifties, William Hindson senior was a much respected master mason and waller who had worked with Sarah and Katharine when they restored Woodside, and on the school and other smaller projects. A generous, well-read man, he lived with his wife Ann in a house overflowing with eight sons and a daughter. Two sons would emigrate, but young William followed his father's trade. In 1835 he was twenty-four, and he and his wife Margaret had a one-year-old son. One story, unsubstantiated, is that Sarah was so impressed she sent William to Naples to study sculpture (although it seems more likely that she sent him as a pupil to Dunbar's Carlisle Academy, and that the story has got muddled with that of Dunbar himself, who had gone to Naples to study in 1825). Certainly she encouraged Hindson, gave him work and admired his skills. Later in life he would be Sarah's tenant in Brisco Hall, and eventually he became a prosperous farmer at Howfield nearby, with nine children and a house full of books, known for his excellent library and his kindness to his in-laws and relatives, some of whom spent their last days with him.

Between the mortuary chapel and the road, Sarah built a cottage for the sexton, low and simple. Its plank door was flanked by two round-headed windows, and on the back wall ran a row of attic windows in the narrow curved arches which would become her signature. Today the chapel stands on the track before the cemetery gate, its weathered wooden doors closed to the light. Inside it is bare and musty, cobweb-hung, like an old barn. But as you walk up the hill from the church, or the other way, from Woodside, it stands out square against the skyline.

16 Extraordinary Power

While Sarah was researching the past and erecting a building that looked back over centuries, five miles away the city of Carlisle was embracing the future. After the troubles of the early 1830s the gentry ventured back to cultural delights, lectures and concerts. The Academy of Fine Arts was finding it hard though to raise funds for its new exhibitions, and its eighth, and last, was held in 1833. But if art was a disappointment, music flowered. The Assembly Rooms behind the Crown and Mitre and the Coffee House had been 'newly and elegantly fitted up', reported the *Journal*, 'and with its brilliant chandeliers it has a rich and beautiful appearance'. It was here, in September 1833, that Paganini, who was making a tour of forty-four provincial towns, 'astonished the people of Carlisle by a display of extraordinary power'.[1]

The great and good of the city − who must have sat open-mouthed at Paganini's fireworks − were soon challenged from other quarters. The Reform Act had dealt a blow to the freemen, the only people allowed to vote in elections under the old regime. Now the Municipal Corporations Act of 1835 saw the end of their power. The eight trade guilds, the Merchants, Tanners, Skinners, Butchers, Smiths, Weavers, Tailors and Shoemakers, from whom the mayor, corporation and bailiffs had traditionally been elected, became a thing of the past. Instead, the new Act provided for annual elections for aldermen and councillors, with the vote open to all male householders with property worth ten pounds or more.

Carlisle was now a full-blown, if small, industrial city. Among its new factories were three companies that would later grow into giants: Joseph Ferguson's mill; Hudson Scott's firm, the forerunner of the Metal Box Company; and Jonathan Carr's famous biscuit factory. But the main industry was still in textiles. On the sky-line, in 1836, the astonishing chimney of the Dixon family's Shad-don Mills was rising between Caldewgate and Denton Holme. Shaddon was the largest cotton mill in the country, seven storeys high, powered entirely by steam, and although the Dixons still employed hundreds of hand-loom weavers who delivered the cloth to their warehouse every Saturday, as the price of coal grew cheaper they expanded the mill and brought in hundreds of new power-looms. Another of the old ways disappeared.

Carlisle from the south-west in 1838, showing Dixon's mill with its high chimney, which Sarah could see as she walked from Wreay to Woodside, standing out against the view of the distant Scottish hills.

Despite the new factories the commercial life of the city was always precarious. A flood of bankruptcies in 1836 caused a run on

Forster's bank, and the stopping of payment. As rumours spread, banks were besieged by people anxious to retrieve their deposits and for their bills of credit to be honoured. Only one local bank survived. As the *Patriot* reported:

> But a week ago Carlisle proudly rejoiced in her prosperity; our manufacturers were fully employed; new branches of trade were every day springing up . . . not a cloud lowered over our prospects, when in a moment the whole was blasted, and that so suddenly and unexpectedly that no one foresaw the calamity which every class from opulent merchant to servant shared.[2]

The alarm here was typical of the country as a whole, and this, combined with a feeling that the Reform Bill had not gone nearly far enough towards democracy, helped to fuel the start of the Chartist movement. The People's Charter of 1838 included in its demands a vote for all men, secret ballots and annual parliaments. When their first petition to parliament was turned down in June 1839, huge, turbulent meetings took place across the country.

Sarah lost money in the Carlisle bank crash, although how much is hard to tell. She was still, however, profiting from the alkali works on the Tyne, of which she was technically the proprietor although the company had been run for her by her uncle William and then by William Septimus. But this too brought some problems: in 1836 she was sued by a local market gardener, whose apples and pears and raspberries had been ruined when they were in blossom the previous May, when gas and fumes from the Walker chimney 'so scorched the blossom, as to discolour it, and caused the leaves to fall to the ground and go hard and, when handled, fell like snuff'.[3] This would hurt Sarah, being such a careful gardener herself.

On the Woodside estate, however, and the other Wreay farms, the agricultural life continued in its steady way. The year's tasks went on: hoeing the potatoes, weeding the corn, scaling dung on the fields and cutting back the gorse, lambing, shearing and taking the sheep to market, putting the cows to the bull and selling the calves. In the village, the Twelve Men held their Candlemas meetings and at Easter there were celebrations and dances on the green. The school was flourishing. On 7 March 1838, when westerlies were blanketing the fells with sleet and Ann Robinson of Scalesceugh was taking potatoes to market in Carlisle, her farmer husband John was busy in his role as one of the Twelve Men, and trustee for the school: 'in the evening at Wreay paying Jos Story Schoolmaster, Quarter Pence for the Schoolers', he wrote in his diary. Next day he went up again to meet his fellow trustee Thomas Slack to talk about taking on more scholars.[4] But the effect of the new Poor Law, which had removed much outdoor relief and established workhouses instead, was felt even in a small village. Seasonal work meant that many country labourers needed help at times and now lived in fear of the workhouse. Down at the new workhouse Robinson settled the election of Poor Law Guardians, while the schoolmaster Mr Story helped him to sort out the poor rate, a tax on local householders, which was gathered in with much grumbling on a cold April day of rain and hail.

Robinson spent other evenings with Richard Jackson, puzzling over the problems raised by the Commutation of Tithes Act that replaced the centuries-old payment of tithes in kind to the church with payments in money. In the past a tenth of the produce of the land – of crops, timber, livestock, eggs – was due to the rector, to pay for his services and for alms. The change to money had already happened slowly when new arrangements were made after enclosures, but now the whole country had to be surveyed, producing considerable headaches for the national Tithe Commissioner, William Blamire. Sarah's own estate was the largest in the village and her name headed the new list of payments, showing an annual rent of £6 10s 10d to the Dean and Chapter in lieu of bushels of corn and oats, milches of milk, numbers of geese and eggs, 'twopence for every Calf, five pence for every foal'.⁵ A special meeting was held at the Plough, called by the local landowners with Sarah once again at the head of the list, to reach an agreement.

There were, however, celebratory moments. On 20 June 1837, William IV died and the accession of the eighteen-year-old Victoria was announced at the Carel Cross in Carlisle's market square 'amidst much cheering'.⁶ Down the road at Penrith, when the proclamation was read out all the church bells were rung. One ringer, Peter Stewart,

upwards of ninety, had acted in that capacity through five successive reigns and tolled the minute bell for the death of four kings. A very fresh man for his years, in drinking Her Majesty's health he wished that she might be a 'good lass' and live to be as old as himself; and then having her lease renewed live longer in the hearts of her people.⁷

Britain was entering a new reign and a new era – the railway age. Sarah saw one of James Losh's dreams come to fruition as the railways drove towards Carlisle from all sides. Her cousin James was now chairman of the Newcastle to Carlisle company and her uncle William a director. Already work had begun on another line westwards to Maryport, and plans were being hotly debated about the best routes to bring lines north from Lancaster and south from Glasgow. The first section of the Newcastle–Carlisle line, from Blaydon to Hexham, opened in March 1835, although services were briefly suspended after a landowner demanded the use of horse-drawn carriages instead of steam locomotives, which had been banned by the original Act of Parliament. In June 1838 the whole route was opened. If she wished, Sarah could travel from Carlisle's London Road station all the way to Gateshead, and the following year a temporary bridge took the railway across the Tyne into the heart of Newcastle itself. To celebrate, the directors put on six early-morning trains from Carlisle and gave the guests breakfast at the Newcastle Assembly Rooms when they arrived.

There was, however, an omen for the future when some of the return trains failed to arrive back on time, shunting into Carlisle in the early hours, fiery monsters in the dark.

A few months after the first train sped across the country another monster roared into the city. This was a gale without precedent, careering in from the Atlantic. In Ireland it was known as the Night of the Big Wind. On the morning of 5 January 1839, snow fell; then the air turned warm and eerily calm, until the wind rose. By evening a hurricane was howling, uprooting trees, tearing off roofs, toppling spires. Blazes started as the wind thrummed down chimneys and scattered fires on the hearth. Houses collapsed. Three hundred people died and thousands were left homeless. A quarter of Dublin was laid waste and forty-two ships were wrecked.

Next day the gale ripped across the Irish sea, blasting the west coast from Scotland to Liverpool. In Whitehaven, the Maryport schooner *John Airey*, which had put in for repairs on her way to Liverpool with a cargo of palm oil, marble, crystal, wool and silk, was driven from her moorings and smashed on the rocks. In Carlisle slates began to fly and chimneys crashed: people trembled through a night of total darkness, lashed by rain and hail. 'The morning', declared the *Journal*, 'dawned upon a scene of desolation such as has rarely been witnessed.' The streets were strewn with slates and bricks, windows were driven in, sheds blown away, factory chimneys toppled – although Dixon's chimney at Shaddon, the wonder of the city, three hundred feet high, withstood the wind. People gathered fearlessly to watch it vibrate and lean backwards many inches. Even the iron-framed carriages from the new trains lay across the track. Several people were killed by falling roofs and the trees around the cathedral 'lay across the street, like temporary barricades against an enemy'.

The wind blew for three days, slackening slowly. In the countryside around, whole plantations were laid waste. At Lowther

Castle chestnuts toppled like ninepins; at Corby the Howards lost their beeches and limes and even the tall Scotch firs. Trees that had 'withstood the storms of a century and a half', intoned the *Journal,* 'have been torn up by the roots as if they were mere twigs'. The hurricane did not miss Wreay: 'At Woodside, the seat of Miss Losh, an immense number of trees have been uprooted.'[8] In the spring and summer of 1840 the ground was cleared. The timber was cut, and left to season; wood for planks, for joists, for roofing timbers, for doors and for pews.

17 Not in the Gothick Style

Having worked on the house, the school and the mortuary chapel, Sarah was becoming an experienced builder, used to imposing her own ideas. For the last two years she had been thinking of building a church, ever since she had persuaded the Twelve Men to move the road and to grant her the land on the south of the old chapel.

To call herself an 'architect' would have been unthinkable: that was a man's profession, and she was a woman and an amateur. No woman would qualify in this sphere until the end of the century. Yet few churches, as one critic has written, 'have ever looked so absolutely one person's creation'.[1] Sarah was a pioneer, with few models to follow. In the past there had been women like Lady Elizabeth Wilbraham, who designed houses for her family and helped Wren with his City churches, but she had never claimed her work. In Bath in the 1790s, Sarah could have heard of Jane Parminter and her cousin Elizabeth, who came back from a Grand Tour and in 1795 built their bizarre, sixteen-sided house, A La Ronde, in Exmouth, based on the Basilica of San Vitale in Ravenna; but the design was then attributed to a 'gentleman architect' from Bath, John Lowder. Shortly after Sarah began work, Elizabeth Simcoe, a wealthy evangelical dowager, and her daughters carved stone and wood, painted glass and designed the decorative schemes for three churches in Devon. More women, as yet unsung, followed suit in the later Victorian period.[2] But in the late 1830s Sarah was on her own. Yet she only had to look locally, in the Eden valley itself, to find a woman builder with dash and courage. This was Lady Anne Clifford who, in the seventeenth century, rebuilt her castles at Brougham, Appleby and Brough, and two fine churches at Brougham and Mallerstang. Like Sarah, Lady Anne 'tended to exaggerate the ruination that preceded her restorations', and she too was a woman of pronounced individual taste, 'not just conservative, but positively medievalising'.[3]

In the mid-1830s, medievalising was all the rage. When Sarah was reading about Perranzabuloe and its chapel in the dunes, and when Lyell and Buckland were gripping public attention with their theories of the earth, new books and tracts were also flooding from the presses on church architecture and its relation to contemporary life and worship, particularly studies of the Gothic. In 1835, booksellers stocked a work by Robert Willis, an affable young cleric who was passionately interested in music, mathematics, mechanics and architecture. He lectured on engineering, and his clearly reasoned book, *Remarks on the Architecture of the Middle Ages, especially of Italy*, reduced elements of building such as vaults, piers and shafts almost to 'parts', rather as one would put together a machine.

The library at Woodside was full of such books. Studies of medieval architecture in Britain and Europe, illustrated with prints and engravings, were now abundant. In 1830, the genial polymath William Whewell had published his *Architectural Notes on German Churches, with notes written during an Architectural Tour in Picardy and Normandy*, and a second edition appeared in 1835. Whewell was a Lancastrian, fond of the Lakes and the northern counties, an admirer of Coleridge and a friend of Wordsworth, well known to the Loshes and their circle. He had travelled in France in 1832 with Thomas Rickman, describing him as an attractive, odd character in his Quaker dress, 'very good-humoured, very intelligent and active . . . a little, round, fat man, with short, thick legs, and a large head . . . he is perpetually running from one side of the street to the other to peep into whatever catches his attention'.[4] Rickman was now back in the area building a new wing 'in the Gothick style' for Scaleby Castle, the birthplace of the writer William Gilpin. The rambling castle had grown piecemeal over the years, with its double moat and pele tower, the small fortified keep of red sandstone, built from stones from the nearby Roman Wall. But by the late eighteenth century it was largely in ruins, and when Gilpin went back, he found two poor families squatting in the lower hall, and the rest of the house, he thought, beyond hope, 'the floors, yielding to the tread, make curiosity dangerous'.[5]

Rickman's new Gothic Reading Room in English Street, Carlisle,
in 1831, dwarfing the surrounding streets.

Rickman's new wing at Scaleby was a careful addition, and his presence was also felt in Carlisle itself, in the new Reading Rooms and Subscription Library – with a billiard hall above – much praised in the city as 'a beautiful example of the Decorated style of Gothic architecture', with oriel windows, pinnacles and 'crocketed canopies'.[6] But Rickman was already being considered as inaccurate, and even dull, in his evocation of past styles. The real authority on the Gothic, even by the mid-1830s, was the young Augustus Welby Pugin. In 1834, after the Palace of Westminster was burned to the ground, the twenty-two-year-old Pugin worked with Charles Barry on the new Houses of Parliament, designing its Gothic interiors and the tower for Big Ben. A genuine iconoclast, loathing the false classicism of the previous generation, Pugin thrilled to the sight of the palace in flames. 'There is nothing much to regret, and a great deal to rejoice in,' he wrote:

A vast amount of Soane's mixtures and Wyatt's heresies have been effectively consigned to oblivion. Oh, it was a glorious sight to see his composite mullions and cement pinnacles and battlements flying and cracking . . . The old walls stood triumphantly amidst this scene of ruin while brick walls and framed sashes, slate roofs etc. fell faster than a pack of cards.[7]

Every false note must be swept away so that 'pure' Gothic could reign again.

Pugin had grown up with Gothic architecture. His father Auguste, a French draughtsman, contributed drawings to Britton's *Architectural Antiquities* and in 1821 published the first volume of his own *Specimens of Gothic Architecture*, with detailed drawings of mouldings and tracery, vaults and fans, 'genuine materials for the Architect to work from'.[8] The text was written by Edward Willson, an antiquary and inveterate collector, who believed that accuracy was not the only vital quality. An architect must also 'endeavour to think in the manner of the original inventors' and understand the ethos of the early works, so that the building would come alive from within. In his teens Pugin contributed to the *Specimens* (later entitled *Examples of Gothic Architecture*) and took over after Auguste's death in 1832.

The urgent search for 'soul' or inner vitality in the new buildings was born of a genuine alarm at an apparent collapse in the Anglican church. Its clergy seemed complacent, often absent

from their parish or keener on hunting and shooting than looking after their flock and their buildings. And while church and
state were still intricately bound together, the Anglican church
had been under pressure in many different forms in recent years.
It was weakened by the repeal of the Test and Corporation Acts in
1828, which removed some of the laws against Dissenters, by the
Catholic Emancipation Act of 1829, and by the bishops' very public opposition to the Reform Bill. Dissenters, who understand-
ably complained about paying church rates, were now building
their own meeting houses while Anglican worshippers in some
slums and in the new terraces of the growing cities had no parish
church to go to at all. At a deeper level, the findings in geology
and the new biblical criticism that presented Jesus as a human
teacher, rather than a divine being, had gnawed at people's faith.
The uncertainty that Carlyle depicted in *Past and Present* when he
wrote of the mechanical age seemed equally true of the spiritual
realm. J. A. Froude – the son of the Loshes' old friend Margaret
Spedding – caught the mood movingly when he looked back,
writing on Carlyle:

All around us the intellectual lightships had been broken from their
moorings, and it was then a new and trying experience. The present
generation which has grown up in an open spiritual ocean, which has
got used to it and has learned to swim for itself, will never know what
it was like to find the lights all drifting, the compasses all awry, and
nothing left to steer by but the stars.[9]

The crisis called forth strong responses. In July 1833 in Oxford,
the Professor of Poetry John Keble preached a sermon on 'National
Apostasy', arguing that the state was trampling on, and demeaning,
the position of the church. This was followed by three *Tracts for
the Times*, unsigned, but the work of John Henry Newman, a fellow of Oriel and vicar of St Mary's, the university church. A third
key figure was the Regius professor of Hebrew, Edward Bouv-
erie Pusey. Successive *Tracts* appeared over the next eight years.

Seeking to revitalise the church from within, the Tractarians, as they were soon known, looked back to the church's relationship with Roman Catholicism, suggesting that the Church of England was in essence still a branch of the original church 'by direct Apostolic succession', with its own continuous history. Feeling that much had been lost at the Reformation, in terms of church design they argued for restoration of the medieval plan, with the nave for congregation and the chancel for priests, divided by a symbolic boundary, traditionally the rood screen, 'with the crucified Christ under a doom painting or last judgement. Thus what stands between the nave and the chancel, this world and the next, are what are known as the four last things – death, judgment, heaven and hell.'[10] They also campaigned for the reinstatement of some parts of the medieval liturgy, a position that eventually drove Newman to convert to Catholicism in 1845.

Pugin, who had already converted in 1835, was sympathetic to these ideas while not overtly adhering to the Oxford Movement. In 1836 he published *Contrasts*, a brilliantly satirical short work comparing the ugly buildings of modern Europe and the stylistic gallimaufry of Regency England to their rich medieval counterparts, and contrasting the neglected poor of London streets with the allegedly contented merchants and peasants of the Middle Ages. His views were widely reported and in a rush of work in the late 1830s he began designing churches, many commissioned by leading Catholics. His *True Principles of Pointed or Christian Architecture* of 1841 protested that Gothic style could be all-embracing, applied to everything from 'a cathedral to a curtain-rail'.[11] Full of wit and passion, this short book was an inspiration to contemporary architects like Gilbert Scott and William Butterfield. Not, however, to Sarah Losh.

Sarah was fully aware that she was taking the plunge at a moment when the arrangement and decoration of churches was a subject of intense scrutiny. She took note of Pugin's strictures

Old and New Towns, from Pugin's brilliantly polemical
Contrasts of 1836.

about accuracy and 'vitality', but firmly turned her back on the
Gothic taste. Indeed, as she planned her stubbornly individual
church, she was working almost deliberately against Pugin's influence. In 1841 Henry and Philip Howard of Corby Castle commissioned him to build a Catholic church, Our Lady and St Wilfrid,
at Warwick Bridge, and Sarah talked to Philip about this and saw
the drawings. Built by George Myers, Pugin's chief associate and
principal builder, this too was a small church, but it was the dia-

metric opposite to Wreay – intimate, romantic, highly decorated and gilded, 'a Pugin jewel-box, dark and claustrophobic, richly coloured and emotional'.[12]

She also resisted the aggressive campaigns of the Camden Society, formed by Cambridge undergraduates in 1839. Their first venture was to collect information about Britain's medieval churches by publishing a handbook, *A Few Hints on the Practical Study of Ecclesiological Antiquities*, with a blank page for notes so that members could send in their findings. Like the Tractarians, the society's members wished to reform both the ritual and the style of building of the Anglican church, but they were far more doctrinaire. Brooding over problems that were at once architectural and theological, they pronounced that Gothic was the only truly Christian architecture, particularly the 'classical Gothic of the Decorated Style'.[13] Church design was not a matter of taste, convenience or caprice, wrote their founder John Mason Neile, but a discipline, a holy science, 'ecclesiology'.[14] Their monthly magazine, the *Ecclesiologist*, whose first issue appeared in October 1841, argued loudly for a return to medieval design, genuinely believing that this would also signal a return to 'medieval piety'.

The movement was staggeringly influential: within three years the society's members included sixteen bishops and thirty-one peers and MPs and was 'dictating ecclesiastical taste to the nation'.[15] The membership were intolerant of all outsiders: they admired Pugin's work but found him suspect because of his Catholicism; they damned Rickman as a Quaker, guilty of 'extreme ecclesiological ignorance'. The more extreme members insisted that churches that did not conform to their rules should be pulled down and rebuilt in the Gothic style – so much so that it has been argued that the Ecclesiologists destroyed nearly as much of the fabric of British churches as Cromwell had done, or, if not, only from lack of funds.[16]

Although resistant to their aesthetic, Sarah was interested in the current debates about the early church and in the new

Anglo-Catholicism. She bought the sermons of the seventeenth-century preacher Lancelot Andrewes, whom the Tractarians had revived, promoting him as a key link in the church's Catholic heritage despite some of his obviously pro-Reformation opinions. She also subscribed to the new edition of *A Plain but Full Exposition of the Catechism of the Church of England* by William Nicolson, a Cumbrian and an antiquarian, Bishop of Carlisle at the start of the eighteenth century. And when, as part of their historical work, the Tractarians began publishing *The Library of the Fathers* – translations of early Church Fathers such as Tertullian, Ambrose, Athanasius and Augustine – her name was on the first list of 2,500 subscribers, and on separate lists for several other volumes.[17]

Yet Sarah had her own ideas of the early church, which she saw as adapting a plurality of beliefs and symbols inherited from classical, Egyptian and eastern religions. She rejected the Camden Society's decree in their pamphlet, *A Few Words to Church-builders,* that the style for a small church must be Early English (and Decorated or Perpendicular for larger ones). When she turned over plans for her church in her head, one thing was clear. It was not in the Gothic style. She wanted something purer, simpler and more 'rustic' – a favourite word of hers, as it was of Wordsworth, conjuring the history of their remote rural area.

Instead, Sarah turned to Romanesque, perhaps with a touch of defiant local pride, a sense that the round arches of Holm Cultram or Warwick Bridge were the 'true' heritage of Cumberland. Romanesque architecture had formed a minor thread in the Gothic revival. As long ago as the 1790s Thomas Girtin had celebrated it in watercolours of Ely cathedral and Lindisfarne; Turner painted Southwell minster and Durham cathedral; John Sell Cotman made ravishing studies of Norman churches in Norfolk and Normandy. Sarah was far from alone in her emotional response to the combination of solidity and delicacy. But although engravings of Romanesque arches and doorways had figured in antiquarian books ever since John Taylor's *Essays on Gothic Architecture* of 1800, writers were puzzled over exactly what term to use. The style clearly pre-dated the Norman conquest – so it could be called 'Saxon' – yet the Normans were also openly proud, as William of Malmesbury had written, of introducing a 'a new kind of building'.[18] In 1814, in *Archaeologia*, the Cambridge librarian Thomas Kerrich had considered this problem of naming: 'the Italians call the old, heavy style of building Lombard Architecture, because they conceive that it was in fashion during the time that the Lombards were powerful in Italy. And we, for the same reason, call it Saxon and Norman, but the architecture is the same'.[19] In the end 'Norman' won out, largely due to its adoption by Rickman in 1817. When William Gunn used the term 'romanesque' in 1819, it was as a pejorative adjective, to describe the way in which this style was 'a vitious deviation from true Roman architecture'.[20] It took a long time to become accepted although it had a useful international dimension, as it could apply to pre-Gothic work in Italy, France or Germany, while also solving the old Saxon/Norman divide in Britain. Sarah herself called the style Saxon, Norman and 'modified Lombardic'.

In Britain, Norman abbeys and parish churches had been repeatedly adapted and modernised: many treasures were lost at the dissolution of the monasteries in the 1530s, and still more with the iconoclasm of Cromwell's Commonwealth. But after the Restoration in 1660, people became interested in placing architectural styles in particular eras. Norman architecture had loyal supporters, like John Aubrey and Christopher Wren, who appreciated its grandeur, although they found it rudely executed and lacking in 'grace', and in the eighteenth century Thomas Warton and Thomas Gray expressed deep affection for what Warton called 'the national architecture of our Saxon ancestors'.[21] In 1795 there was a chorus of protest when James Wyatt, nicknamed 'the destroyer', dared to 'restore' Durham cathedral, attacking the Norman apse and the vault of the chapter house and even threatening to demolish the Galilee Chapel to make a carriage drive.[22]

By contrast, at Tickencote, near Stamford, a village on the Great North Road well known to travellers, the small Norman church with its beautiful quintuple chancel arch and elaborate arcades on the west front was sensitively restored in the 1790s. If Sarah read about Tickencote in the *Gentleman's Magazine*, she might have noticed that although the architect was a man, Samuel Pepys Cockerell, the sponsor was a woman, Eliza Wingfield, whose family had been important local figures since the sixteenth century, just as the Loshes were in Wreay. And an article in Loudon's *Architectural Magazine* in 1834 might also have caught her eye, recommending the Norman model, partly because it was cheap compared to Gothic (a point she made herself to Bishop Percy) and its simple mouldings were 'such as any country mason might easily execute'.[23]

But the Romanesque was still a minority interest. Germany seemed to be the only country where the round-arched style was openly admired, and here it was called 'Byzantine'. In the 1830s Frederick William IV of Prussia, inspired by histories of the Byzantine empire and by his own travels to Vienna and Ravenna, commissioned architects to build simple Roman basilicas in Berlin and Potsdam with an externally arcaded apse and a separate campanile. Very occasionally the builder of a new English church leant in this direction. William Whewell's protégé, the Lancastrian Edmund Sharpe – a true original – returned from a series of Continental tours determined to become an architect and built a 'German Romanesque' church at Witton near Blackburn in the late 1830s, and in 1840–2 he was working on the simple Gothic church at Calder Bridge, beyond the fells on the western plains of Cumberland.[24]

Sarah did not see the new German churches, but she was able to read one book that excited all those who were interested in architecture and romantically inclined. This was Thomas Hope's *Historical Essay on Architecture*, with nearly a hundred illustrations, published by his son in 1835, four years after Hope's death. Hope wrote wittily, informally and eloquently, considering Egyptian, Greek and Roman architecture before turning to the domes and cupolas of Byzantium, and the triumph of the arch: 'Arches thus rising over arches, and cupolas over cupolas, we may say that all which in the temples of Athens had been straight and angular, and square, in the churches of Constantinople became curved and rounded – concave within, and convex without.'[25] He also traced a descent from Constantine's use of a hall with a baptistery attached to the first Christian basilicas, and from Hagia Sophia to the cathedral of Torcello and the early French and German churches. But his main emphasis was on the transmission through Italy, and in describing it he stuck to the old term, 'Lombard'.

Hope's forebears were Scots who settled in Amsterdam and became enormously wealthy merchants and bankers. His father had a fabulous sculpture collection, and Hope built up his own collection on a spectacular Grand Tour through Europe, Asia and Africa. In 1796 he fled the French occupation of the Netherlands with his two brothers and settled in London, decorating each room of his house near Cavendish Square according to the different countries he had visited and opening it to elite visitors. Soon he began a second Grand Tour, exploring the Ottoman empire, making drawings and notes and collecting innumerable treasures. Back in England, he entertained connoisseurs in his new Surrey mansion, providing books in different languages in each guest bedroom. His novel *Anastasius*, set in the Ottoman empire, was published anonymously in 1819 by Byron's publisher, John Murray, causing such a sensation that it was attributed to Byron himself (who allegedly wept with jealousy when he read it).

Hope was often in Italy, especially from 1815 to 1817, the same time as the Losh sisters. He saw Lombardy, 'the country in which associations of freemasons were first formed', as:

the first after the decline of the Roman empire, to endow architecture with a complete and connected system of forms, which soon prevailed wherever the Latin church spread its influence, from the shores of the Baltic to those of the Mediterranean; in part adopted from the more ancient Roman and Byzantine styles, in part differing from both – neither resembling the Roman basilica, nor the Greek cross and cupola.[26]

As the style spread, Hope wrote, it was 'modified' by local conditions. Henry Lonsdale, who knew and talked to Sarah in her later years, pointed out that the arcade of small arches following the slope of the roof at Wreay resembles those 'met with in Lombard and Rhenish churches, and notable in those of San Michele in Pavia, and the Duomo of Parma', while 'the entrance doorway is in the Lombard style, recalling that of Santa Maria della Piazza, Ancona'. Sarah may have seen these on her Italian trip, but all three examples and others like them, including St Augustine's in Pavia, are beautifully illustrated in Hope's book. He also shared her interest in the 'primitive' church architecture of Britain, noting that the churches described by Bede and others were all 'built in the Roman style', claiming that St Wilfrid, who built the first abbey at Hexham, on his route between Carlisle and Newcastle, in 674, had learnt architecture in Rome and brought over Roman workmen, and adding that in the time of Alfred new churches were always called *opus Romanum*.

In 1841 yet another book appeared on the subject, the Rev. J. L. Petit's *Remarks on Church Architecture*, illustrated with atmospheric sketches made on tours in Britain and abroad. Here at last, in Petit's appreciative studies of older churches, and in his refusal to accept any doctrinaire rules for restoration, was a clear suggestion that the round-arched style might be used for English churches. Petit was roundly rebuffed, especially in the *Ecclesiologist*. 'The

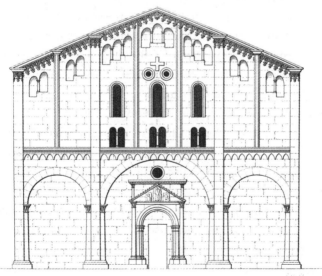

Thomas Hope's drawings of the facade of San Michele and the church of the Augustines, both in Pavia, published in his *Essay on Architecture* in 1840, nine years after his death.

proposed introduction by Mr Petit and his followers', it declared, 'of a new style, whether Romanesque, Byzantine or Eclectic, is to be earnestly deprecated, as opening a door to the most dangerous innovations, and totally subversive of Christian Architecture as such.'[27] But Petit's views, like Hope's, bolstered Sarah's decision. She knew her own desires, and she did not give a fig if peopled labelled her as dangerous, or subversive.

Sarah's church would be simple, a rectangular nave with a chancel apse, strikingly different from anything else in Britain at the time. Sarah used Hope's term 'Lombardic', and her triangular facade did remind people of the small churches of northern Italy, or of the deep south, of Puglia, and of Sicily. But Wreay also had echoes of local Norman churches, like St Leonard's at Warwick-on-Eden, with its deep blind arches around the outside. It was plain and direct, mysterious and exotic, northern and southern, all at the same time.

She chose this disregarded style because it was early and simple. But she did not merely copy the Romanesque. Like a geologist demonstrating the strata of belief, she decorated the church with symbols that looked back to the earlier religions, myths and cults that lay buried beneath Christian imagery and ritual, as the wheat of Demeter and the grapes of Dionysus lay behind the bread and wine of the sacrament. On her carvings, pillars and altar she placed the lotus, one of the early symbols of creation. The myths of the Nile told that before the universe existed there was only an infinite ocean, the primeval being, Nun. Out of Nun a lotus flower arose on a patch of dry land and as the blossoms opened a child stepped out, the self-created sun god Atun, or Ra. The lotus was the womb of earth and light, its petals closing at sunset and opening at dawn. In eastern religions, Sarah knew, the lotus, whose flowers were untouched by the water around it or the mud from which it grew, represented detachment from worldliness. To the Romantics and to Sarah it was a symbol of light, its petals representing the rays of the sun, and also of receptivity, reproduction and continuing life.

Hindu mythology was one source for the Romantic quarrying of myth, and in 1810 Robert Southey – influenced by Sir William Jones's translations from Sanskrit – wrote *The Curse of Kehama*, describing the lotus floating on its lagoon, fed by perpetual springs. The influential work of Max Müller on comparative mythology, religion and Indian culture was still to come but many articles and books discussed early religions and cults. Friedrich Creuzer's hefty, four-volume *Symbolism and Mythology of the Ancient Peoples* of 1810–12 was translated in 1829, linking Greek myth to Indian sources and arguing that fertility symbols were the earliest expressions of deep truths about nature, pre-dating language.[28] Then in 1836, when Sarah was planning the church, a new edition appeared of Richard Payne Knight's 1818 *Inquiry into the Symbolical Language of Ancient Art and Mythology*, which pointed to the resemblance between all ancient religions and argued that all the gods were personifications of nature, with oppositions of male and female, heaven and earth. We cannot know if Sarah read this but it has been noted that her chapel is full of the symbols that Payne Knight mentions, from the cockerel, snake and tortoise – often seen at the feet of classical gods and acting as 'the support of the deity', as in Hindu stories of the world being created on the turtle's back – to the lotus and the pomegranate, the Old Testament image of abundance and Persephone's fruit of summer and winter, day and night.[29]

The lotus, pomegranate and barley-corn, Payne Knight thought, were emblems of the female 'passive generative power'. Their counterpart, the 'male, or active generative attribute', was the pinecone.[30] In Assyria the pinecone was a token of reproduction; in Babylon it was carried by the creator-god Marduk; in Egypt a pinecone staff was a symbol of Osiris: papyri showed the dead bearing pinecones on their heads before they received

Osiris's judgement. In ancient Greece, a pinecone-tipped staff marked the cult of Dionysus, and in Rome the cult of Bacchus. Pinecones abounded in the decoration of Catholic churches, as Sarah had seen in Rome, and in Masonic halls. For the Masons they were linked to the notion of enlightenment, associated with the pinecone-shaped pineal gland which Descartes had suggested might be the 'abode of the spirit of man'. 'The soul', he wrote, 'has its seat in the little gland which exists in the middle of the brain, from whence it radiates forth through all the remainder of the body by means of the animal spirits, nerves and even the blood.'[31] The cone's slow ripening and opening to release the seeds came to stand for the expansion of consciousness.

So Sarah's church would not be Gothic, or even pure Romanesque. Its simple form would be wreathed by images that conjured up buried connections with ancient religions – Greek, Roman, Egyptian, Hindu, Buddhist – the strata of spiritual rather than geological time.

18 Stone by Stone

The new year of 1841 was fiercely cold, with ice floating down the Petteril, and on 2 February the Twelve Men trudged to their Candlemas meeting at the Plough Inn through a snow storm.[1] The snow lessened slightly before the Wreay Hunt met a fortnight later, but when the thaw came the Petteril flooded its banks. Amid another burst of wild weather six weeks later Richard Jackson and his churchwarden, James Longrigg, landlord of the Plough, called a special vestry meeting on Lady Day, 25 March, to 'consider certain Propositions that will then be made for rebuilding the Chapel'.[2] This was a matter for the whole congregation, Jackson insisted, and 'It is particularly requested that all Landowners and others, who hold sittings in the Chapel, will attend.' John Robinson, whose men were busy with spring work on the farm – hedging, threshing barley, getting oats ground for the cattle, loading turnips, laying up dung and beginning to plough – wrote tersely in his diary 'Self in Turnip Field. Aft. At Wreay about a meeting for a new chapel. Wind south, came on heavy shower at 4 o'clock.'[3]

After the meeting Jackson jotted down the minutes. 'Resolved unanimously', he noted, 'that the kind proposal made by Miss Losh to rebuild the chapel at Wreay be accepted.' When they appointed a committee to push this forward, Sarah's name headed the list, with Jackson and Longrigg, followed by John Robinson of Scalesceugh, Thomas Slack of Intack, William Carrick of New-biggin Hall and Joseph Scott. Sarah seems to have been the only woman present, but all the local landowners were represented. No one raised the thorny issue of architectural styles, as most people assumed that the church would be rebuilt in its old form, and much of the meeting was taken up with the issue of the pews.

This was not, to those present, a trivial question. Pews and benches were introduced to British churches after the Reformation, with families having permanent 'title' to pews according to what they contributed, often boxing them in to make them more private. Paid pews were anathema to Pugin and the Ecclesiologists, who regarded them as a post-Reformation intrusion, a secular invasion of the sanctuary. But in Wreay, a traditional place, the family pew was valued not only for seating but for status. Although the old boxed pews were to go, Jackson's minutes recorded, new ones would be made, 'of yellow pine & instead of doors have a piece of wood fixed to one end of the back of the seats with a little ornament on the top, such as may be agreed on by the Committee'. (Another prescription that Sarah ignored.) There were to be separate pews for the 'singers', the schoolmaster and the clerk's family, but otherwise the arrangement would stay the same as before, '& the expense borne by the owners of the respective seats according to the number of sittings'. Sarah's own pew would be free, and the expenses of consecrating the chapel would be contained in the general account.

This important matter settled, the way was clear to move ahead. Now that she had the goodwill of the Twelve Men, they could jointly approach the cathedral authorities for permission to 'repair' the church. The next three months were full of negotiations. A vital stage was winning the acceptance of the Bishop, Dean and Chapter of Carlisle. She had evidence, she said, that the old chapel was almost falling down – indeed villagers had been seen taking stones to repair their own homes. It was, she wrote later, in a very dilapidated condition. The slate was much broken, the timber of the roof was in a dangerous state of decay and the walls were in many parts mouldy and green from the moisture which trickled down them. Interments had taken place not only close to the walls but even within them, so that in consequence of these various circumstances, the air of the building had become so vitiated as to prove injurious to the health of many of those who remained in it during the time of service.[4]

A mild restoration seems to have been, at first, the under-standing of the bishop, dean and chapter. They consented and as patrons of the living agreed to give £30 to restore the chancel. When he saw the plans, however, Bishop Percy was taken aback, regarding the proposed style as crude and the lighting inadequate. A great deal of argument and frustration on both sides was hidden beneath Sarah's laconic, and slightly evasive, account of what happened. At the end of her notes she wrote:

The unpolished mode of building adhered to in the new chapel, most approximates to early Saxon or modified Lombard, which was preferred to a more improved style, as less expensive and elaborate. In conformity to this primitive manner of building, large windows could not have been made in the absis, but the Bishop fearing a want of light, gave only a conditional assent to the plan as it now stands, desiring that it should be so contrived that larger windows might be opened if found desirable. These, however, he afterwards dispensed with.[5]

Her next move was to offer to bear the whole cost herself. Economy was hardly a credible argument for her 'modified Lombardic' plan, given that the rebuilding took £1,100 of her own money compared to the bishop's £30, but once her money was on the table the bishop's conditional assent evolved into a reluctant, permission. Without the cathedral authorities fully realising it, she got these powerful men to agree, in the end, that she could do exactly as she wanted. She offered, she wrote briskly, 'to furnish a new site for the chapel and to defray all the expenses of its re-erection, on condition that I should be left unrestricted as to the mode of building it'.

Unrestricted she was. The faculty to rebuild Wreay Chapel, granted on 20 May 1841, allowed her to take down the present fabric 'and to erect a new and more commodious structure' within thirty yards of the old church, 'so as to make and render the same fit and convenient for the celebration of Divine Service and hearing sermons therein'. In fact the work had already begun. Three days earlier, shivering in the late spring wind, with the mountains behind them still covered in snow, the trustees had turned up to lay the foundation stone.

By now a report had appeared in the *Carlisle Journal* that Miss Losh, 'with her usual munificence', was planning to build a new church. The next issue carried a firm letter to the editor saying that 'Miss Losh will be much obliged' if he could put right a statement in the previous paper 'respecting a building commenced at Wreay, at which place it is not intended to erect a Church, but merely to re-edify the old Chapel'. In this context, 're-edify' was a splendidly slippery word. 'Although regretting to call attention to so trivial an undertaking', she continued:

She considers it due to the various parties, who are concerned most, to place the affair in its right point of view. The expense of replacing the seats &c, will be defrayed by the Chapelry at large. The Dean and Chapter of Carlisle (who are the Patrons of the living) gave thirty pounds for the construction of the Church, for the rest, she has been kindly assisted by some of her own relations.

On the occasion of laying the first stone of this rustic structure, an appropriate prayer was offered by the Rev. R. Jackson; and some coins were deposited in the foundation by the hands of his infant son.[6]

She was lucky to have Richard Jackson to support her at every move. He was keen to make a mark on his new parish. In addition, his family came from Torpenhow (or 'Trup-en-ah' in local speech) near Wigton on the Solway plain, and he had grown up with its church, built in 1120, one of only six Norman churches in the country to survive unspoilt, with a magnificent chancel arch, elaborately carved with entwined figures in dark red sandstone on the north side, and human and animal figures in paler sandstone on the south, the side of light. Jackson had no problems with Sarah's round-arched style.

Once the foundation stone was laid, like magic, the weather turned. It was dry, sunny and even hot and Sarah and her workmen plunged into action. Only a week later, the village congregation left the old church for good and gathered for the Sunday service in the mortuary chapel instead. 'Self, Mary & Margaret at the new Chapel in the new Cemetery', wrote John Robinson in his diary. They continued to meet here every Sunday, although usually it was the women who went, while the men stayed at home or worked their fields. Baptisms and burials took place at High Hesket church until the following year, when the graveyard was clear of builders' ladders and carts.

The old church at Wreay in 1836, looking quiet and atmospheric despite its dilapidated state.

William Hindson, whose sons had been busy working at John Robinson's farms, now gathered his workforce and, stone by stone, they demolished the old church. In Sarah's notes – which Richard Jackson copied carefully into his notebook, to answer any criticisms of vandalism from the antiquarian community, or questions about money from the Dean and Chapter or the Twelve Men – she described what they found, belittling the poor workmanship and revealing her own architectural knowledge on the way. 'The destruction of an ancient structure, however necessary, must always afford cause for regret', she agreed, 'but the Chapel at Wreay had apparently little claim to respect, whether in an antiquarian or an architectural point of view.' Although it was thought to date from the time of Edward II – the late thirteenth to early fourteenth century – they found no coins to substantiate or refute this. There was one Tudor window but the other windows were later, 'with coarsely hewn mullions', and the only visible door was a recent one, 'of miserable workmanship'.

In the course of demolition, however, they found a small narrow door near the east end of the south wall, and when Sarah noticed that this had 'the flat-headed corbel arch so common in the time of Edward', she had it carefully removed and set aside to top the doorway to the new crypt. The workmen also uncovered traces of a larger doorway in the west wall, which had clearly once been the main entrance but had been walled in long ago and coated with plaster inside. When the plaster was removed, Sarah wrote, you could see 'large projecting stones, constituting a solid corbel arch as seen in the annotated sketch made by Mr Hindson, the builder'. A note on this sketch read: 'Inside of the old Chapel doorway only visible on removing the plaister. The outside was totally defaced.'

The church, Sarah reassured any doubtful readers of these notes, had obviously been altered at various stages and rebuilt relatively recently, 'but marred and spoilt by unskilful hands'. All it was good for was building materials. Hindson made use of the stones and flags, and took the slates to line the drains. The good window was 'set aside to be used at the parsonage', but the rest were broken up to be used as common stones: all the glass was shattered, and was valued at fourteen shillings, which the glazier – who could use the fragments – deducted from his bill. As for the timber, some could be laid as sleepers beneath the seats, 'but it was of little value, the spars were indeed so much decayed as to be taken for firewood by the workmen who required large fires within and without the building'. When they came to build the new roof, the men used the dismantled pews as extra supports, hidden behind the wooden ceiling. Some things were beyond hope, like the pulpit and reading desk which 'fell to pieces with age and dampness and were quite useless'. Others posed problems that Sarah never solved, like the communion table, which could hardly be broken up, and was simply kept, jammed into the tiny crypt. The old bell-gable she placed by the pond on the road to Southwaite, to 'remain as a relic of the former chapel' – today it still stands in the ditch, almost hidden by wild flowers.

Orders were sent to the quarries, timber merchants and glaziers. Soon the churchyard was a mess of ladders, buckets, canvas and rope and tools, and piles of stone. Most of the yellow sandstone came from the local quarries owned by John Robinson, who was paid £16 19s 10d for the lot, with a smaller amount from Shawk Foot quarry for the apse and the finely worked arches of the windows and doors. Then, when they dug the foundations, the workmen met trouble: they found water – copious springs, seeping and flowing.

'The ground was very uneven,' Sarah noted, 'and had formerly several pools of water, on which, when frozen, the schoolboys skated. On levelling, the water gushed up and filled the new-dug foundation so rapidly, that it was necessary to fill it with stones, and to commence further to the eastward.' Sarah knew about springs and revered them. This churchyard was a sacred place, perhaps a place of worship far older than the Christian cell and chapel that had stood there since the thirteenth century. Local builders had always respected their springs, like the one that flowed beneath the church of Kirkoswald, tucked beside a dome-like hill in the meadows beyond the river Eden, where the mayflies rise in clouds and the sand martins swoop and skim across to their nests in the sandy bank. There the masons built a well against the church's western wall, round, narrow and deep, with an iron lid and a cup on a chain that could be let down to scoop the clear water. Sarah too made a well of sorts by the western door, square in shape, with steps down one side, turning towards the spring, topped by a lion's head, enclosed in a fence of iron arrows. Today this is usually dry, a mere gesture to the power of the waters below.

Eventually the builders managed to divert the flow from the springs into a large drain below the small crypt under the chancel, which also received the water from shallow drains dug around the walls. From here the channel ran north-east under the churchyard before flowing beneath the road 'and thro' the orchard opposite, whence there is a good descent for it down the bank'. Once the drainage was dealt with, the stone flags that Sarah thought came from the old pele tower were laid in place, and to keep the chapel floor dry it was raised on 'dwarf walls' with an entrance platform built up on dry-stone chippings.

From the gate they made a raised path like a causeway leading to the door. The gate itself opened through a wall built in the old dry-stone manner with huge blocks of sandstone, rough-hewn and heavy. The gate posts were upright blocks, jagged at the top, the kind you might find on a field near a Cumberland fell, where the farmer had dragged blocks from the hillside, or on a Cornish moor, using standing stones from a nearby stone circle. On each side of the gate the stones became smaller, the wall lower. It was both a barrier and an invitation, a boundary between church and village and countryside beyond.

Sarah was on site almost every day, watching, mulling over problems, and talking to Hindson, whose skill and advice she greatly valued. She had no architect and although her eagle eye and constant presence may have irritated the men at times, her grasp of practical details impressed them almost more than her ideas. 'Bound by no commonplace rules', wrote Lonsdale,

and following none of the stereotyped lines of masonry, she directed the workmen in their operations from day to day. Like a master-mind, loving her work, she carried her church-building and other designs in her brain, and from the foundation to the finishing of the super-structure never had to undo what had been done according to her directions.[7]

The villagers appreciated her dedication. From June to August people gave their labour free, not only those closely involved, like the Robinsons, Longriggs and Slacks, but labourers like Henry Gill and farmers from nearby Brisco, Foulbridge and Burn-thwaite. In the summer months, in between harvesting, they lent their carts to haul stone and timber. Even Henry Aglionby – the new heir to the estates at Newbiggin Hall and Nunnery – came up trumps with two cartloads of gravel.[8]

Stone by stone, the church rose. The shape of the nave was so simple, with its long walls and gable ends, that it could almost be a local fellside barn. But the apse took it into another realm. Curved and round, its shape was that of a small Byzantine basilica.[9] Yet the building was local as well, its arcade reminding people of St Leonard's at Warwick-on-Eden, which also had thirteen tall arches. These, Samuel Jefferson had written recently in his *History and Antiquities of Carlisle*, were 'intended to signify Christ and his twelve apostles'. As always, Sarah modified the model: where St Leonard's had three small windows set into the arches, Sarah had seven, each filled with small orange lights. And above them, like a frieze below the curving roof, she placed a semi-circle of small windows, later filled with the strange tracery of fossil forms.

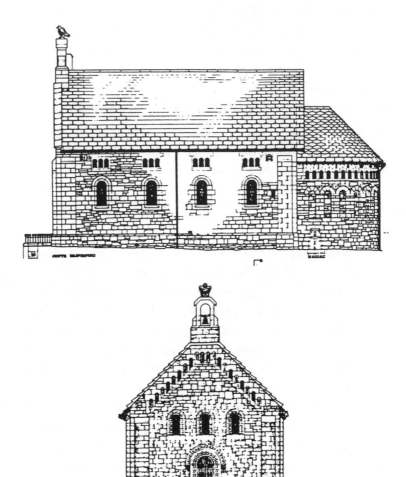

The south and west elevations of Sarah Losh's new church,
drawn by the architect John Robinson.

On the west facade, with its tall, plain buttresses, the triangular gable rose to a belfry topped by 'an alert, proud and aspiring, almost Napoleonic eagle', an echo of the one that guarded the twin bells at Holm Cultram.[10] Following the gable line was a series of small stepped windows, nine on each side, in the Italian style that Hope had so often illustrated. At the apex, in two niches, the men placed statues of St Peter and St Paul, their origin unexplained, perhaps brought from Sarah's travels abroad, or from a church demolished elsewhere.

The facade was also rich with carving. Around the door young William Hindson carved four enfolding arches, in the Norman style. The outermost arch was plain, and the next and innermost were narrower, carved with regular fillets. Between these was a slightly wider band, carved with twenty-five stylised water lilies, cousin to the lotus. On the curving dripstone, supported on pinecones, he carved the lotus again, thirteen times, with a stylised leaf between each. On one leaf only he carved a tracery of veins – the rest were left plain, leaving us a mystery. Was this a sign of haste to get the church finished? And if so, why did he never finish the rest?

Above the doorway three windows were set in triple bands of stone. Once again the outer and inner arches were plain, carved with regular panels, but the middle arches bore the imagery Sarah loved. Hindson carved them to her designs in sections in his workshop, before they were carefully put in place. Around the central window a chrysalis rested on an oak leaf at each side, with six butterflies above, separated by poppy-heads, ripe with seeds, reaching up to lilies curving round two butterflies – their wings outspread and their antennae touching a band of ripe wheat. All these, including the butterflies, symbols of the soul, from their Greek name *psyche*, spoke of the earth. By contrast the carvings on the left-hand window conjured ancient oceans, with ammonites and nautilus fossils and staghorn coral. On the right, they took to the air. Fir branches met at the top and between the cones perched a raven, a scarab with open wings, a bee and a small, wise owl.

The carving has a direct, childlike, almost two-dimensional quality. The crudity could have come from inexperience, but it seems deliberate. Lonsdale tells us that Sarah herself was 'the moulder of the natural-history forms . . . As she only engaged country operatives who had never shown the slightest feeling for art, she made her mouldings in clay and then taught the mason to work them in stone; and marvellously well did she succeed.'[11] The very formality makes them feel archaic, as if the flowers and beetles, fossils and birds were on the verge of being transformed into abstractions, or absolutes of their type. All the carvings at the entrance burst with life yet carry their own resonance: the poppy that brings sleep, the lilies of the field, the wheat that gives flour, the cones that keep their seeds safe in their patterned bracts.

The side walls were plainer, with four arched windows set in filleted bands, each with a trio of small windows above, matching those on the facade. The only oddities were two small, plain glass windows letting light in on to the pulpit, a concession to Bishop Percy's complaint that the church was too dark, but also a copy of the narrow slit windows at Newton Arlosh church. The arrangement of the windows fascinated the people of Wreay. Canon Hall, who was rector here for nearly fifty years, came to believe they had a numerical significance:

The symbolical numbers are three (for God), four (for creation), and seven (for completion or perfection). So at the west end of the Church there are three times three small windows at each side, climbing up to the apex of the roof, and three large windows below, making in all seven times three windows in that wall. At each side of the nave there are four windows, with a group of three above. All the windows in the Church, including the two small ones near the pulpit and the reading desk and those round the apse, number eighty-four, i.e. three, four, and seven multiplied together.[12]

It is a nice thought – three, four, seven, God, creation, completion – and the play with numbers would have pleased Sarah's mathematical mind, but there is nothing at all in her notes to suggest that the canon was right.

Finally the walls were finished. But before the glaziers or roofers could begin, the men had to fix her 'emblematical monsters' as she called them, 'which are placed like gargoyles'. These endearing, rather than threatening, creatures charge from the corners of the wall as if about to take flight. With their folklore appeal and dinosaur echoes, they were born, perhaps, from her reading of Buckland's fossil monsters and their tracks. They are huge, almost too heavy for such a small church. On one side, a great snake curls its head forward, peering with wide-open eyes: it has the serpent-like neck of a plesiosaur, and jaws filled with triangular teeth. Elsewhere a crocodile sticks out, with tiny feet and open mouth; a winged turtle launches itself into the void and a tortoise seems almost on the verge of falling, its whole chubby body extended, and all four feet in the air – ready to make tracks.

These had a practical purpose. They did not drain water from the roof like traditional gargoyles – Sarah and Hindson had taken care to avoid the need for guttering and spouts by making the roof project well over the walls. Instead, the four monsters on the corners hid ventilators while the dragon on the north-west corner was 'for the emission of smoke' from the boiler below the floor of the nave. (Not many churches have a dragon that breathes fire, its smoke spinning across the road in the westerly winds.) While the others balanced easily on the wall, the dragon, as Sarah said, was too heavy, and was 'kept in place mainly by the stones above it':

Should any repairs be required here, great caution should be used to prevent its falling. The iron bar inserted in its jaw, is to prevent the starlings from making nests in it. A fine brood of young birds was hatched here soon after its erection, and the flue was completely choked up by the sticks and rubbish of the nest.

She enjoyed the 'fine brood' even if they were a nuisance.

The next big project was the roof. For some of the struts they could use wood from the old church, but the main beams were all made of oak cut down at Woodside itself. Each massive cross-beam was carved with a different pattern, though all had a pinecone pointing down from the centre, like a medieval boss. When the timbers were in place, instead of the fashionable Borrowdale slates, the tilers laid heavy flags from Lazonby, the kind that were used on many local houses and barns, red sandstone flecked with quartz that glinted in the sun. These were practical, being extremely hard-wearing and rarely needing repair, as well as being part of local history, but they were a big expense and Sarah carefully noted down the cost, £33 13s, plus £3 12s 11d for lead and £14 9s 8d for the slater's work.

By September 1841, only five months after they began, work had progressed so well that the Committee for Building the Chapel – John Robinson, William Carrick, Joseph Scott and Thomas Slack – could start thinking about the interior, especially the familiar vexed question of the pews. The wood for these had now moved up a grade from yellow pine, and it was unanimously resolved 'that the framing of the panels for the seats be of the best Danzig oak, and that Spanish chestnut be used for the Pannels, Newel posts and seats'. The floor below the seats was to be laid with inch-thick 'Memel boards', oak from Memel in Lithuania, long imported for use by the British navy. Below these would lie oak sleepers, using wood from the old church. That settled, their minutes ended, it was resolved that 'Miss Losh & Revd. Jackson have the liberty of making any alteration respecting the choice of wood, and that they determine the dimensions & width of the seats – and any other matters respecting the Chapel'.[13] With that 'any other matters', the committee lightly relinquished control to their vicar and the indomitable Miss Losh.

19 Jubilate

In January 1842 there were deep snow drifts in the lanes and on the fields, followed by an iron frost that made the roads treacherous. 'Too hard to plow,' groaned John Robinson in his diary, day after day. For two months the fierce cold made it impossible to plaster walls, or work on the church.

Sarah and her craftsmen were forced to work inside, the woodcarvers on the lecterns and pulpit and other carvings and the glaziers on the stained-glass windows. The smaller windows were put together by a local firm, Geoffrey Rowell of Grey Goat Lane in Carlisle, including the high, narrow windows for the nave, in which different flowers – rose, lily, poppy – were set within dark circles that made them stand out against a background of fragments. For the large windows Sarah commissioned William Wailes of Newcastle, who would later become a famous maker for Victorian churches across the country, including the huge, intricate west window of Gloucester cathedral and several in Carlisle cathedral. In 1841, in his early thirties, he was just at the start of his career. Wailes had begun his working life as a tea merchant and grocer, but he had a passion for medieval glass and set up a kiln in his backyard, making decorative enamels for his shop. In 1830 he went to study glass-making in Italy and eight years he later sold his grocery business to his partner and set up his workshop.

William Bell Scott, who came to Newcastle to work at the new

School of Design around this time, found Wailes an odd character, a tradesman with no background in art but a passion for churches, especially those of France. He was determined to make his windows in the old style, which suited the vogue for the medieval, and would soon employ the talented artist Francis Oliphant and begin working, not altogether happily, with Pugin. The workshop was a down-to-earth, business-like place:

Here was the Scotch Presbyterian working-artist with a short pipe in his mouth cursing his fate in having to elaborate continual repetitions of saints and virgins – Peter with a key as large as a spade and a yellow plate behind his head – yet by constant drill in the groove realising the sentiment of Christian art, at last able to express the abnegation of self, the limitless sadness and even tenderness in every line of drapery and every twist of the lay-figure.[1]

This kind of artisan workmanship was just what Sarah wanted. Her craftsmen were not 'artists' and sometimes their work was crude, but it was heartfelt and, as Bell Scott said, it was tender.

Sarah may have been told about Wailes's work by William Septimus, who kept up with the art world in Newcastle while running the alkali works. In Sarah's plan stained glass filled the large windows that pierced the walls, with groups of small clerestory windows above. The design of these was formal, with panels inset within circles, but the overall ground was made up of fragments of broken glass, held together in webs of lead like surreal mosaics. Some of the glass fragments were new, imitations of medieval glass picked up from the floor of the glazier's workshop. Among them were plain, glowing pieces in deep red, blue, amber and emerald green; others showed peering faces, curling leaves, broken crosses or swirls of foliage, and here and there words appeared, or parts of words, 'MEMO' or 'ATE', hinting at a text lost for ever in fires or tempests, riots or wars.

This was one of many ways that Sarah reused old material that would otherwise have been cast aside. It was one of her forms of resurrection, creating beauty out of destruction, form out of chaos, picking up scraps from the past to make new forms and puzzles. One window, the most easterly window on the cold northern side, nearest to the chancel, contains genuine medieval glass – the precious fragments that William Septimus had brought back from Paris when the windows of the Hôtel de Sens were shattered during the fighting of 1830. These were put together to make up an image from nature, like so many of the images in the church. But this image was not benign. The flower made from the fragments was deadly nightshade, named by Linnaeus as *Atropa belladonna*, the devil's herb and witch's berry which can lead, if eaten, to delirium, coma and death. It is *Atropa* after Atropos, the oldest of the three Fates, who cuts the thread of each mortal life with her shears while her sisters spin the thread and measure its length. It is *belladonna* because it makes the pupils dilate, creating a dewy-eyed loveliness. It is death in life.

William Septimus was an artist as well as a scientist. The Paris-born artist Joseph Bouet, son of a refugee from the revolution, had taught him to draw while he was at school in Durham.[2] Remarkably, Sarah now set to work as a sculptor herself, and William Septimus worked with her on the fossil cut-outs for the narrow, deep windows of the apse and some of the higher clerestory windows, and helped her with the lotus candlesticks and the font. All these were carved from alabaster. Here Sarah was ahead of fashion, as this soft form of gypsum, a favourite for medieval and Renaissance tombs, saw a revival in Victorian times. But she was also following her habit of using local materials, especially ones that had history buried within them; there was an alabaster quarry, where the Romans had made their tiles, on the edge of Wragmire Moss.[3] Alabaster needs to be kept out of the weather, indoors, but away from an open fire, and the big, airy outhouses at Woodside were perfect for a studio, with large tables and room for stone and tools, and a brazier if the frost was too sharp.

The stone was not only translucent but so soft that Sarah could easily cut it with a knife, and for her windows, she turned for designs to the fossils found in the Northumbrian and Cumbrian mines. Among those that she copied and turned into near-abstract patterns, cut out of thin sheets of alabaster, were *Neuropteris acuminata* and *Pecopteris heterophylla* from Felling Colliery, the fern *Sphenopteris dilata* from the Bensham seam, and the broad-leaved, palm-like *Sphenophyllum Schlotheimii*.[4] The windows' references spread further. On her travels she had seen the sixth-century basilica of San Vitale in Ravenna which was built before the use of glass was common: it is filled with an amber light, filtered through alabaster sheets. In the windows at Wreay, her cut-out forms of fossils from deep below the earth could be encased in glass and held up to the light. After a thousand ages the sun would shine through them again.

The lotus candlestick, carved in rose-pink alabaster.

She carved the lotus candlesticks in pale rose alabaster, making them formal rather than naturalistic, a solid base of leaves with the plump bud reaching up, about to open. The font was more delicate and complicated, cut from a single block of alabaster, with tapering sides and a wide brim. William did most of the work on the cover, where a mirror made a gleaming surface for alabaster water lilies. The sides were cut in ten panels, with a border of Norman zig-zags at the top and Greek fluting at the base. Each panel was different, some flat and formal, others naturalistic and precisely observed: the curving spores of a fern, water lilies and lotus flowers, a butterfly above a leaf, hairy ears of wheat and barley, a hovering dragonfly, a curling grapevine, a pomegranate, a feathery dove with an olive leaf. Where the candlesticks were solid and serious, the font was a work of relaxed accomplishment, shared delight.

The first stage was to make a clay model to work out the form and then mark up the details. Alabaster was not hard to carve, but it scratched easily and could bruise if hit too hard with a mallet or chisel, crushing the crystals. The work was dusty, and the carvers wore old clothes and gloves with the fingers cut off to protect their hands from sharp slivers of stone. First they dampened the stone to show fault lines that might help to direct their design, then they roughed it out, drawing straight on to the alabaster. The block was placed on bags filled with sand, to dull vibrations and prevent breaks. Then they took their tools and began, digging in with the chisel, hitting it gently at an angle with a mallet to remove large pieces to make the relief, before taking up the 'claw' – a wide-headed, toothed chisel – sliding it along the grain and beginning to shape the outline. It was hard, long work, carving the stone out a chip at a time. When the broad outline was done, they used finer tools, thin chisels and points, and files. The next, tedious process was sanding it, wetting the stone and wiping away the paste from the mix of dust and water. Finally, when it was dry, they smoothed on a clear wax and buffed it with a cloth, gently, again and again, to bring out the shine.[5]

The work took many hours and much patience and elbow grease and unladylike sweating. But Sarah was a hard worker, and while she and William Septimus carved the alabaster, others worked in wood. These were local people, unsung artists. Robert Donald, Sarah's own gardener, carved the intricate gourd and vine around the inner frame of the door, with its tendrils and flattened leaves, fluttering butterflies and fat grub, the gardener's foe. He knew just what he was doing, carving the stem in a concave section rather than convex as in real life, 'a practiced carver's trick as the concave cuts reflect light in such a way as to make them appear more realistic'.[6]

Another craftsman, John Scott, a crippled man from Dalston, carved the lecterns. Here powerful soaring birds are worked in clean, long strokes that show long-practised skill – a stork stretching its neck and arching its wings, an eagle with hooked beak and scaly claws gripping the bog-oak stand. Scott was clearly a professional, although his other work is not known. He was also responsible for the iron-work arrows with their feathered shafts and may have carved the owl and the cockerel, the dragon and winged bat that support the archangels, and the striking pulpit in the shape of a ringed fossil tree, a calamite, with a primitive horsetail for a candlestick. The wood used for the pulpit was bog oak, from a tree that had lain submerged in a bog for three thousand years or more until it took on the darkness of the peat itself: it was hard and black and heavy, and Sarah paid a guinea to have it dragged from the moss and carted up the hill.[7] The carving was a playful conceit, turning an ancient tree into something older still.

While this work was going on the frost lingered, but in March the sun arrived, the peas and beans were planted, and the workmen came back to Wreay. All through the year the usual cast of village day-labourers, Henry Gill, William Bowman, John Dixon and others, worked alongside the builders, clearing, levelling, draining the village green and putting stones on the new road, known as the Chapel Walk. After Easter the dry east winds arrived and the late spring was unseasonably hot. In Newcastle Wailes packed the fragile windows and put them on the train to Carlisle, and these and the windows from Rowell's workshop were brought by cart to Wreay and fixed in place. The fossil windows were particularly delicate and Sarah noted that 'some caution will be needed in repairing such of the windows as are made of alabaster which is exceptionally brittle'.

Once the building work was finished the Hindson family went back to walling ponds and repairing farm buildings. In the church the floor was laid and the walls plastered with 'Parker's Roman cement' from Nelson's marble works in Carlisle. This was a special mortar made of burnt nodules of clay, ground down and mixed with sand, which had been patented by James Parker in the late eighteenth century. It set very quickly and gave a hard stone-like surface. 'This is a superior covering if not broken into,' wrote Sarah with her usual firmness:

but its liability to crack unfits it for any wall designed for the reception of monumental tablets. These I would earnestly hope would not be introduced into this rustic chapel, the simplicity and uniformity of which would be totally destroyed, by the glaring aspect of black, white or coloured marble, with the usual decorations either heraldic or mortuary. Indeed I would hope that the time is not distant when Christians will have too much reverence for their places of worship, to fill them with memorials of their dead, and that the pernicious practice of interment within these sacred buildings, will soon be entirely abandoned.[8]

In October the first snows came, promising a hard winter ahead. Over the next six weeks the final touches were made. The carvings, lamps and marble altar were placed in position and two ebony-backed chairs brought from Woodside. Outside the ground was cleared and James Dalton was paid three shillings and sixpence for 'clearing away boards etc'. The pathway was made across the causeway to the door and near it Sarah put up a sundial, inscribed 'Do today's work today'. Her own work was nearly done.

At Woodside Sarah, her cousin Alicia and their aunt Margaret – a striking figure in her seventies, with her high-waisted black dress and her keys hanging by a rope-belt like a grand chatelaine or lady abbess – got together the things they would give to the church. For 'the Gospel and Epistle lights' at each side of the apse, they brought out the 'bronze candelabra of Pompeian design' with lamps from Pompeii that Sarah and Katharine had bought in 1817, attached to the stands by gold chain-necklaces of Renaissance design, also bought on their travels. These candelabra, wrote Lonsdale cheerily, 'when decorated with ivy at Christmas-tide, have a very pretty effect'.[9] Other treasures from abroad included a fourteenth-century bronze holy-water pail from Normandy, with an inscription to pray for the donor's soul, '*Prie pur l'alme G. Glanville*', and reliefs of figures of death, 'one blowing a horn and ringing a bell, a second as a reaper or grape-cutter, the third perhaps pouring water from a vessel'.[10] The two oak chairs inset with Italian ebony panels, one showing the shepherds at the Nativity and the other the Wise Men, were brought from Paris, possibly part of the *spolia* of woodwork scooped up by the British antique dealers who followed the Napoleonic armies like hawks.[11] Sarah's maternal aunt Ann Bonner gave two brass eagles to support the altar table, a slab of green Italian marble.

Sarah thought of every detail. She had the Bible, the Book of Common Prayer, the psalter and service book bound in polished wood with brass clasps, in the traditional way. She found bearskins to place on the floor by the altar – perhaps those that George had brought back from Russia in his youth – having heard that these were present in early churches, as votive offerings from Christian converts. She arranged for stoves to heat the church, but even these, so necessary for the freezing northern winters, sound strange; one was made of iron cast in the form of the stem of a *sigillaria* – a tree-like plant found in the Northumbrian coal-measures.

★

Finally, on Thursday 1 December, John Robinson wrote in his diary: 'Wm. Watson Plowing in Tree Field. Jos Sowerby thrashing Wheat and loading Turnips. Jno. Bell thrashing Wheat. Self Ann Sen., Ann Jn., Fanny at the Consecration of the Chapel at Wreay. Wind South East, fair.'[12] After last-minute polishing the day had come. At ten o'clock, the *Carlisle Patriot* reported, the church door was opened '& very shortly afterwards the area of this extremely handsome structure was crowded with the elite of Carlisle & the neighbourhood'. The clergy waited at the parsonage for Bishop Percy and his chaplain, the Rev. Chancellor Fletcher. At eleven, the bishop led them across to the church; the lawyer Mr Mounsey read out the petition for consecration, and the bishop proceeded to the altar, reading the twenty-fourth psalm, alternately with the clergy:

> The earth is the Lord's, and the fulness thereof; the world,
>   and they that dwell therein.
> For he hath founded it upon the seas, and established it upon
>   the floods.

The bishop read the dedicatory prayers, then the chancellor proclaimed the sentence of consecration, which Bishop Percy signed and handed back to Mounsey for enrolment. There was no specific service for consecrating churches, but the ceremony used here followed the form devised by Lancelot Andrewes and accepted by the Anglican Convocation in 1712. Andrewes had also set the reading, describing Solomon's dedication of the temple, and his doubt at the impossibility of such a venture: 'But will God indeed dwell on the earth? behold, the heaven and heaven of heavens cannot contain thee; how much less this house that I have builded?'

The morning service that followed was taken by Richard Jackson, with Bishop Percy giving 'a highly impressive and forcible Discourse' on the reading from Kings. From their special pew at the west end, the chapel choir led the psalms, ending with the Jubilate, the favourite 'Old Hundredth':

> Make a joyful noise unto the Lord, all ye lands.
> Serve the Lord with gladness: come before his presence with singing.

The rain held off as Bishop Percy strode outside and – with more psalm-singing – consecrated a new extension to the burial ground. Then the massed clergy and the great and good got back into their carriages and headed off for a 'sumptuous collation' at Woodside.

'Although we are aware', wrote the *Patriot*, 'that the unobtrusive and truly Christian character of the Lady's benevolence makes her prefer to do good by stealth, it is only right to add that the inhabitants are wholly indebted to the munificent liberality of Miss Losh of Woodside, for the Erection of this Elegant and Convenient place of worship.' This is noncommittal praise, standard for the day. It could be that many who entered the chapel for the first time, adjusting their eyes to the dusky light, felt a shiver of uncertainty, or even shock. The first surprise was the sense that although this was unmistakably a church, something was missing. There seemed, at first glance, to be no Christian symbols at all. The cross was banished to sporadic appearances in the windows, as a small red cross in a high oval or a Maltese cross surrounded by decorations. In its place on the altar stood two foreign, indeed pagan, candlesticks. The Bible stories of the Nativity were hidden on the ebony chair-backs. There was no image of Mary, whose name the church carried. Instead of saints and miracles, the windows shone with flowers and plants from past millennia.

Sarah did however follow the Tractarian ruling that the design of a church should make each stage clear, proceeding from baptistery to nave to altar, a movement that reflected both the stages of human life and the progress from the Old Testament law to the promise of the New and the mystery of Revelation. At Wreay, the Mosaic Tablets of the Law were hung on the walls each side of the font, one lit by a 'Jewish Lamp', the other standing above a bracket carved with the owl and cock, 'emblems of vigilance'.[13] At the other end of the church, between the pillars of the apse, the globes of amber-coloured glass set into the walls, graded from pale gold to deep red, represented the seven burning lamps of the spirit of God in Revelation. But there was one crucial difference: at the boundary between the nave and chancel there was no rood screen and no imagery of doom. Just as Sarah had wanted to move her church away from the graves, so she would have no judgement or death within it. Instead the chancel arch curved upwards, broad and open, with the head of a man and woman – 'the male and female principles' – on either side.

This posed problems for later vicars like Canon Hall, who worked hard to give every aspect of the church a conventional Christian meaning. The stork lectern, he decided, was actually a pelican, the bird of charity; the vine and grub round the door referred to God planting a gourd to shelter Job and withering it with a worm in the night. The lotus candlesticks, an uncomfortable excursion into orientalism, could be overlooked if the two candles themselves were stressed as 'types of our Lord as the Light of the World, in his two-fold nature of God and Man'.[14] The eagles were 'emblems of aspiration', and the Holy Table, borne on eagles' wings, is an invitation – *Sursum corda*, 'Lift up your hearts'.[15] The butterfly and chrysalis represented 'one of the fundamental ideas of the Church – that of the resurrection'.[16] But there was nothing to reassure him of this in Sarah's own notes.

In 1842, when Ann Robinson of Scalesceugh and her girls came to chapel, they stepped through the door on to the narrow platform of the baptistery, with the alabaster font and the tablets of the Law. Before them was the well of the nave, and just at the height to rest a hand as they stepped down were two large pinecones standing on square pediments, 'viewed', wrote Lonsdale later, with a more pagan understanding than Canon Hall, 'as emblematic of the passage through death to immortality'.[17]

Eleven rows of pews, resting on low oak platforms, provided just enough seating for the village families. The frames were oak and the panels and seats were of Spanish chestnut, blown down in Lowther Park in the storm of 1839. Before them rose the chancel arch, broad and simple, with its inner arch resting on the two profile heads, carved by William Hindson, of a man and a woman gazing across at each other, perhaps Adam and Eve, but serene, classical, archaic. On the walls at each side were the wooden archangels, one with a palm frond, one a flower, their heads tilted, their drapery sweeping in some invisible wind.

The chancel arch, rising before the villagers in their pews.

The apse ceiling curved upwards, striped with light wood and dark battens. The deep windows gleamed with alabaster ferns, and the pillars below them each had a different carved capital. But the position of the altar table was startling, completely contrary to Anglican practice: instead of being placed against the east wall it was free-standing in the chancel, so that the priest could minister from behind it. 'How did the church authorities react?' gasped Pevsner when he saw it a century later. 'Was this not popery? Perhaps they were not on their guard yet.'[18] In fact Sarah was just in time. The significance of her church, as Lonsdale noticed shrewdly, 'was hardly comprehended by Bishop Percy and his episcopate supporters'.[19] Later in the century the evangelical reaction to Tractarianism led to such panic about 'Popery' that some ministers were actually imprisoned for taking up the wrong position at the altar and other divergences from Anglican rules.[20]

The surprises went on. The whole small church was filled with a play of colours from the stained-glass windows. In Wailes's glass there were no figures, but underlying patterns reaching from top to toe – roundels and quatrefoils, circles and ovals and St Andrew's crosses. Within this tracery was a kaleidoscope of quarry glass – brilliant emerald, ruby red, ochre yellow and mauve – and clear glass where pictures had been painted and then fired, full of odd details like an acorn, a trefoil, a bishop's mitre, a leaf, or a medieval face with a rough beard. The small windows above glowed with flowers, and in those of the western gable the alabaster cut-outs showed wheat and grapes, elements of the bread and wine of the Last Supper, but also the symbols of Ceres and Bacchus.

The stone and wood carving was equally intricate and strange. Most of the capitals of the pillars in the apse were bold and formal, with symmetrical patterns, abstractions from nature, but the last one on each side was different. On one a bat spread its wings, guardian of the night and symbol of death and rebirth, and on another side a bird held a lizard in its curved beak, perhaps the ibis

of Thoth, devouring the creatures of chaos. On the column opposite another fierce bird struggled with a snake spiralling out from
beneath its wing. In front of the chancel arch, the eagle and stork
and bog-oak pulpit shone dark against the lamps of the apse. And
if the village children, restless in their pews, craned their necks
and looked up above the arch, in place of a painting of the Day of
Judgement stood a row of angels, almost fading into the shadows
of the roof. The shelf that supported them was carved with oak
leaves and acorns, grasshoppers, flowers and grapes. Separated by
primitive palms, they formed an archaic procession, two praying,
four carrying palm branches or lilies and the central one spreading her banner of good news. Surely these angels and palms, like
the open lilies on the columns, were a nod to the supposed origins of all church building, Solomon's temple, where 'he carved
all the walls of the house round about with carved figures of
cherubim and palm trees and open flowers, within and without'.[21]

20 Remembering

There was one more mystery to Sarah's church. When the oak doors were closed, narrow wooden panes could be lowered in the door panels, leaving two iron arrows on each side silhouetted against the light. There were arrows, too, forming railings around the well by the door, and more disconcerting still, one arrow was fixed, point first, as if its feathers were still quivering, in the inside wall to the left of the baptistery. Sarah left no explanation, or none that has survived. Despite all her banishment of mortality, had death leapt through the door and fired a bolt into the wall, like a border raider? Did the arrow suggest that life could be assaulted, even in a sanctuary? The arrows pierced the imagination of the village, almost asking for a legend to be woven around them. One was soon found.

Although Wreay had been caught up in the work on the chapel, it could not altogether turn its back on the world. It was the start of the 'Hungry Forties', and the fourth year of bad harvests. Trade and manufacturing slumped and industrial towns saw lock-outs and strikes: when the second Chartist petition was roundly rejected, Chartists and anti-Corn Law campaigners called for a general strike and two thousand troops marched to Manchester, in fear of more riots. Abroad, the British flag rose in Hong Kong, and New Zealand was proclaimed a colony. But there was also humiliation and despair at Britain's fortunes overseas, particularly in Afghanistan.

British rule was firmly established in India but in the late 1830s there were fears of a Russian invasion over the Khyber pass, and after failing to make an alliance with the Afghan warlords the British sent an army to install a puppet ruler in Kabul. As their stay in the country stretched into months, the British envoy William Hay Macnaghten allowed the troops to bring their families up from India. Seeing this as a sign of a permanent occupation, the Afghans rose in rebellion. General Elphinstone was in command of the Kabul garrison, 4,500 troops of whom seven hundred were European and the rest Indian. With him, as his aide-de-camp, went William Thain, fondly remembered in Wreay and at Woodside, where he had stayed as a boy and which he had often visited in later years, and in Newcastle where he was a close friend of James Losh's children.

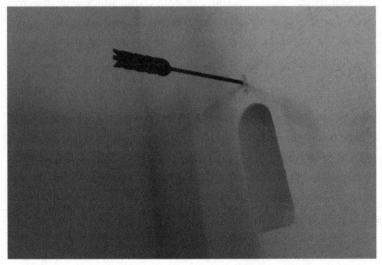

The mysterious arrow in the wall of the baptistery.

William had been with Elphinstone in India for two years, writing home jovially to his sister Sophia of the monsoon and the heat, the punkahs and palanquins, the tents of striped cloth

Sarah herself, with the help of her cousin William Septimus, carved
the octagonal alabaster font and the strong, lotus-shaped candlesticks
for the altar.

The powerful eagle and stork lecterns were carved by a Dalston man,
John Scott.

The angels processing on their beam above the chancel arch, and one of the archangels that guard it on each side.

At the other end of the church, Sarah's gardener, Robert Donald carved the inner frame of the western door with a vine and gourd.

The interior of the church, looking towards the apse and the green marnle altar table, supported by eagles.
The chancel arch is supported by the heads of a man and a woman, while the apse pillars are carved with formal designs, like this lotus bud and leaf.

Returning to ancient designs: the church at Newton Arlosh restored from the ruins, and Sarah's copy of the Bewcastle Cross.

Sarah never recovered from her grief at her sister Katharine's death.
The 'druidic' mausoleum, sheltering Dunbar's marble statue of Katharine,
is both a refuge and a cell.

The Losh grave enclosure in Wreay churchyard. The grave of Sarah and
Katharine bears the inscription, 'IN VITA DIVISAE, IN MORTE CONJUNCTAE'
– 'Parted in life, in death united'.

This later plan shows the central part of Sarah's Woodside Estate – coloured
in pink, with yellow and blue for fields mortgaged by her heirs –
and suggests the dramatic impact of the railway, cutting through her land,
the invasion of a new age.

lined with printed chintz, and the camels lying round the fires at nights.¹ But he was tired and homesick, dreaming at times of Wreay. 'I long excessively for a cottage & a garden & a pig in the stye,' he wrote from Jalalabad, before he marched north, '& I think if I were honorably out of the service tomorrow nothing (if it pleased the Almighty) should stop me till I got to the banks of the Peteril. But the world is very wicked and war seems brewing all around to punish us for our sins.'² In Kabul Elphinstone was elderly and ill, 'Unfit for it, done up, in body and mind,' as he described himself in a letter of October that year, and William took much of the burden.³

Two days before Christmas, at a meeting with the Afghan leader, Macnaghten was murdered and his body dragged through the streets and displayed in the bazaar. Soon the British position was untenable and in January 1842 Elphinstone negotiated an agreement for the safe departure of the British and all their dependants. As they struggled through thirty miles of dangerous passes and rocky gorges, deep in snow, with no shelter and little food, hundreds froze to death and more died in the constant attacks. On 8 January, as they tried to climb the Khoord Kabul pass, more than three thousand were killed or wounded, and many women and children and soldiers were taken hostage. The remaining troops pushed on by moonlight to the Jagdalak pass, where they made their last stand. All were massacred. Out of the sixteen thousand people who had left Kabul only one, the surgeon William Brydon, survived to reach Jalalabad.

On the first day of their flight William Thain's horse was shot from under him and later he received a deep flesh wound in the shoulder, but he went on, leading repeated charges, until he was killed in the final pass.⁴ The news did not reach England until late spring, when work on the chapel at Wreay was reaching its last stages. This was the reason, the villagers said, that Miss Losh put the arrows there, with their message of violent death. Shortly before his death, William had sent home a pinecone. The seed from this was raised, and a tree was planted in his memory beside the burial ground at Wreay.[5] Next to it Sarah placed a memorial stone with a sculpted pinecone, remembering him not in his final regiment but in the one he had fought with at Waterloo:

This Khelat pine is planted in memory of Wm Thain, Major of the 33rd, and was raised from seed transmitted by him to England. He perished in the fatal pass of Coord Cabul, esteemed and lamented by all who knew him.

★

The people of Wreay remembered the boy they had known, who had been to their school, who had spent holidays here, and had died in the icy passes. But the horrors of Afghanistan were remote from the village. The church was soon part of normal parish life. As if the poorer inhabitants had been waiting for it to be finished before they christened their children, there were three quick baptisms in December 1842: 'Robert, son of William and Esther Birkbeck, labourer; Isaac, son of Christopher and Elizabeth Scaife, labourer; Matthew, son of Matthew and Ann Monkhouse, labourer.'[6] Before Christmas 1842, Margaret Longrigg spent a week polishing the pews, at a shilling a day. A new communion cloth was ordered and a new surplice for the vicar, and more mundane things needed to keep the church going: kneeling stools, mats for people to wipe their muddy boots, coke for the boiler and '2 spades for digging Graves'.[7]

Drawing a line under their great venture, in June 1843 Sarah Losh and Richard Jackson drew up the accounts for approval by the Twelve Men, with each payment listed, for carving and glazing, stones and slates, foundry work and plastering, sawing and carting. The suppliers were named, including the timber firms: Richardson's in Carlisle, for the Lowthers' chestnut; Walker's in Tower Street, for the American elm and Memel boards; and

	£	s	d
Larch & sawing it at sawmill for flooring	4	0	0
Oak wood cut at Woodbank & Woodside say	150	0	0
J. Macdonald contract for seats	20	0	0
Scott sawing for ditto	1	7	0
Scott sawing for ditto	8	10	0
Richardson Chesnut wood for seats	28	7	0
Nicholson (Annan) Dantzic oak	13	6	9
Leading Dantzic oak & Woodside sawpit		4	0
Leading Chesnut wood from Carlisle	1	16	0
Advertizing work		4	6
Horsing planks		1	0
Moving old seats		8	9
Chesnut wood for carving	2	4	0
Scott carving eagle & carriage thereof	5	1	6
Scott for Stork	5	0	0
Scott for other carving	2	4	0
Stone eagle	2	1	6
Black oak – expense of getting from the Moss	1	10	0
Total	1092	7	4
for Chesnut slabs remaining valued at			

A page of the building accounts, copied from Rev. Jackson's notebook, showing some of the wood ordered, and Scott's work on the carvings.

Nicholson, across the Solway at Annan, for the Danzig oak for the pew frames. The charge of £150 – a very modest price – for cutting timber across the Woodside estate was duly noted. Many sundry items jotted down at the end of these accounts were paid for by Sarah herself, including the alabaster and the talc for dusting it as she cut her windows, the stove ornaments and books, the carving by her gardener Robert Donald, the additional railway carriage to bring the windows over for Wailes's workshop and the 'wear and tear of carts, barrow ropes & scaffold bands'.[8]

That June, Sarah was no longer supervising workmen or fretting about windows and carving. In the early summer she, Alicia and Margaret could sit on the terrace looking over the valley to the grey shoulders of the moors and the distant Cross Fell, shimmering in the haze like a great sleeping animal. In midsummer, while the hay was cut and the fruit ripened, they retreated to the cool of the house or the little hermitage and walked under their fine Woodside trees. In September, before the frosts and the first snow, the long grass on the hillsides became bleached and pale. In the low sun, ponds and becks glittered and fields shone green against the brown bogs and moorland, tawny as a lion's back. When storm clouds gathered over the fells to the west, velvety slants of light caught the marram grass, the cobwebs filled with dewdrops, the shining bracken and rough drystone walls.

This was Sarah's landscape, changing with the seasons, following the rhythm of the farming year. But her church had not satisfied her passion for working in stone. Over the next few years, she moved outside, into the churchyard, and then across the county to the family's old home, Newton Arlosh.

Her first ambitious undertaking was the copy of Bewcastle cross which she and Katharine had long ago planned as a memorial to their parents. Her model was daunting. Fourteen foot high, the Bewcastle cross was carved on all sides. On the west were the dignified figures; on the north and south were scrolls and inter-lacing patterns and on the east a rhythmically twisting vine, home to beasts and birds. The knots and scrolls and vines linked Bede's Northumbria to the carvings in the early churches of Rome, while the style of the figures recalled Syrian sculptures and the ivories of the eastern Mediterranean; perhaps a craftsman had travelled from there to work on the stone. It was local and familiar, yet it crossed the boundaries of nations and time, blending Coptic and Celtic, East and West. With its sundial on the southern side, divided into the four 'tides' that governed the day, it asked people to look up from earth to sky, from birth to death, from past to unknown future. And the cross might have been set up, some scholars thought, by St Ælfflæd, the half-sister of the Northumbrian king Alchfrith to whom it was dedicated, and the friend of St Cuthbert and succes-sor of St Hilda as abbess of Whitby. Could it be women's work?

Sarah managed to find a quarryman who could cut a single great block of sandstone to the measurements she gave, load it on to a cart and bring it to Wreay.[9] Antiquarians were puzzled at the time, and later, as to how these Celtic crosses had been carved. Some believed that they were laid on trestles and turned, but most thought that they were carved when vertical. Sarah's venture was thus a true antiquarian quest, the first serious scientific attempt to solve this puzzle. Philip Howard lent her drawings, and she also looked carefully at the engravings in Daniel and Samuel Lysons' *Account of Cumberland*: some details of her carvings are much closer to these than to the original. It looks as though an expert, probably William Hindson, carved three of the sides, where the knots and lacing and chequers are crisp and fine, but Sarah probably carved the figures on the west side herself. To do this, she needed to redraw the sketches to scale, mark the outline on the stone and then clam-ber up the ladder with her hammer and chisels, day after day.

The Wreay cross was the same shape and the same size as that of Bewcastle, apart from a cross placed on the top of the obelisk.

North Side   South Side   East Side   West Side

The drawing of all four sides of the Bewcastle obelisk, engraved
for Lysons' *Cumberland* in 1816, provided a pattern-book for Sarah's
pioneering adaptation.

But as with all Sarah's work, she subtly adapted her model. The figures have a freedom of outline that looks unmistakably of the Regency, like the drawings of Hope or Thomas Stothard, with draperies in easy folds. At the bottom stands the man with the hawk, his plump bird perched on a stand facing the falconer, not gripping his hand and looking forwards as at Bewcastle; in the centre, Christ stands firmly, no longer floating above the lions' heads; at the top, as in Smith's drawing of a century before, the Virgin Mary – to whom Wreay church was dedicated – stands with her baby in her arms, his hand touching her face.

Since this was a memorial to her parents, Sarah replaced the Bewcastle runes with lines from Psalms 27 and 57. The inscription on the stone is in Latin, but the King James version runs 'The Lord is my light and my salvation', and 'Be merciful unto me O God, be merciful unto me: yea, in the shadow of thy wings will I make my refuge.' Images of light and shadow, salvation and reunion also echo through the lines on the eastern side, translated as 'May this sign of consolation cast its shadow on the grave of John Losh and his wife Isabella. May you walk safely, beloved souls, through the midst of the shadow of death. Farewell, till the times of refreshing in the presence of the Lord.'[10] For the psalms and the dedication to her parents, *animae carissimae*, Sarah did not turn to the English Bible, beautiful as its prose was, but to the Vulgate, the pre-Reformation Bible used in the Catholic church, with its ringing phrase from the Acts of the Apostles about the 'times of refreshing', *ut cum venerint tempora refrigerii a conspectu Domini.*

On the base of the cross was written '*Hoc saxum poni duae filiae sibi proposuerunt: una maestissima effecit*', 'Two daughters proposed that this stone be set up: one, greatly sorrowing, performed it.' In her mind Sarah undertook this work with her sister. Now she would build a memorial to Katharine herself. This would be different. Katharine's death had scarred her and she could not make it beautiful. It had to be fierce, strong, even ugly. More cartloads of stone were brought to the churchyard, this time weighty blocks of sandstone, rough and unfinished. Between the copy of the cross and the churchyard wall Hindson's men used these to build walls without mortar, and roofed them with heavy flags set on great stone beams, to form a huge box, a chest to hold grief. Startled commentators called this mausoleum Druidic, semi-Celtic, Cyclopean, archaic, even 'Archaean', as if it dated from an era before human time began.

Light filtered in through two narrow windows on the north and south, and on the east, facing the rising sun and the Bewcastle cross, was a rough oak door protected by an outer door of copper. Inside Sarah placed a white marble statue of Katharine, glimmering like a ghost in the shadows. The sculpture was carved by Dunbar, working from a sketch that Sarah had made of her sister on the beach at Naples in 1817. Katharine sits on the sand with bare feet, her ankles crossed. She is half smiling, and her head is bent as if reading, except that she does not hold a book but a pinecone, resting in the folds of her dress. On the plinth, at Katharine's feet, a Latin inscription was carved, giving her name without the K, which is not in the Latin alphabet: *Catharina Isabella soror placens amabilis, semper mihi carissima, cara nunc tua pallida imago*, a last cry to her sister, 'pleasing and lovable, always most dear to me, dear now is your pale likeness'. An *imago*, it must be said, can also mean an idea, an echo – a ghost. The statue has a date on it, 1850, but perhaps this was when Dunbar came back to make some finishing touches, since it was certainly there in 1847, when Mannix and Whellan's gazetteer described it as a 'chaste' bit of sculpture, within 'a cell in the Druidical fashion'.

With its thick stone walls, the mausoleum does feel like a cell, where Sarah could at last contain her grief, holding Katharine forever in this pose. In three of the corners Sarah put marble relief portraits of her parents and her uncle George, Alicia's father, sculpted by Dunbar in 1845. These too seem to have been made from her drawings. The fourth corner stayed empty, perhaps waiting for a portrait that was never finished – of her uncle James, or George's wife Frances. The roughness of the stone and the haphazardly placed portraits make the whole mausoleum feel provisional, despite its solidity, as though its maker could not bear to go on.

When Bishop Percy consecrated the new part of the graveyard in 1842, where the cross and mausoleum would later stand, the singers intoned the dark Psalm 39, with its warning to bridle the tongue against wickedness and its prayer to prepare for the end:

> Lord, make me to know mine end, and the measure of my days,
>   what it is: that I may know how frail I am.
> Behold, thou hast made my days as an handbreadth; and mine age
>   is as nothing before thee . . .

In the early 1840s Sarah spent much of her furious energy on pinning down the dead, as if refusing to be haunted any more. Among the leaning tombstones of long-dead parishioners, she walled in the Losh family graves, building a low balustrade with round arches. This would enclose some of the oddest, heftiest, most strangely carved gravestones in England, laid out in an irregular pattern. It seems likely that she tackled the carving herself, and if not, she gave firm instructions. Her models were the weighty medieval grave slabs found in many Cumbrian churches, reinterpreted in a highly individual style. She began with her parents, placing a massive lump of sandstone, heavy enough to deter a vampire, on the grave that they shared with their infant son John. She left the surface rough, unshaped, uncarved, deprived of images of consolation: on the south side a plain inscription recorded their names, dates of death and age, and Isabella's status as 'daughter of Thomas Bonner of Callerton'.

On 29 December 1845 her aunt Margaret died, aged seventy-seven. She had often been downcast and ill and her inscription, a

Traditional grave slabs, found near the medieval churches of Cumbria.

diagonal banner biting into the stone, with its claim of steadfast faith even in 'the dark house of mortal dissolution', sounds as if she chose the words herself.[11] Almost in defiance Sarah had the slab carved with a pinecone and branches, and a butterfly, tokens of continuing life. Her other aunt, her mother's sister Ann Bonner, died the following August. The two Bonner sisters had gravestones in the old Cumbrian style, like the Templar and crusader slabs of Bridekirk or Kirkoswald, but almost every other stone carried potent symbols of enduring, primitive life, corals and branches, scallops and cones. No angels looked heavenwards. The dead were all metaphorically returned to the earth. Even Katharine lay beneath her weighty stones, eternally part of the turning world, like Wordsworth's Lucy:

> No motion has she now, no force;
> She neither hears nor sees;

Rolled round in earth's diurnal course,
With rocks, and stones, and trees.

★

If the stones were heavy with death, the church behind was full
of reminders of the regeneration of the natural world and the way
that human ideas and beliefs flowed through time, rich and alive.
Sarah's successful management of this large project prompted her
to take on another. She looked back to the place that her family
had come from, Newton Arlosh on the Solway plain, where the
flat, square fields were bordered, as they still are today, on one side
by wild peat mosses and on the other by tidal salt marsh, riven by
winding, sluggish channels. Local farmers held grazing rights to
'stints' on the marsh, and peat rights, by which they let the villagers cut and dry peat for their fires.[12]

The church here had its own long history. Local legends held
that St Ninian had founded a chapel on his way home from
Rome at the end of the fourth century, before he crossed the
Solway to build his white church, his Candida Casa, at Whithorn.
In recorded history, the long, straggling village was really born in
1303 when the small port of Skinburness on the estuary sands,
where Edward I's small fleet had gathered to invade Scotland, was
swept away in a storm. After the dykes were destroyed the refu-
gees moved to a safer place where the ground rose slightly above
the flooded lands. Here they built Newton Arlosh, their new
town; the chartered market for Holm Cultram moved from Skinburness and was held for fifteen days each June. In 1304 Bishop
Halton of Carlisle gave the abbot permission to build 'one chapel
or church afresh' and obtained a licence to crenellate, accepting
from the start that this would be a refuge from raiders.[13] When
it was finished, the new St John the Baptist, built of cobbles and
sandstone, was 'Half church of God, half castle 'gainst the Scots',
as Walter Scott wrote of Durham cathedral.[14] Like the church at

nearby Burgh-by-Sands it had a tower at the west end, with thick walls, vaulted rooms and battlements: the door was only two feet six inches wide, making it easy to defend, and the nave and tower had narrow slit windows for the defenders to fire their arrows – even the main east window was only eleven inches across, and all the windows were high off the ground, above the reach of a man's hand. The church fended off attacks for two centuries, but after the dissolution of the monasteries, when Holm Cultram became the parish church, St John's lay abandoned. The roof fell in, the lead was taken for salt-pans, and the nave was a shelter for sheep.

The roofless tower and church of Newton Arlosh at the start of
the nineteenth century.

Sarah was allegedly appalled, on one of her visits in 1843, to find the villagers carting away the stones as if it was a quarry, and, supported by Canon Simpson of Holm Cultram, offered to restore it. When she assured Bishop Percy that she would pay, he granted permission. The builders moved in. As they worked on the foundations, they found piled-up skeletons, casualties of some border skirmish, and Roman coins, some dedicated to Jupiter

Ammon, the Roman form of the Egyptian Amun, creator of life and protector of the poor.[15] The workmen patched up the ruined tower and battlements, and doubled the width of the nave by adding an extra area on the northern side.[16]

Sarah thought the plan out carefully, so that the silhouette of the church against the western sky as people approached from Burgh and Carlisle would stay unchanged, or rather would recover the old outline that had crumbled away. She stuck to the Anglo-Norman style, adding an apse with a scalloped stone roof, like that of Wreay, and a magnificent west door with two mighty wedge-shaped stones forming the arch, as in early Mediterranean churches. Many of her characteristic touches were here, like the sandstone flags instead of roof tiles and the eagle standing guard on the roof. Inside, a Hindson palm tree formed the lectern, a bog-oak pulpit (long since stolen) gleamed dark against the walls and two ram's heads supported the chancel arch. These were doubtless a nod to the coins marked with Jupiter Ammon, since the Egyptian Amun often appeared as a man with the head of a ram. The reference was typical of her interest in the overlapping of old beliefs but the rams' heads, with their demonic connotations, 'gave rise', as Lonsdale put it diplomatically, 'to some discussion'.

Sarah did not mind if she upset people. She had built her memorials to those she loved and walled in their graves. She knew that her work at Newton Arlosh was good, although progress was slow and the church was not consecrated until July 1849 when Robert Whiteman was appointed vicar.[17] The following year, the marriages and baptisms and burials began, and here, as at Wreay, village life flowed on again.

21 Living On

Almost everyone in Wreay worked on the land. Sometimes three generations lived on a farm and many had families of six children or more.[1] The schools that Sarah and Katharine had built were packed. But when Sarah drove into Carlisle, or walked up to Brisco, she touched a different world.

There were farms here and in the next village of Upperby, but as the hill dipped down towards the Petteril, farm workers gave way to the weavers, calico printers, colour mixers, bleachers and 'washers of prints' from the Woodbank works. Although the works were managed by the local firm of Harrington and Pattinson, Sarah was the ultimate owner of the land, the print works and the workers' cottages, and felt a responsibility for the unemployed. All the textile workers in Carlisle were suffering from the arrival of the new machine looms, and from the fierce variations in trade which could make four or five hundred weavers at a time suddenly destitute. The city workhouses could not cope with the numbers or the cost, and the Poor Law Commission made a special exception, allowing the Board of Guardians to apply an 'outdoor labour test', giving relief as long as people undertook hard labour like stone-breaking in a special yard. Few would accept this.

In Denton Holme the calico printers, William Losh & Co, went bankrupt and eventually moved their business to Manchester. At the auction in November 1841 everything was for sale,

'Machinery, Utensils, Implements etc', from the latest engraved copper rollers right down to buckets and blankets, wheelbarrows and the pony and cart. A month after this, the Carlisle corporation sent a petition to the House of Commons, through Philip Howard, saying that there were now 389 families living on 'casual charity', while nearly six thousand people in all had weekly earnings of no more than one shilling and sixpence, including cotton spinners, bleachers, tailors, shoemakers, bricklayers and labourers. Two years later, when James Harrington died, the Woodbank print works was closed. Sarah sold part of the printfield to the Lancaster and Carlisle Railway, and the lease was taken over by the engineer William Bouch to make railway equipment – the industry of a new age.[2]

Sarah helped the weavers where she could and worked hard to ensure that a new use was found for Woodbank. She was not a Lady Bountiful, wafting into cottages. She kept her giving quiet although her name was on every subscription list, for the infirmary, the institute for the blind and for schools in High Hesket and Upperby as well as Wreay: in the freezing January of 1844 she gave fourteen carts of coal, as well as clothing, to the poor of Upperby alone.[3] She was on hand when needed and could drive a cause with steely determination, as she did in the case of a poor woman unable to afford a lawyer, setting out the case so clearly that the plaintiff's solicitor advised his client to withdraw.[4] She was a local character, admired and held rather in awe.

In Wreay Sarah could now turn from the church, the cross, the mausoleum and the graves and walk across the road into family life. In the mid-1840s, William Septimus built a large house, Wreay Syke, down the lane opposite the church with terraced gardens looking far out over the valley. He chose a decidedly Sarah Losh style with narrow round arches everywhere, even on the orangery and the gallery above, and when all was ready he moved in with his wife Sarah and their son James, who was then about twelve and loved roaming the fields and the gardens at Woodside. He grew up to be a keen naturalist, and in a talk in Carlisle many years later he remembered his childhood discoveries: the frog whom he named Pharoah and set free into a wayside marsh, the beautiful cream-coloured mole that was caught at Woodside, and the toad who came out every evening for his shower-bath 'which was given him tenderly from the fine rose of a watering can'.[5] Above all James loved birds: the redstarts that came to Woodside year after year; the whinchats and stonechats on Wragmire Moss; the flocks of hen chaffinches in the winter. This delight was something that Sarah could share. Down by the Petteril where the kingfisher swooped 'with open wings, head downwards, ready for his rapid plunge', one could walk from Newbiggin to Wreay Hall Mill through woods carpeted with 'blaeberry, cow-wheat, wood-rush, dog-mercury, saxifrage, water avens, anemone, and other shade-loving herbs, with clumps of primrose, blue-bells, ferns, wild raspberries or iris appearing here and there'.[6] The sunshine filtering through the leaves sparkled on the water and the trees rising high on each side seemed to shut the world out.

But the world could not be shut out. In the mid-1840s the valley of the Petteril was a building site, with cranes and carts, and gangs of navvies. Over the past ten years the railways had crept north from London – the London and Birmingham, the Grand Junction and the North Union – and the people of Carlisle had lobbied strongly for a continuation north from Lancaster that would link them to the capital. The difficulty lay in finding a route. George Stephenson proposed a line around the west coast to avoid the fells, while his pupil, the engineer Joseph Locke, looked for inland routes, despite the steep gradients. The local papers were full of arguments and reports of meetings, and in January 1839, at the height of the great storm, the men of Penrith had formed a company for the inland route, selling shares at £50 each.[7]

While the surveyors worked, local people sought anxiously for news, some hoping for the railway to come as near as possible, others fearful of its encroachment on their land. After long debates and a royal commission in 1840, Locke's plans for the inland route won through. The line would run along the coast from Lancaster then climb to Oxenholme, from where a branch line would head north-west to Kendal and Windermere. The main line would tackle the steep climb over Shap Fell before running down to Penrith and along the Petteril valley to Carlisle. In other words, right past Wreay.[8]

The bill giving the Lancaster and Carlisle Railway permission to build was passed in June 1844. That autumn Wordsworth, who had become poet laureate on Southey's death the previous year, began his campaign in the *Morning Post* to stop the branch line to Windermere. Trainloads of uneducated crowds would, he feared, utterly destroy the lonely grandeur of the lakes. He attacked the railway with the same desperation with which he had inveighed against the larch plantations fifty years before:

> Is then no nook of English ground secure
> From rash assault? . . .
> . . . Plead for thy peace, thou beautiful romance
> Of nature; and, if human hearts be dead,
> Speak, passing winds; ye torrents, with your strong
> And constant voice, protest against the wrong.

Wordsworth and the torrents protested in vain: the extension to Windermere was approved in June 1845.

By then work on the main line was well underway. The stupendous cost was borne largely by the railway companies, but local landowners like Sarah, and grandees who held shares, also had their say.[9] In July the first sod was cut at Shap Summit, the highest point on the line, nine hundred feet above sea level. Thousands of labourers were hired, building bridges and viaducts, embankments and tunnels, and cutting through solid rock at Shap. In late 1846 when they were rushing to the finish there were nearly ten thousand men and a thousand horses up on the fell. A report in the *Carlisle Patriot*, from someone who had walked the line, declared:

I never saw a line better stocked with materials of the best kind and most modern construction, nor did I ever see so great a number of the finest and stoutest workmen together. They are the admiration of all. They seem very happy and contented, great attention having been paid by Mr. Stephenson, the contractor, to provide for them houses and lodgings. There are hundreds of neat dwellings erected, the comfort of which surpasses all belief. The country is so wild and solitary, that it is absolutely necessary to supply provisions for the men, otherwise the work could not proceed.[10]

Shap cutting, where thousands of navvies and their families camped for months in 1844.

Not everyone was so admiring. Many visitors were shocked by the sight of men sleeping rough in turf huts and the ragged women and children who camped with them. The Irish potato crop failed in 1845 and again the next year and as people died in their thousands in Ireland, and many more were evicted from their homes, men fled to England to work on the railways. To stop trouble, the nationalities were separated. In January 1846, however, disputes broke out between English crews at Yanwath, just south of Penrith, angry because the Irish undercut their wages, and Irish gangs labouring at Plumpton, six to eight miles from Wreay. The Irish took over Yanwath and the English looted and burned the Irish settlement. In the rioting in the narrow streets of Penrith an Irishman was brutally killed. The Westmorland Yeomanry, drawn from the local gentry, seemed powerless to stop the fighting, but eventually both sides fell back before troops sent from Carlisle. At the subsequent trials the *Patriot's* description of the English ringleader evokes the image of the navvy that people feared so much – short, broad, immensely strong, with rough matted hair:

We understand he has said that for nine years he has never slept in a bed, or worn a hat: that his custom was to put on his boots when new, and never remove them until they fell to pieces, and his clothes were treated very much in the same way, except that his shirt was changed, once a week.[11]

The navvies worked with incredible speed. When they brought their picks and sledgehammers to Wreay, where many men and their families were billeted in the farms and cottages, there was no violence, just noise and dust and the occasional brawl outside the Plough. The new line curved across the high bank above the Petteril opposite Wreay Hall before running along the slope below the Plough, and then straight through Sarah's fields, past Spoilt Bank Wood to the Bells' farm at Low Hurst. The navvies then dug 'the great cutting' between the parkland of Woodside and Newbiggin Hall, a mile long, forty-five feet deep and troubled by constant landslides.

The first section of 'The Lanky', from Lancaster to Oxenholme with its branch line to Kendal, opened in September 1846. In December the line from Oxenholme to Carlisle was ready, double track all the way except for a stretch in Wreay cutting which had been delayed by the landslides and would take another month to finish. On 17 December, although snow covered the hills and icicles hung from the rocks of the cuttings, the first train from Lancaster groaned slowly over Shap. Steaming downhill, it crossed the Lowther Viaduct, where the view of Lowther Park, declared the *Illustrated London News*, 'with its thick and massive Woods – the clear winding river, 100 feet below – the stern grandeur of the distant mountains, just tinted with the last farewell rays of the setting sun – formed a beautiful picture'. Then came the Eamont viaduct and the sight of Brougham Hall, whose pleasure-grounds 'looked gloomily with their winter's clothing'.[12]

Meanwhile, in a scattering of snow, a train was still waiting in Carlisle station to head south towards Penrith to meet the Lancaster train. After an hour, the *Journal* reported, 'the passengers began to amuse themselves and endeavour to warm their toes by a general pattering of feet such as is sometimes heard in theatres when an audience becomes impatient'. Peals of laughter followed each bout of tapping, until the train eventually set off. As it steamed into Penrith the band struck up 'See the Conquering Hero Comes'. After an hour both trains chugged slowly north along the double tract down the Petteril valley. Just past Barrock Lodge, 'on the borders of a vale of remarkable loveliness', the papers announced, 'a high embankment passes Wreay Hall and village, noted for the beauty of its Chapel'.

There are no records of jubilant celebrations in Wreay, but in Carlisle more crowds met the trains and more bands played. There was a banquet at the Athenaeum and a grand contractors' dinner at the assembly rooms of the Crown and Mitre, where Sarah and Katharine had smiled their way through so many assize balls. For nine months the line ended at London Road, the station for the Newcastle trains, but in September 1847 the Citadel station was opened, where the line joined the new southern section of the Caledonian Railway. The delighted Losh families could now travel

by train from their own nearby station all the way to London or
Glasgow. At first the 'Newbiggin and Wreay' station was at Brisco,
but after much lobbying from the Rev. Jackson in 1852, this was
closed in favour of a halt at Wreay itself. The whistle of steam
engines became as much a part of life as the lowing of cattle.

With her long experience of working with her uncle James
over the Newcastle–Carlisle railway a few years before, Sarah
made sure that she got good money for her land, both the route
across her own park and the land she sold to the railway company
below Brisco, nearer Carlisle. She also made her own distinctive
mark on this enterprise. When the navvies were digging the great
cutting at Woodside, she discovered that they planned to fell one
of the large oak trees her father had planted. Incensed, she tackled
the builders, who built a special retaining wall, like a great flower
pot, around the oak, thereafter known as 'Miss Losh's Tree'. It was
still remarked on in a railway guidebook of the 1920s.

Sarah was sixty in 1846 when the first engines hooted past. Her
brother Joseph, 'poor Joe', was still living at Ravenside, still looked
after by Sarah Gaskin who had moved there after the old vicar's
death. Joseph died in January 1848, aged fifty-nine. He was buried
in the churchyard, under an unshaped grave slab with an inscription across one corner and a design of fossil mosses and cones.

Far from being a sole survivor, Sarah was surrounded by her
extended family as never before, a tangle of names, a dance of
families. Her cousin Alicia was now forty-five: she had lived at
Woodside for several years and it was clearly destined to be her
permanent home. Alicia's younger sister Sarah, William Septimus's
wife, was now living down the road and in this decade two more
of George's daughters settled nearby. The first was the invalid Jane,
who died at Wreay Syke in 1847. Then the following year Frances
came back from the Isle of Man with her doctor husband, Francis
Coleridge Hutchinson, and moved into The Cottage in Brisco,

the Bonner sisters' old house. By 1849 Wreay was thus home to three of the six girls who had traipsed after George from Newcastle to Scotland and France: Alicia, Sarah and Frances. A few years later their older sister, Mary Kemmis, also came to live at Wreay Syke. Only the youngest, Georgina Cussans, stayed in France. Her story had a flash of daring reminiscent of the wayward father after whom she was named. At twenty-one she had embarked on marriage to Thomas Cussans, forty-two years her senior, the son of a Jamaican plantation owner, 'soldier, captive of the French, Regency rakehell – fast women and slow horses – debtor exile', and father to several illegitimate children whom the determined, colourful Georgina looked after carefully in her will.[13]

George himself had come home from France to live at Low Heaton near Newcastle, where he died in 1846 at the age of eighty. The last survivor of the dashing Losh brothers was William, who was still going strong at Walker, and carrying on as the port's vice-consul for Prussia, Sweden and Norway. A hero on the Tyne, held in great affection until his death at the age of ninety, William was a craggy, eccentric figure down at the works in his old clothes. An oft-repeated story tells how the captain of *The Ark*, lying in the river off Walker, got talking to a 'loafing old fellow' in a seedy coat and was staggered to discover that this was the great Mr Losh. He and Alice were living at White Hall, Benton, not far from the works, where they had largely brought up their daughter Margaret's children, Spencer and Alice Boyd, now in their twenties. Later they moved back to Point Pleasant and then into Newcastle.

By now, Losh, Wilson & Bell was the largest engineering firm in the north, making iron rails, castings, machinery and pumping engines for mills, collieries and iron works. The Wreay legacy extended further: Thomas Bell's son, Isaac Lowthian, left Walker to run a blast furnace in Washington, County Durham, founding the great Bell iron- and steel-making dynasty on Teesside. Another Wreay son, William Armstrong, George's first partner in the corn merchant's on the quayside, became a powerful local politician, whose son, William George Armstrong, would be one of the Tyne's great tycoons, engineer, arms manufacturer and shipping magnate – an extraordinary thought that such an array of industrial might should come from one small village.

The chemical experiments of John Losh and Dundonald had grown into a huge industry. By now there were soda factories all along the Tyne, employing three thousand people and producing over seventy thousand tons of alkali, crystal soda and bleaching powder.[14] In 1850 William Septimus was still involved at Walker, taking out a lucrative new patent for converting the evil-smelling soda waste into 'hypo', used in paper-making for removing chlorine traces after bleaching. His oldest brother James was also living in Newcastle, practising as a barrister on the Northern Circuit, as his father had done, and later as a judge. Although James never married, he had a long relationship with a young neighbour, Mary Lindsay Brown, and by 1850 they had three small children.[15] They were a devoted couple, and although they could not make their relationship public, James's brothers all knew and lent James money, and acted as trustees for his children after he died.

The Wreay Loshes often visited Tyneside or headed in the opposite direction to visit William Septimus's sisters, Cecilia, Margaret and Jemima, who lived south of the Lakes around Ulverston and Cartmel, where their mother Cecilia had settled until her death in 1841. In turn, these relations and their children came to stay and Wreay became a hub of family gatherings. At The Cottage in Brisco, the Hutchinson children included Anna and Celia, both in their late teens, Francis, who was eleven in 1848, and little Louisa who was only six. Across the road in Langarth Cottage was William Septimus's brother Robert. Almost next door, Sarah's land agent William Moffit lived with his ten children, ranging down the years from a son of twenty-one to a small baby.

Woodside, just up the lane, was full of young people again: Hutchinson girls in tight-waisted crinolines playing the piano, boys charging across the lawns, toddlers clambering up the terrace steps. Fringed shawls and ribboned bonnets were thrown on the Chippendale chairs in the drawing room. The village was full of Losh family news, of moves and marriages and deaths and births. At Wreay church in August 1846, the youngest child of William Losh's daughter Margaret and her second husband Henry Mayhew was baptised. The baby's name was Catherine.

In 1847 Sarah sold her share in the Walker alkali works to her uncle William. With the railway money and shares and income from her lands and farms, she was happy to stop calling herself a 'soda maker' on official forms, and just to be a landowner. She was still building, in a small way, creating a landscape full of memory. Over the brook near the village she set the stone arch from the door of the old Wreay chapel. Down a lane at Brisco, she built a more formal well in dressed sandstone with a square flagged trough and a round, carved arch, over the spring of St Ninian. The saint was said to have rested here on his way north from Rome, baptising the local people, before he crossed the Solway. To Sarah these springs were still sacred. William Septimus followed her lead, building a large well with her typical rounded arches at a bend on the Southwaite road, known as 'Katharine's well'.

Involved with the new railway, working on the memorials in the churchyard and the renovation of Newton Arlosh, Sarah was busy. She still read voraciously. 'She relished a good book of the thoughtful, suggestive, and historical stamp', remembered Henry Lonsdale, 'and was not slow to appreciate the capital novels of Scott, Lytton, the Ostade pictures of Dickens, and the satirical hits at modern society by Thackeray.' She and her friends had been reading Dickens since the mid-1830s, and now Thackeray's novels were appearing, with *Barry Lyndon* in 1844 and *Vanity Fair* four years later. There were new novels too, clearly written by women even where pseudonyms were used: *Jane Eyre* and *Wuthering Heights* in 1847, Gaskell's *Mary Barton* the following year.

Books also kept arriving on archaeology and architecture, politics and theology, literature and geology. In 1844 Robert Chambers' *Vestiges of the Natural History of Creation* was published, at first anonymously. Combining astronomy and geology with anthropology it suggested, sensationally, 'that the planets had originated in a Fire-mist, that life could be created in the laboratory, that humans had evolved from apes'.[16] The message of transmutation from simple forms to complex was like a vindication of Sarah's ideas, so visible in her church, harking back to Hutton's words, 'no vestige of a beginning, no prospect of an end'. For Eliza Lynn Linton, granddaughter of Samuel Goodenough, the Bishop of Carlisle who had stuck to his old ways and his wigs, *Vestiges* provided vital ammunition in her battle with her clergyman father in his Cumberland parish: 'giving, as it did, the first idea of cosmic continuity, and the consequent destruction of the bit by bit creation of Genesis, it was a priceless treasure to me, to him a deadly and diabolical sin'.[17]

Sarah kept up her interest in theology, particularly in the High Church, Anglo-Catholic writings of the Oxford Group. The Woodside library contained a rush of books from the mid-1840s, including the many volumes of the *Lives of the Saints* by Alban Butler and by Newman (who gives a long and tender account of St Ninian), and Palmer's *Origines Liturgicae, or Antiquities of the English Ritual*, the fourth edition, published in 1845. There were history books too, such as Joinville's *Chronicles of the Crusades*, and books on antiquities, like Collingwood Bruce's study of the Roman Wall and a revised edition of Brand's *Popular Antiquities of Great Britain*.

The doctor Henry Lonsdale − or Harry, as his friends called him − got to know Sarah in the late 1840s. Lonsdale had graduated in Edinburgh, and practised there after a short spell in a country practice at Raughton Head a few miles from Wreay, where he lectured on scientific subjects and started the local agricultural society. In 1846 he came back to Carlisle as physician to the infirmary, publishing influential articles on medicine and being closely involved, as Sarah was, in public health campaigns. After he married in 1851 he travelled widely, concentrating on his love of Italian art, another interest shared with Sarah. A radical, friend of Mazzini and Garibaldi, he was interested in her politics and in the fusion of myths and symbols in her work. Her male and female symbols showed, he thought, 'Nature in her broader, genetic aspects', and her church displayed, he added with dry amusement and a rare exclamation mark, a regard for 'the development of different Cults, from the time of Osiris and his Nilotic nymphs' to the wisdom of Solomon and 'the monogamic, non-virtuous Anglo-Saxon, accredited with representing the latest phase of civilisation!'

At Woodside, Lonsdale found that in contrast to the galleries crowded with paintings and the elegant drawing rooms, Sarah's own rooms were plain. She had polished floorboards, engravings on the walls, a deal table for her books and needlework and a basket of logs for the fire:

Only special friends were admitted to this sanctum in the upper storey, where I found her one morning in a laughing humour from reading Baron von Reichenbach's 'Researches on the Dynamics of Magnetism, Electricity &c in their relation to Vital Force' – a highly theoretic work pertaining to physiology and psychology, if not divination, that did not comport with the fine logical acumen of Miss Losh.

Reichenbach's *Researches* was published in English in 1851. He was a respected physicist, chemist and geologist who threw himself, after his retirement, into researching a field of energy which he believed flowed through all living things: he called this the Odic force, from the Norse god Odin. Sarah laughed – she could detect 'pseudo science' when she saw it – yet her own work too had been concerned with the vital energy of the natural world, linked to myths and beliefs.

Intellectual and forceful as she was, in person Sarah was reserved. She avoided confrontation and kept her voice clear and tone even, 'yet, if needful, in discussion she could maintain her own lines of thought with firmness'.[18] She was witty, enjoyed a joke and was never sentimental. Initially her reserved, formal manner could intimidate strangers, said Lonsdale (clearly meaning himself), but this quickly disappeared once the conversation flowed. In 1852 he introduced her to Father Gavazzi, a friend of Garibaldi, attacker of papal corruption and campaigner for Italian independence who had fled to England after the defeat of Garibaldi's troops in 1848, and had since travelled the country, 'giving to English audiences a description of Italy's miseries and necessities'.[19] Sarah talked with him in French, then in Italian, to make him more at ease. When Lonsdale met Gavazzi again eleven years later on the banks of the Arno, she was the first person he asked about.

She was still good-looking, with a face full of character, dressed in the dark colours she had worn since Katharine died. When she went out, she put on a black bonnet 'of cottage shape', with a shawl over her plain merino gown: this was how the villagers saw her as she walked down the old road, Waygates, to the church and the enclosure and mausoleum where her parents and her sister were buried, and back home to Woodside again.

She walked more slowly now, sometimes out of breath. She suffered from bronchitis in the winters, and in early 1849 was dangerously ill. That March Mary Wordsworth added a postscript when she wrote to Isabella Fenwick, 'Wm. has just mentioned to me that Miss Losh is in a dangerous state – seemingly sinking from weakness without any apparent cause'.[20] The summer of 1850 was warm and mild even into September, and Sarah recovered well. For the next two years she was busy giving dinners for family and friends, walking in the garden, tending her trees, reading the new books of theology and science – and pseudo-science. Friends came over to visit the church. It was not to all tastes: Henry Lonsdale noted that 'On entering the church, visitors are struck with the "dim religious light" as vastly too dim', but admiring comments came from a younger generation. William Bell Scott, researching his *Antiquarian Gleanings in the North of England*, published in 1851, took advice from Sarah, 'the first good friend I made in these northern parts'.[21] She had, he decided patronisingly, 'a thoroughness of taste and power of intelligent design altogether singular among women'. Sarah introduced Bell Scott to Philip Howard, and among his 'gleanings', which ranged from Roman stones to copes that had lain untouched for centuries in Carlisle cathedral, he noted several antiquities from Corby Castle as well as the copper vessel from Normandy that Sarah had presented to the church.

Although Sarah kept active, she was tired. She found the piercing cold of winter increasingly hard. Just before Christmas 1851 she made her will, scratched in black ink and signed with a flourish, and in the following September she added a detailed codicil. In early March 1853, a month of biting east winds, she collapsed. After two weeks of severe illness she died on 29 March at Woodside, with her old servant Joseph Scott at her side. Lonsdale, who witnessed her last hours, wrote that she was 'calm and dignified', but the death certificate, chillingly, says she died of 'dysentery'. A few days later she was buried next to Katharine in Wreay churchyard. The gravestone, with its scallop shells and primitive plants, says simply 'Katharine Isabella Losh, died February 1835, aged 47. Sarah Losh, died March 29, 1853. *In vita divisae, in morte conjunctae*' – parted in life, in death united – 'Lord Let thy Mercy lighten upon us.'

Epilogue

Three years after the church at Wreay was finished, two notable Byzantine-style churches were built, James Wild's Christ Church in Streatham, south London, with its tall campanile, and Sidney Herbert's St Mary and St Nicholas, at Wilton in Wiltshire. But Wreay came first, and as William Bell Scott pointed out, 'before the revival of church architecture in connection with ritual and reactionary theology, her little Byzantine Church of Wreay was a notable performance. Its general simplicity and able symbolism introduced into its modest decorative features show some of the highest qualities of art.'[1]

Sarah's church was all about beginnings: lines, forms, shapes; triangle, rectangle, semi-circle; cube and sphere. She looked back to the early Christian churches, the plain box with an apse, the low Roman columns, the light through narrow windows. This was something very early, very pure, before the Celtic churches, the Romanesque and Gothic and the protestant Perpendicular. In her decoration, she hunted for origins, in living creatures and in myth. But in nature she found no 'beginnings'; Genesis was a story, as the fossils proved. Instead, there were unending cycles, seed and plant, pinecone and tree. Buried things emerged with time, like the Roman finds in Cumbrian fields or the fossils in the mines, or the lotus, whose seed can lie dormant for a thousand years, and the scarab that buries itself in desert sands, emerging at dusk, its green coat catching the light.

Sarah wrote poetry, though none has been found. If we think of the church as a poem in three dimensions, its puzzles fall into place, adding depth without demanding explanation. Like Tennyson, who began publishing when she began building, on the brink of the Victorian age, she grew up with a Romantic love of legend, but with a world-view changed by new ideas and fractured by loss. Her family were eager readers of Byron and Scott; she knew the *Lyrical Ballads* as a girl in 1798 and read Coleridge's poems of 1816 just before she left for Italy. She has been compared to Wordsworth, and it is true that she deliberately chose a simple, traditional style, just as he adopted subjects of 'humble and rustic life' (words she often used), because, he wrote, 'in that condition, the essential passions of the heart find a better soil in which they can attain their maturity, are less under restraint, and speak a plainer and more emphatic language'. Like Wordsworth, too, Sarah took familiar elements and threw over them 'a certain colouring of imagination, whereby ordinary things should be presented to the mind in an unusual aspect; and, further, and above all, to make these incidents and situations interesting by tracing in them, truly though not ostentatiously, the primary laws of our nature'.[2]

As Wordsworth reworked local ballads so Sarah drew on the familiar Norman churches, grave slabs and Celtic crosses of Cumberland. Her materials were vernacular: sandstone from the quarry, wood from trees felled in a gale. She transformed these 'ordinary things' through a lexicon of imagery drawn from nature, from the new language of geology and from the symbolism of Greece and the Orient, and did indeed attempt to trace 'the primary laws of our nature'. But there is something dark, troubled and visionary about Sarah's work, more like Coleridge than Wordsworth. Her church was a defiant celebration of life and art, summoned by her own decree, standing on the brink of mortality and time, like Kubla Khan's secular pleasure dome above the chasm, echoing with ancestral voices prophesying war.

Sarah Losh found building seductive, an exercise of power, and some of her work is disturbing. We have no note of her personal theology. The imagery of the church suggests she was a deist, not holding to doctrines of the Trinity, grace and redemption, but a believer in an *Ens Entium*, a Supreme Being who had set the universe in motion, renewing itself in measureless time. Just as the physical world was so much older than was once believed, so she knew that the human compulsion to touch the infinite was far older than Christianity. Hence her pantheistic imagery. She did not deny an afterlife. The cross and graves at Wreay suggest that beyond this world lies a mystery exceeding comprehension, and that despite our rational selves we still cling to dreams of light and reunion: 'Lighten our darkness we beseech thee O Lord'.

The week after Sarah's death, the *Carlisle Journal* reported,

On Monday, April 4, the day on which the late lamented Miss Losh, of Woodside, near Carlisle, was interred, a very large number of poor weavers, with their wives and families, assembled on the Village Green, and there planted a tree to perpetuate the memory of that excellent lady, and to convey an expression of their gratitude for the many gifts and favours that they had received from her, and also of the high esteem in which they hold her memory. By uniting together their penny subscriptions they have since had the tree fenced round. Miss Losh's admiration of trees is well known. This, therefore, they consider the most suitable memento within their means.[3]

In April 1853, the villagers and schoolchildren of Wreay also planted two lime trees on the village green, in memory of Sarah and Katharine. This was still her village.

In her will she left her Wreay relatives the houses they were living in: Wreay Syke to William Septimus and The Cottage to Frances Hutchinson.[4] Ravenside went to Alicia, with its fields and plantations, plus £3,000, an annuity of £100 a year and most of Woodside's silver, glass, china, linen and 'household stores'. All the rest of her land and buildings, including Woodside itself, was left to her cousin James and then, if he had no sons, to the other sons of James Losh and their heirs. The only one omitted was the errant Baldwin, who by a nice irony inherited it from his brother James and was the only one of the brothers who actually lived at Woodside, being firmly settled there with his wife Gertrude in the late 1860s, taking a benevolent interest in the school, as Sarah had done, and also cheerily taking out mortgages on her land.

Large sums went to Frances Hutchinson and to Sarah's cousin John Warwick, to pay off a debt. Smaller sums went to all her female cousins and to the children of William Gaskin. All the Woodside servants were left money and annuities: Hannah Shepherd, who had worked for Sarah since she came from the Isle of Man with the Hutchinsons; her gardener Robert Donald, and servants Joseph Scott, George Davidson and John Armstrong. Each was given furniture, Hannah receiving a 'mahogany chest of drawers . . . & my clothes', while the maid Mary got the bedding and washstand. Small legacies of £20 went to a charity for blind orphans at Newcastle, the school at Upperby, the dispensary at Carlisle and 'ten pounds to Mr Jackson and five to the Wreay poor at my funeral which must be private & inexpensive as possible'. A host of small sums of money, paintings, prints, brooches and books were distributed among friends and relatives. Mary Kemmis and Georgina Cussans got 'my Roman mosaics to be set for a broach', while the Newcastle doctor's wife, Mrs Ramsay, received, whether she wanted it or not, '£10 & large inkstand made at Birmingham after that of Petrarch'. The will's final words were 'I desire the old poney may be taken care of as at present & the old carriage horse also.'

Sarah left all the 'chests & closets with all articles, writings, drawings of my own, to my cousin Alicia M. Losh', apart from an oak desk and iron chest containing papers concerning the estate. She had burned many papers and letters and notebooks but several of these writings and drawings must have survived, like the travel journals which Henry Lonsdale read in the 1870s. After that, they vanished.

Across the road at Ravenside, Alicia lived on in some style, looked after by the devoted Hannah Shepherd, who would be the only person outside the family to be buried in the Losh grave enclosure. As she grew older Alicia paid long visits to her younger cousins, who saw her as a benign, impulsive, whist-addicted spinster aunt. The most creative of this next generation, with a style as independent as Sarah's, were her uncle William's grandchildren, Spencer and Alice Boyd. Alice was a talented painter while Spencer, who had inherited the near-ruined Penkill Castle in Ayrshire, was a woodcarver and an antiquarian. With William's encouragement

Alice Boyd, Rossetti's drawing, etched by William Bell Scott.

and money, they began restoring the medieval castle, filling it with old oak furniture, tapestries and armour. Then in 1859 in Newcastle Alice met William Bell Scott, now master of the School of Design: they lived together in a virtual *ménage à trois* with Bell Scott's wife until the end of his life. When Spencer died suddenly in 1865 and Alice became the new laird, she and Bell Scott continued the restoration, 'turning Penkill into a summer residence, where they generally lingered until the first frosts'.[5] Bell Scott covered the walls and staircases with murals and elsewhere they hung embroidered cloths, including the beautiful William Morris tapestries, *Qui bien aime*. Morris was enchanted by Penkill with its views across the Clyde, 'the great wide firth, Ailsa Craig plain to see, and the mountains of Arran lying in the distance: there were beautiful daffodils out in the woods, and more blackbirds than one could count'.[6]

Their Pre-Raphaelite friends, especially Christina and Dante Gabriel Rossetti, also loved Penkill, with its 'relaxed atmosphere of art and animals, whisky, friends and endless talk'.[7] Alicia met Rossetti here in 1868 and offered to lend him money to free him from work until his bad eyesight improved, feeling sympathetic as she had cataract trouble herself. According to Bell Scott, Alicia enjoyed playing the two men off against each other, and to his fury Rossetti accepted a partial loan.[8] In August the following year, he stopped at Ravenside for two nights on his way to Penkill. Afterwards he wrote to his mother, his 'Good Antique', telling her that he had seen 'some most remarkable architectural works by a former Miss Losh':

She must have been really a great genius, and should be better known. She built a church in the Byzantine style, which is full of beauty and imaginative detail, though extremely severe and simple. Also a mausoleum to her sister – a curious kind of Egyptian pile of stones with a statue of the lady in the centre, and opposite a Saxon cross – a sort of obelisk, reproduced from the old one, but with restorations by the lady herself.[9]

Rossetti described the Pompeiian cottage, the cemetery, the mortuary chapel based on the lost church in the dunes, and the Tudor wing at Woodside: 'All these things are real works of genius, but especially the church at Wreay, a most beautiful thing. She was entirely without systematic study as an architect, but her practical as well as inventive powers were extraordinary.' In his excitement he also wrote to Jane Morris: 'The works are very original and beautiful, very much more so than the things done by the young architects now . . . I was very much interested in them and should like Webb to see them.'[10] Philip Webb, the designer of Morris's Red House, may well have seen Wreay as he designed two houses for George Howard, Earl of Carlisle, and in the 1870s, in Brampton, he built his only church, with its grand windows by Burne-Jones.

For the next two years Rossetti wrote to Alicia, accepting more small loans and filling his letters with tumbling news.[11] In 1871 Alicia travelled to London for an operation on her eyes, and following complications, she died of pneumonia the following March. Her property, including a large amount of money still held by the alkali company at Walker, went to her nieces.[12] Like Sarah, Alicia had culled her papers and her executors destroyed more, although Rossetti's letters survived, marked in a shaky, elderly hand 'no use I am afraid except to me'.[13]

Across the road from Ravenside, Woodside was rented out by James Losh, who contined working as a judge in Newcastle. In his will, made in 1854, four years before he died, he made a handsome provision for his illegitimate children but placed an entail on Woodside so that it would pass down in sequence among his brothers, from Baldwin to John Joseph, Robert and William Septimus and then to the latter's son James.[14] Then came a trio of deaths: James in 1858, John Joseph – who came back from Madras to live in Wreay before he died – in 1862 and Robert in 1867. In the next decade Baldwin and his wife Gertrude moved to warmer climes in the Isle of Wight and, since William Septimus had no desire to leave Wreay Syke, his son James took over Woodside. James had trained for the church and held the living of Ponsonby in West Cumberland, but gave this up when he became a Unitarian. He also gave up his name, or rather changed it back: in 1870, when his son Godfrey was born, he took the name Arlosh.[15]

In Carlisle James was known and liked as a naturalist and a Liberal campaigner for reform. He loved the house, and when he made his own improvements and finally inherited it after Baldwin's death, he was delighted to discover the stones of an old pele tower below the building, just as Sarah had found the slabs beneath the church. But Woodside's later history was sad. In 1890, when he was twenty and a student at Brasenose College, Oxford, Godfrey died after falling from his horse in Port Meadow. Grief-stricken, his parents James and Isabella stayed near Oxford, only returning to Wreay at the end of the century. James died on a visit to Oxford in 1904, and Isabella followed him within a fortnight. To the wider family's fury, he left everything to Oxford's Manchester Unitarian College, to whom he had already given a magnificent set of Burne-Jones windows in Godfrey's memory. The college needed money, not an empty house in the north, and over the years they disposed of the estate, farm by farm. Of the Loshes' splendid library, all they took were a hundred books.

In 1912 Woodside was sold, with a great auction of all its contents, room by room, paintings, dinner services, snuff-boxes and rings, and a separate three-day sale of the books. The house was bought by Andrew Gibson, the newly married son of a Liverpool ship owner, but on the eve of their move Gibson's wife Florence died. Distraught, he moved into Ravenside, leaving Woodside empty, and to avoid paying rates he had the roof removed. Rain and snow ruined the rooms and the garden became a wild playground for the village children. It was rescued in 1933 by Geoffrey Carr, of the Carlisle biscuit factory, whose brother lived at Newbiggin across the Petteril. Only one wing could be saved, and the house looks strange now, with a squat 1960s extension, but inside it is full of character, flooded with light, its northerly windows looking over the fields towards Carlisle and the Scottish hills, and its south-facing terraces gazing across to the Pennines.

Three years after Sarah's death, Henry Lonsdale suggested that she was one of the local people who most deserved a memorial in Carlisle cathedral, describing her as unassuming, generous and impressively intellectual, 'well informed in architecture, and history and English lore; – the beautifullest of women, – a study for the historian and philanthropist'.[16] In 1873, helped by James Arlosh and building on his own memories of her at the end of her life, Lonsdale wrote a chapter on Sarah to follow those on her father and uncles in his *Worthies of Cumberland*.

By then the school that Sarah and Katharine had built in Wreay was growing: it soon took girls as well as boys and the small dame school was closed. William Septimus built a library next door, a reading room for working men, run, as all things still were, by the vicar and the Twelve Men. Until the village hall was built in the 1950s, in the field next to the schoolmaster's 'Pompeian Cottage', the school was the only place for village meetings. There were sports and wrestling matches. Dances were held there, the wooden floor scattered with French chalk, and during the war the Ministry of Defence put on films, like a memorable showing of *In Which We Serve*, with Noël Coward in the lead. The school, across the road from the churchyard with its flowering cherry trees, is still full of children.

The landscape that Sarah created survives, but after she died the church went on evolving, as a parish church must do. In 1884, when James Arlosh employed the architect C. J. Ferguson to help with the Woodside improvements, Ferguson called in F. R. Leach, who often worked with William Morris on internal decoration

A wrestling match at Wreay school.

schemes. The year before, the two men had redecorated St Cuthbert's in Carlisle, and Leach's diary notes 'Rev Arlosh. Woodside – Carlisle', and then, the following May, 'to Wreay, called at Ch. & on Mr. Arlosh fare 1/-'.[17] That September the *Carlisle Journal* noted the new heating at Wreay, a new path around the church, and the 'interior decorated by Leech [*sic*] of Cambridge'. Leach's team painted Sarah's Roman cement walls in dull pink and cream, decorated the apse with leafy scrolls in pale umber colours, and ornamented the wall behind each of the thirteen sedilia, the stone seats between pillars. The central panel shows the Lamb carrying a banner with the monogram IHS; the other twelve bear the emblems of the twelve Apostles, with the articles of the Apostles' Creed below.

There were other changes. An altar rail blocked off the apse; the bearskins disappeared and a red carpet was stretched over the flags; the chairs with their fine ebony backs were stolen; the 'Jewish lamp' disappeared. Sarah's strict rule against monuments was bro-

Wreay church on the day of Edward VII's coronation, 26 June, 1902.

ken, and memorials appeared on the walls. A makeshift vestry was erected beside the font, where one of the Tablets of the Law used to hang, and a harmonium occupied the opposite corner. The church remained a focus of village life, a place of baptisms and burials, private and public celebrations. But time took its toll. At the start of this century the oak pegs that held the heavy Lazonby slabs on the roof began to rot and the loose slabs left holes open to the rain. In a major restoration in 2006, the roof was repaired, the stained glass restored, the wood carvings cleaned and oiled, and the blistering, peeling paint was replaced with a white mineral-based alternative that allowed the walls to breathe.[18] At the same time the old harmonium gave way to an Edwardian pipe organ.

If some of the mystery disappeared with the mould, the church is still distinctly strange, resting in the heart of the village, a sheltered oasis of quiet between the railway line to the east and the M6 that roars behind the hill to the west, and circles across between Sarah's houses, Ravenside and Woodside. All visitors to

Wreay are struck by the church, as I was when I saw it as a girl, and again years later, crossing the road from the green in a haze of Cumbrian rain, when I became curious about its creator. I love the exuberant church but I shudder at the graves with their primitive forms, and at the statue of Katharine trapped for ever in her sunless box of stone. I am intrigued by Sarah Losh's deliberate withdrawal from view, the sense of a driving will and flowering imagination beneath her cloaked reserve. She destroyed many papers but, despite hunting in vain, I am sure her journals are still lying in some attic or uncatalogued archive, perhaps even in the iron chest mentioned in her will. I hope some day they will emerge into the light.

This enigmatic quality is built into her work, making it hard to place her church in any accepted canon or chronology. When Pevsner saw it in 1967 he was as astonished as Rossetti had been, almost exactly a century before. In an article for the *Architectural Review*, he noted how the rising arches of the facade echoed 'the dwarf gallery of Italian Romanesque churches', but pointed out that some features were more French than Italian, while the windows, with their triple clerestory windows above, were entirely her own: 'Miss Losh was quite free in her interpretation and quite original'.[19] Had she, he wondered, known anything of the German revival? It seemed unlikely, but even if she had seen prints:

Wreay has a solidity all of its own, and in any case its symbolic carvings have no parallel at all. In fact one might make the mistake of dating St Mary as one of the examples of the Early Christian or Byzantine revival which took place about 1900 and its carvings as Arts and Crafts. The latter is indeed almost unavoidable.

The decorations, naturalistic yet 'flatly carved', were also 'of a stylization which would be expected of 1900 but is unique in the 1840s'. The furnishings were unexpected too, and the stained glass, and the mausoleum.

Some commentators have linked the church to the ideas of Ruskin, but it was built a year before *Modern Painters* burst on the scene in all its lyrical power, transforming British attitudes to landscape, art and architecture, and seven years before *Seven Lamps of Architecture* in 1849, with its interest in the 'Pisan Romanesque' and its exhortations to draw on local traditions, train craftsmen, be humble, and study nature.[20] As the writer Jane Stevenson put it, 'By a wonderful irony, one of the greatest of all Ruskinian buildings pre-dated the Ruskinian revolution by a decade, and was built by a woman.'[21] Pugin's biographer, Rosemary Hill, has noted how the sympathetic relationship between the designer and craftsmen at Wreay anticipates the work of Ruskin and the architect William Lethaby. But above all she sees the affinity with Ruskin in the way that Sarah Losh's imagination, 'like his, had been fired by Romanticism, by a desire to express in architecture the sympathy of humanity and the natural world'.[22] How important, she asks, is Sarah Losh's work? 'If artistic feeling is to be measured by an ability to seize the currents of thought and feeling that flow through the age and give them fresh and vital expression, Sara Losh and her church are very important indeed.'

Yet Sarah, as Pevsner noted starkly, 'died in 1853 and was soon, except strictly locally, entirely forgotten'. Strictly locally, however, up to the end of the nineteenth century older villagers remembered her walking down Waygates in her black cloak and bonnet. As the century turned, there were changes in Wreay: in the early 1930s, when the houses were connected to the water mains, people stopped collecting their water from the pump. In 1943 the station was closed, and Wreay slipped back into a sleepy quietness. By the 1940s the churchyard within its paling fence was so dense with elderberry, holly and brambles that it was impossible to see across it from the school. One evening in 2011, a group of village people gathered at the Plough Inn – where the Twelve Men still meet to dispense local charities, as they did in Sarah's day – and sat round the table for an evening going over their memories, recalling that when they were children the overgrown churchyard was a great place for collecting eggs, as the village hens much preferred it to their coops. Then in 1956 the tangle was drastically cleared. The old gravestones, pulled up to make it easier to mow the grass, should have been set behind the church against the wall: instead, by some accident or misdirection, 'the whole ruddy lot' were tipped into the quarry at the end of the road, except for a couple that turned up in the garden of Forge House, the old blacksmith's shop. The Losh graves alone escaped. Behind them were the cherry trees planted along the school side of the churchyard. But between the graves and the mausoleum stood a fir tree. It had been there a long time – it can be seen faintly in an old sepia photograph of the 1880s. 'Big Tree. Roughly three or four yards off roadside. Blew down 20 years ago,' remembered one Wreay resident. 'Was sold. Blew into church yard. Can't say whether it hit the graves.'[23]

So William Thain's pine tree, if that was it, has gone too. But the pinecones remain, on the graves, held in Katherine's hand in the mausoleum, and on the windows, door, steps and roof beams of the church, with their promise that life and art and creation will go on.

Acknowledgements

My first thanks go to my colleague and friend Clara Farmer, who shared my fascination with Wreay church and wanted a book about it: this is for her. I am also grateful to Rosemary Hill for encouraging me from an early stage. Once I began, many people helped me and made my work highly enjoyable: the words 'immense generosity' apply to them all. In Carlisle I would particularly like to thank Celia Lemmon, who shared her unique knowledge of the James Losh manuscript diaries; Stephen Matthews of Bookcase, editor of the *Sarah Losh Journal*, who drove me around north Cumbria and provided constant information; and the local historian Denis Perriam, who taught me with great good humour about every aspect of Carlisle life. All three have saved me from errors, large and small.

In Wreay itself I owe special thanks to Raymond Whittaker, architect and Chairman of the Friends of St Mary's, who introduced me to local people and answered many questions. I am also grateful to Lois Whittaker for her hospitality; to Tony and Patricia Harrison of Wreay Hall for Canon Hall's book and the portrait of James Losh; to Michael and Violet Liddle of Woodside, for their warm welcome and books, and to Peter Strong for educating me about stained glass.

Marie McCulloch from Canberra kindly provided information about her ancestor George Losh and the family, while Tony Flowers in Newcastle shared his research into the Thains and William's tree. Angela Thirlwell passed on sources for Alice Boyd and Penkill; David Gardner Medwin answered queries about Thomas Coulthard Heysham, Simon Bradley lent Hope's works, and offered invaluable help with architecture and railways; Michael Hall and Ric Leach solved problems about the date of the apse paintings; Felix Stirling traced information in High Hesket records. Many ideas came from good conversations with John Barnard, Mary Evans, Rona Sulkin and Stella Tillyard.

I would also like to thank Stephen White of Carlisle Library, Jeff Cowton of the Wordsworth Trust, Grasmere, and David Bowcock of Cumbria and Westmorland Archive Service. Other helpful archivists chased queries, in particular Elaine Archbold of the Robinson Library, University of Newcastle; Melanie Gardner of Tullie House Museum, Carlisle; Pat Gundry of Carlisle Cathedral Archives; Kay Easson and Alison Gunning of the Newcastle Literary and Philosophical Society; June Holmes of the Natural History Society of Northumberland; Sue Killoran of Harris Manchester College, Oxford; and Fiona Tait of the Soho Archives, Birmingham. I also received kind directions in my hunt for papers from Canon David Weston and the Rt Rev. David Thompson, Bishop of Ely.

My thanks, too, to Sandra Oakins for the maps, Ray Nichol for his sketches and Sara Crofts, Phil Rigby, Claire Storr, Raymond Whittaker and Tom and Steve Uglow for the photographs.

As always, I am more than grateful to my agents, Deborah Rogers, Mohsen Shah and Melanie Jackson, and to my publisher, Jonathan Gallassi, at Farrar, Straus and Giroux. And I would like to thank the whole Faber team, especially my amused and supportive editor Julian Loose, the perceptive Kate Ward in production and the brilliant copyeditor Eleanor Rees. Finally my thanks go to Alison Samuel for her warm interest and comments, and to Hermione Lee and Steve Uglow, both of whom are the best of readers and acutest of critics.

Abbreviations and Notes

BL   British Library
CJ   *Carlisle Journal*
CL   Carlisle Library
CN   *Cumberland News*
CP   *Carlisle Patriot* 1815–90
CWAAS   Cumberland and Westmorland Antiquarian and Archeological
     Society
CRO   Cumbria Record Office, Petteril Bank, Carlisle
HRO   Hertford Record Office
JLD   James Losh's diaries, 33 MSS vols., 1787, 1796–1833, Carlisle Library
NA   National Archives, Kew
NHSN   Natural History Society of Northumberland
NL&P   Newcastle Literary and Philosophical Society
ODNB   *Oxford Dictionary of National Biography*
Robinson Library   Bell Collection, Robinson Library, University of Newcastle
Soho   Soho Archives, Birmingham Central Library
WT   Jerwood Library, Wordsworth Trust, Grasmere

Short titles

Some works are abbreviated throughout the notes, as listed below. Otherwise a full reference is given the first time a work is cited in each chapter; thereafter it is in a short form.

Bell Scott   W. Bell Scott, *Autobiographical Notes*, ed. W. Minto, 2 vols (1892)
Bullen, *Cross-Currents*   J. B. Bullen, *Continental Cross-Currents: British Criticism & European Art, 1810–1910* (2005)
Gent. Mag.   *Gentleman's Magazine*
Gilpin   William Gilpin, *Observations on Westmoreland and Cumberland* (1786 edn.)
Hall   A. R. Hall, *Wreay* (1929)
Hill   Rosemary Hill, *Pugin* (2009)
Hill, *Crafts*   Rosemary Hill, 'Romantic Affinities', *Crafts* 166 (September–October 2000)
Hughes   E. Hughes, *North Country Life in the Eighteenth Century*, 2 vols (1965)
Hutchinson   William Hutchinson, *History of Cumberland* (1794)
Hyde, *Cumbria*   Matthew Hyde and Nikolaus Pevsner, *Cumbria: The Buildings of England* (2010)

Jefferson, *Carlisle*   Samuel Jefferson, *History and Antiquities of Carlisle* (1838)

JLD Surtees   *The Diaries and Correspondence of James Losh*, ed. E. Hughes, Surtees Society (1962)

Kemp   Laurie Kemp, *Woodside* (1997)

Lonsdale   Henry Lonsdale, *The Worthies of Cumberland*, vol. IV (1873)

Lysons   Daniel Lysons and Samuel Lysons, *Magna Britannica*, vol. IV (1816)

Mannix and Whellan   Mannix and Whellan, *History, Gazetteer and Directory of Cumberland* (1847)

Matthews   Stephen Matthews, *Sara Losh and Wreay Church* (2007)

Pevsner   Nikolaus Pevsner, *The Buildings of England: Cumberland and Westmorland* (1967, revised edn ed. Matthew Hyde, 2010)

Pevsner, *Architectural Review*   Nikolaus Pevsner, 'Sarah Losh's Church', *Architectural Review* 142 (July 1967), 65–7

SLJ   *The Sarah Losh Journal* (Carlisle, 2011–)

Woof   Pamela Woof, *A Portrait of a Friendship* (2008)

Notes

Epigraph and Prologue

1 Jane Gary Harris (ed.), *Mandelstam: The Complete Critical Prose and Letters* (1979), 355

2 Rossetti to his mother, August 1869, O. Doughty and J. R. Wahl, eds, *Letters of Dante Gabriel Rossetti* (1967), II, 716; Simon Jenkins, *England's Thousand Best Churches* (Penguin edn 2000); Pevsner, 40; see also Pevsner, *Architectural Review*, 65–7

1 The Walk

1 CRO PR 118/9 Minute Book of Wreay, 1729

2 CRO PR 118/30 Jackson Notebook: Notes of Rev. R. Jackson, transcribed by his nephew, 1906; Mannix and Whellan, 173

3 Anne married William Parker, 14 August 1735: three sons and three daughters; Margaret (1713) married John Bell of Haltwhistle, 7 April 1740: three sons and two daughters; Elizabeth (1718) married Edmund Wilson of Hesket-in-the-Forest, 4 October 1744: two sons and three daughters.

4 For Joseph, see *Gent. Mag.* 2 (1784), 557; information from Marie McCulloch. The note about the walking match is inscribed on the reverse of the portrait of his brother Robert, Scottish National Portrait Gallery.

5 CRO D/Sen 5/5/1/8/33, 6 July 1789, Kitty Senhouse to Wilhelmina
  Beloches
6 JLD 3 November 1824
7 T.W. Thompson, *Wordsworth's Hawkshead* (1970), 74–6
8 From the late seventeenth century the British iron market was dominated
  by bar-iron from Sweden and Russia. For the brothers' studies and travels,
  see Lonsdale, who also mentions Margaret in Rome being asked by 'Cav-
  aliere Lande' to model for 'Valeria' in his painting of Coriolanus. Gaspare
  Landi's *Veturia at the Feet of Coriolanus* (Pitti Palace) is dated 1804, an unlikely time for British travellers to be in Italy, although Landi worked on
  it for some years before. On the other hand, it might have been a family
  joke that turned into a 'fact', after the sisters saw the painting in 1817.
9 Lonsdale, 149
10 WT 2004.L1/2 Jane Christian (senior) diary, 7 May 1796

2 City and Strife

1 Kenneth Smith, *Carlisle* (1984), 45–6
2 *The Poetical Works of Robert Anderson* (1820), xxi
3 Railton Longrigg, 14 December 1791, quoted in Denis Perriam, 'When
  Carlisle was "nothing but cotton mills"', *CN* 16 July 2004. See also Jefferson, *Carlisle*, 88
4 Woodbank, 1797, sale notice, *Cumberland Paquet* 22 August 1797: see also
  Denis Perriam, *CN* 23 December 2011
5 *CJ* 11 February 1832; 'The Bonny Stampt Gown', *The Citizen*, 1 November 1829
6 Mary Milner, *The Life of Isaac Milner* (1842), 130
7 William Paley, *Natural Theology: or, Evidences of the Existence and Attributes of
  the Deity* (1802), 3–4. Paley was first chaplain to his friend Edmund Law,
  Bishop of Carlisle, vicar of Dalston and, in 1782, Archdeacon of Carlisle.
8 Lonsdale, 203
9 Lonsdale, 201–2
10 In 1799 Carlyle went to Constantinople when Elgin was appointed am-
  bassador, and travelled through Asia Minor, Palestine, Greece and Italy,
  collecting manuscripts for a new version of the New Testament. On his
  return he was given a living in Newcastle, where he died in 1804. *Poems
  Suggested Chiefly by Scenes in Asia Minor, Syria, and Greece* appeared in
  1805, with extracts from his journal.
11 CRO PR118/9 Minute Book of Wreay, 1792, 1793: see Hall, 36–7
12 CRO PR118/9 Minute Book of Wreay, 1795, 1808
13 1780 Committee. Sarah's great-uncle, the lawyer Joseph Liddell, a firm
  Whig, was urged to stand against Lowther in an election. Lowther's route
  to power was helped by his marriage to Mary Stuart, daughter of George

III's prime minister the Earl of Bute. (Mary, a talented artist, left him after fifteen years of misery.)

14 Curwen represented Carlisle from 1786 to 1821, and was then one of the county MPs for Cumberland until he died in 1828.

15 Henry Lonsdale, *Worthies of Cumberland*, vol. III, Howard

16 *Bulmer's History & Directory of Cumberland*, 1901

17 Coleridge retitled this as 'Themes to debauch Boys' minds on the miseries of rich men & comforts of poverty'. See S. T. Coleridge, *Note Books*, ed. K. Coburn (1957), 1. 75

18 CRO Ca/2/100

19 Lancashire Record Office, DDTY 4/1

20 Lonsdale, 198

21 CRO D/Cart/11/70 Grant of land by tenants of Wreay to Bacon of Foulbridge, 1782

22 WT E761, Red Book, Blamire Family MSS

3 Foundations

1 CRO PR 118 /30 Jackson Notebook. For the history and antiquities I have used many works from SL's lifetime, and the later 19c. In addition to Hutchinson, Jefferson, Lysons, and Mannix and Whellan, these include Joseph Nicolson and Richard Burn, *History and Antiquities of Westmorland and Cumberland*; M. Creighton, *Carlisle* (1889, 1906); Samuel Jefferson, *The History and Antiquities of Cumberland: Leath Ward* (1840); Daniel Scott, *Bygone Cumberland and Westmorland* (1899); R. S. Ferguson, *Diocesan Histories: Carlisle* (1889).

2 Andrew of Wyntou, *Orygynale Chronicle*, 142; For Arthur, see Stephen Matthews, *King Arthur in Merrie Carlisle: Carlisle in the Arthurian Literature of the Middle Ages* (2009). At one point, the manors of Penrith and surrounding villages, known as the Honour of Penrith, were given to Scottish monarchs in return for their relinquishing their claim to the whole of Cumberland.

3 Ritson Graham, 'Wragmire Moss', *CJ* 24 July 1962; John Miles, 'Moss that was tamed by Rome', *CN* 11 October 1991; Denis Perriam, 'How they carried a Bishop from old oak tree', *CN* 20 November 1998

4 Hutchinson, I 44–54; editor's note: 'We are under great obligation to John Losh Esq. of Woodside, for the valuable assistance he has rendered in this part of the work.'

5 Gilpin, II 105

6 Gilpin, II 104–5

7 Gilpin, II 107, 109

8 Hutchinson, II 235

9 Kemp, 13. Marie McCulloch: Margaret, daughter of John Losh, d. 1639, was married twice, to John Robinson in 1626, and then Thomas Slack.

10 G. G. Mounsey, *Authentic Account of the Occupation of Carlisle in 1745* (1846), 246–59

11 Lonsdale, 144

4 Fields and Woods

1 JLD 30 August 1824

2 Norman McCord and Richard Thompson, *The Northern Counties from AD 1000* (1998), 178

3 M. E. Turner, *English Parliamentary Enclosure* (1980), 50, 60–1, 77–9. 'sterks' or stirks: cattle, bullocks. See McCord & Thompson, 181.

4 Turner, *Enclosure*, 90. In 1803 around fifty thousand acres of Inglewood Forest were enclosed.

5 Hughes, I 379

6 Private Act, 17 George III, c. 60 HL/PO/PB/1/1777/17G3n121 (1777)

7 CRO D/DHK 9/5/228 Henry Howard to John Losh, 8 April 1811

8 Hutchinson, 680

9 Richard L. Greaves, *Dictionary of Modern British Radicals* (1984)

10 'Account of the Larch Plantations on the Estates of Dunkeld and executed by the late John, Duke of Atholl', *Transactions of the Royal Highland Agricultural Society of Scotland*, 1832, 165–235. These were European larches, with spreading branches, not the tall, thin 'Dunkeld Larch' that developed when a later duke crossed the European and Japanese varieties in the 1880s.

11 *Gent. Mag.* 159 (1836)

12 Thomas de Quincey, *Literary Reminiscences* (1851), 200

13 *Description of the Scenery of the Lakes in the North of England* (4th edn 1823), 81

14 H. A. Macpherson, *The Vertebrate Fauna of Lakeland* (1892), 136

15 CRO D/HE/1/3 1829 Thomas Coulthard Heysham to SL

16 CRO D/HE/1/3 SL to Heysham, 17 April 1829

5 Springs, Fresh and Salt

1 Hughes, I 174–5 (CRO Curwen MSS 1789)

2 George Topping, *Rambles in the Borderland with the 'Clan'* (1921)

3 Denis Perriam, *CN* 15 April 2011

4 Thomas Crawford, *Nineteenth-Century Notes on Walker* (1904), 8

5 *Directory of Newcastle*, 1778, cited in John Baillie, *An Impartial History of the Town and County of Newcastle upon Tyne and its Vicinity* (1801), 520

6 'The Tyneside Chemical Industry', pamphlet, NL&P, 10

7 Cheshire County Archives, D 3075/21

8 L. F. Haber, *The Chemical Industry during the Nineteenth Century* (1958), 16

9 See A. & N. Clow, *The Chemical Revolution* (1952), 100–3

10 Soho, MS 3782/12/41/30, 26 Jan. 1796

11 H. L. Pattison, 1841; William Fordyce, *The History and Antiquities of the County Palatinate of Durham* (1857), 190

12 Eneas Mackenzie, *A Historical, and Topographical View of the County Palatinate of Durham* (1825), 463

13 See Archibald Dundonald, *The Present State of the Manufacture of Salt Explained* (1785)

14 NL&P: see R. C. Clapham, 'An Account of the Commencement of the Soda Manufacture on the Tyne', *Transactions of the Newcastle upon Tyne Chemical Society*, I (1868–71), 29–45. For the copperas works next door, from where they obtained their sulphuric acid, see correspondence of James Watt junior and Thomas Barnes. Soho, MS 3219/6/30 and 3219/6/2/37b

15 J. T. Hoyle, *Newcastle Weekly Chronicle*, 1876. With thanks to Tony Flowers.

6 Friendships

1 *Morning Chronicle*, 8 March 1793; see *Dictionary of British Radicals*.

2 See Nicholas Roe, *Wordsworth and Coleridge: The Radical Years* (1988)

3 Godwin Diary 27 Feb 1795,; Woof 1–2

4 For JL and Wordsworth, see Woof.

5 Gavin Kennedy, *Captain Bligh: the Man and His Mutinies* (1989), 116, 223

6 Benjamin Constant, trs. James Losh, *Observations on the Strength of the Present Government of France, and the necessity of rallying round it* (1797); E. L. Griggs (ed.), *Collected Letters of Samuel Taylor Coleridge*, 6 vols (1956–71); see Woof, 6. James Losh's inscribed copy of Coleridge's 'Ode on the Departing Year', printed in Bristol, is in the WT Collection.

7 JLD 17, 21, 23 August, 5, 9 September, 12, October 1796. See *Dictionary of British Radicals*.

8 JLD 15 June–11 September, 3–5 October.

9 WT Spedding letters, Margaret to William Spedding, 6 February 1797

10 JLD 12 June 1798

11 JLD 17 March 1798. With thanks to Celia Lemmon for her study of JL's reading.

12 Woof, 8. *The Letters of William and Dorothy Wordsworth, The Early Years, 1787–1805*, ed. E. De Selincourt, rev. Chester L. Shaver (1967), 212–14

13 JLD February–September 1798

14 Abbé Giovanni Mariti, *Travels through Cyprus, Syria and Palestine* (1792), II 49

15 Lonsdale, 199

16 Robert Southey, July 1799: Barbara Wedgwood and Hensleigh Wedgwood, *The Wedgwood Circle, 1730–1897* (1980), 112. For Beddoes, see Mike Jay, *The Atmosphere of Heaven* (2009)

17 WT Spedding letters, Margaret to William Spedding, 15 November 1796

18 Joseph Wilkinson senior, d. 1787, left both sisters £5,000 in government securities, and adjoining houses in English Street, Carlisle. Will, 25 October 1786. Information from Marie McCulloch.
19 *Newcastle Chronicle* 28 June 1794, *Directory of Newcastle upon Tyne and Gateshead* 1801, 1807. See Nigel Tattersfield, *Bookplates by Beilby and Bewick* (1999), 165–6
20 For the Bigge family, and JL's impressions of them, see Tattersfield, *Bookplates*, 65–8
21 JLD 12, 18 September 1799
22 JLD 16 July 1799
23 WT 1998.60.34 Jane Blamire to Jane Christian Blamire, 9 May 1806
24 JLD 10 October 1799
25 Carl Ketcham (ed.), *Letters of John Wordsworth* (1970), 105
26 JLD 12 April 1801
27 JLD 11 February 1802
28 JLD 6 March 1802
29 R. Tweddell (ed.), *The Remains of John Tweddell* (1815). See JLD 30 January, 4 March, 23 June 1816
30 Robert Southey to Tom Southey, *JLD* Surtees, ix

7 Family Matters

1 JLD 31 May 1801
2 JLD April/May 1799
3 Kemp, 76
4 Henry Lonsdale, *The Life of John Heysham, MD* (1870), 101. Even Leblanc was there in 1799: 'Le Blanc appears to be a man of a mild disposition with a clear head, but no very extensive knowledge beyond the bounds of his profession.' JLD 29 July 1799.
5 Mary Milner, *The Life of Isaac Milner*, 1842. After an unhappy stint teaching in America, Leslie became tutor to Josiah Wedgwood's son Tom, publishing *Experimental Enquiries into the Nature and Properties of Heat* in 1804.
6 C. M. L. Bouch, *Prelates and People of the Lake Counties: a History of the Diocese of Carlisle, 1133–1933* (1948), 379
7 *Gent. Mag.* 172 (November 1808), 1044; *European Magazine and London Review* 54 (1808), 402. See also Denis Perriam, *CN* 28 April 2006
8 WT 5/5/1/8/334 Letters to Humphrey Senhouse III and to his wife Kitty. Miss Aitkin January 1802
9 *Jollie's Carlisle Guide and Directory* (1811)
10 Lonsdale, *Life of Dr Heysham*, quoted in Laurie Kemp, *From Carlisle and Old Cumberland* (2008), 157
11 JLD 22 January 1803

12 CRO D/Sheff 1/14/1 6 and 7 September 1803; see also Denis Perriam, 'Speculation and perversity ruins city bank', *CN* 15 April 2011

13 JLD 6 July 1803

14 JLD February 1804

15 See Nigel Tattersfield, *Bookplates by Beilby and Bewick* (1999), 165. For Losh, Lubbren & Co., see Northumberland County Archives, SANT/ BEQ/26/1/7/14/a. One dissatisfied creditor was Sir James Lowther, to whose agent James wrote in 1805. CRO Lowther/Newcastle

16 JLD 12 November 1801

17 JLD 6 August 1804; Lonsdale, 201

18 JLD 27 November 1804

19 CRO PR118/9 Minute Book. John was not present at meetings in 1797, 1798 and 1799, and from 1803 to 1807, and 1810–11.

20 WT 1998.60.35, 45 Jane Blamire to Jane Christian Blamire, 3 December 1806, 23 January 1807

21 JLD 3 August 1807

22 JLD 10 August 1801

23 WT 1998.60.34 Jane Blamire to Jane Christian Blamire, 9 May 1806

24 Lonsdale, 204

25 CRO D/Sen 5/5/1/9/73 Mary Warwick to Kitty Senhouse, 27 December 1810

26 George Eliot, *Middlemarch* (Penguin, 1965), 117

27 JLD 28 January 1811

28 JLD 25 March 1811

29 *CJ* 1 March 1806, collection £579 18s 10d; also booklet on Hudson Scott & Sons, showing the mayor's advertisement, May 1949. Information from Denis Perriam.

30 Denis Perriam, 'Forgotten Trafalgar already?', *CN* 16 May 2003

31 Robinson Library, Bell Collection, William Losh to William Charlton, 15 November 1806

32 Robinson Library, Bell Collection. William Losh, 19 June 1808

33 Dorothy Wordsworth, *Journal* 16 August 1803

34 K. W. Bond, *Freemasonry in Cumberland and Westmorland* (1994), 63–4; W. F. Lamonby, *A New History of Craft Masonry in Cumberland and Westmorland* (1879), 8

35 *The Literary Panorama*, ed. Charles Taylor (1808), IV, col. 1294. For the Covent Garden ceremony, see *The European Magazine and London Review* 55 (1809), 54–6

36 JLD 30 June 1809

37 JLD 24 April 2011

38 Kenneth Smith, *Carlisle* (1984), 49

39 WT 1998.60.36 Jane Blamire to Jane Christian Blamire, 22 May 1812

40 CRO D/Sen 5/5/1/8/44, Kitty Senhouse letters

41 JLD 4, 13–18 June, 27 November 1812

42 JLD 23 March 1813

43 JLD 18 October 1813

8 Wanderings and Waterloo

1 JLD 28 March 1814

2 JLD 29 March 1814

3 JLD 31 March 1814

4 John Losh, will, Newcastle 24 February 1811, codicil 8 October 1813. With thanks to Celia Lemmon.

5 Joseph James was born in Stanwix and baptised at St Cuthbert's, Carlisle, on 3 March 1810. He was married twice, to Mary Morley in Stanwix in 1837, and Martha King in Lewisham in 1847, with whom he had six children. In London he worked as a clerk, was declared bankrupt again in 1866, and died in Camberwell in June 1881. Information from Marie Mc-Culloch. Kemp, 36, suggests that his mother was the daughter of Thomas James, a maltster, baptised 6 March 1784 at St Cuthbert's, and thus about twenty-four when Joseph was born.

6 JLD 2 April 1814

7 JLD 25 July 1814

8 Hall, 61. Hall writes that the book is marked 'William Thain, 1802'; William would then have been five, and this is probably a mistranscription of '1812'.

9 William Thain to John Bruce, 8 March 1814. John Bruce Williamson, ed., *Memorials of John Bruce, Schoolmaster in Newcastle upon Tyne and of Mary Bruce, His Wife* (1903). With thanks to Tony Flowers.

10 Hall, 61–4

11 Lonsdale, 205

12 JLD 3 October 1814

13 JLD 9 October 1814

14 CRO D/Sen 5/5/1/9/73 Jane Harrison 1815

15 JLD 25 March 1815

16 JLD 11 May 1815

17 JLD 16 August 1815

18 Patents 31 May 1815 and 30 September 1816. See *CP* 11 January 1817

19 *JLD* Surtees, I 73, 13 November 1817; JL letter 13 November 1817; Lonsdale, 191–2

20 JLD October 1815

21 Denis Perriam, 'Survivors of Waterloo battle', *CN* 13 September 2002, 26 October 2007

22 HRO DE/Ml/86378 William Thain to James Thain, 16 June 1815

23 *Memorials of John Bruce*, quoted in unpublished paper by Tony Flowers

(2010), 'A Fine Soldier and a Moral Philosopher? William Thain, *c.*1796–1842'

24 *CP* 3 June 1815, quoted in Barbara Melaas-Swanson, *The Life and Thought of the Very Reverend Dr Isaac Milner and His Contribution to the Evangelical Revival in England*. Doctoral thesis, Durham University (1993), 136. See Mary Milner, *The Life of Isaac Milner* (1842), 612

9 Italy

1 Church calendar 1817
2 'He dared to consecrate his life to glory and to truth, and was always persecuted, by himself, or by envy.' In her journal Sarah made some errors in her transcription from memory, transposing the first two lines; Lonsdale 209.
3 Anna Jameson, *The Diary of an Ennuyée* (1826), 21–8
4 Shelley, 20 November 1818, *The Complete Works of Percy Bysshe Shelley*, Roger Ingpen and Walter E. Peck (eds), IX, *Letters* (1965), 344
5 Byron to John Murray, 30 May 1817
6 Shelley, *Works* IX. See Bullen, *Cross-Currents*, 18–19
7 Shelley, *Works* IX: the painting was *Madonna che allatta il bambino*: see Bullen, *Cross-Currents*.
8 Virgil, *Aeneid*, Book VII: translation adapted from Joseph Davidson, 1770
9 Jameson, *Diary*, 272–3
10 François Hagnere, Sansevero Chapel, trifter.com/europe/italy/naples/sansevero-masonic-chapel
11 W. M. F. Jashemski, F. G. Meyer and M. Riccardi, *The Natural History of Pompeii* (2002), 134, 144, 362, 383
12 JLD 28 March 1823: see also 27 January 1822

10 Mullioned Windows

1 WT 2004 E653, Jane Blamire diary 1814
2 WT 2004 E761 Red Book, MS journals of Blamire family
3 JLD 26 January 1819
4 See Rosemary Sweet, *Antiquaries: The Discovery of the Past in Eighteenth-Century Britain* (2004), 325–8. Other significant works included Taylor's *Essays on Gothic Architecture* (1800, often reprinted), and John Milner's *Treatise on the Ecclesiastical Architecture of England during the Middle Ages* (1811). For antiquarianism in relation to national identity, and collections, see Arthur MacGregor, *Curiosity and Enlightenment: Collectors and Collections from the Sixteenth to the Nineteenth Century* (2007), 281–94
5 John Britton, *The Architectural Antiquities of Britain*, IV (1814), vii

6 Unidentified notes by James Arlosh, c.1880.With thanks to Celia Lemmon and Laurie Kemp.

7 William Cobbett, *Rural Rides* (1912 edn), I 5, 30 October 1821

8 These included Peter Frederick Robinson's *Designs for Ornamental Villas* (1825) and *Domestic Architecture in the Tudor Style* (1837), and Thomas Frederick Hunt, *Half-a-dozen Hints on Picturesque Domestic Architecture* (1825) and *Exemplars of Tudor Architecture Adapted to Modern Habitations* (1830).

9 *Building News and Engineering Journal* 37 (1879, and 1887).With thanks to Steve Matthews.

10 CL 2B9 WRE9 Woodside sale catalogue, 1908; Kemp, 14–15

11 Quoted in Chris Brooks, *The Gothic Revival* (1999), 192

12 JLD July 1828

13 Marjan Sterckx, 'The Invisible "Sculpteuse": Sculptures by Women in the Nineteenth-century Urban Public Space—London, Paris, Brussels', *Nineteenth-Century Art Worldwide*, 7 ii (2008)

14 JLD 14 September 1826

15 Hughes, I 380

16 JLD 26 May 1821

17 CRO D/Ing 187/4

18 CRO D/Hud 13/10 Elizabeth to Andrew Hudleston 27 January 1820

19 JLD 19 April 1820

20 JLD 25 October 1820

21 JLD 22 April 1823

22 JLD 13 September 1821,Wordsworth to JL 4 December 1821.Alan G. Hill, *Letters of Dorothy and William Wordsworth: The Later Years 1821–1828*, III, Part I, 96–9;Woof, 27–30

23 For Antiquarian Society correspondence see Northumberland County Archives SANT/ADM/4. For St Mary's Chapel and well, see F.W. Dendy, *Archaeologia Aeliana*, 3rd series, i (1904), 122–48

24 JLD 31 August 1821.After her death he wrote:'As far as I am able to judge from conflicting accounts, the late Queen was a woman of considerable talents with an ardent and active mind . . . But she was used ill from the first day of her arrival in England, married to a heartless debauchee, surrounded by cunning and profligate courtiers and finally hunted to her death by every kind of ill usage and unfeeling persecution.'

25 William Farish, *Autobiography: The Struggles of a Handloom Weaver* (1889), 23; CRO D/Hud 13/10, to Andrew Hudleston 17 March 1820

26 *CJ* 29 May 1820

27 JLD 31 July 1821

28 *CP* 22 September 1821. For the Academy see Denis Perriam, 'The Carlisle Academy of Fine Arts', *The Connoisseur*, August 1975, 300–5

29 John Chapple and Alan Shelston (eds), *Further Letters of Mrs Gaskell* (2000), 8

30 *Carlisle Express*, 4 June 1857

31 JLD October 1820
32 Quoted by Bob Teevan, 'Letters to the East Lothian Banking Company', www.bankingletters.co.uk.
33 JLD 14 April 1822. For the bank collapse, see www.bankingletters. co.uk and *CJ* 23 May 1822; see also *CP* 16 January, 25 April, 26, 29 July, 5 August 1826 and 23 June 1829. For Elliot's stoppage, *CJ* 19 April 1822 and Denis Perriam, 'Brief life of city's Scots-trading bank', *CN* 3 June 2011
34 HRO DE/Ml/86383, 86401, William Thain to James Thain 2 March 1823, 14 May 1828

11 The Misses Losh

1 JLD 5, 27 September 1827, 6 May, 28 June 1829. With thanks to Celia Lemmon.
2 JLD 30 September 1825
3 Kemp, 145
4 JLD 6 August 1821
5 JLD Monthly summary for February 1824
6 Lonsdale, 236
7 *CJ* 29 December 1826; Norman McCord and Richard Thompson, *The Northern Counties from AD 1000* (1998), 246
8 JLD 1826; Hughes, I 360
9 *CJ* 9, 21 December 1826
10 JLD 6 October 1824
11 Peter Connon, *In the Shadow of the Eagle's Wing, The History of Aviation in the Cumbria Dumfries & Galloway Region 1825–1914* (1982), 2–5
12 JLD 22 July 1826
13 JLD 19 August 1826
14 JLD 20 August 1826
15 Carrick exhibited a 'Portrait of a Young Lady' at Carlisle Academy in 1828: he turned professional in 1833 and left for Newcastle in 1836. Denis Perriam, see articles on T. H. Carrick, *CN* 23 May 2008, and his son, the Pre-Raphaelite and Newlyn School painter J. M. Carrick, *CN* 30 July 2010.
16 JLD 20 October 1826
17 JLD 2 September 1826
18 CRO DRC/6/162 Bishop's transcripts 1776–1872
19 *CJ* January 1831
20 CRO DX 92 Sale particulars 1908
21 CRO DX 1314/19 Harrison Family of Wreay, John Robinson cash book, February 1838
22 JLD quoted in Hughes, I 383

23 CRO PR 118 Minute Book
24 Joseph Nicolson and Richard Burn, *The History and Antiquities of Westmorland and Cumberland* (1777), II 33
25 Nicholas Carlisle, *Concise Description of the Endowed Grammar Schools in England and Wales*, vol. I (1818). Carlisle is quoting from the account of Wreay School in the Rose Castle manuscript Visitation Book of the Revd Walter Fletcher, Chancellor of Carlisle Cathedral and Vicar of Dalston: with thanks to Canon David Weston.
26 Transcription of letter, December 1844. CRO PR 118/30 Jackson Notebook, 52: see also Hall, 94–6
27 *JLD* Surtees, II 28 September 1830
28 CRO PR 118/30 Jackson Notebook, 53
29 Hall, 98
30 CRO PR 118/30. The letter is pre-November 1832, as references to Gaskin show he is still alive. The subject came up again when the dean and chapter wanted to build a new parsonage in 1844, and enquired about school stock.
31 Mannix and Whellan, 174
32 CRO PR 118/ 30 Jackson Notebook

12 'The Antient and Present State'

1 Mannix & Whellan, 133. See also Hutchinson, II 439
2 CRO D/Sen 5/5/1/9/49 Jane Blamire to Kitty Senhouse 7 February 1809
3 CRO D/Ay/6/23 Jane Matthews' letters to friends
4 For the attitude towards women see Rosemary Sweet, *Antiquaries: The Discovery of the Past in Eighteenth-Century Britain* (2004) 69–79
5 Northumberland County Archives SANT/ADM/4/1/2/94
6 Hyde, *Cumbria*, 183
7 P. Henderson, ed., *The Letters of William Morris to His Family and Friends* (1950)
8 *Archaeologia* 2nd ser., 14 (1903), 109–18
9 Rev. James Hewison, 'Notes on the Runic Roods of Ruthwell and Bewcastle', *Transactions* of CWAAS, 10 March 1913
10 Camden, *Britannia* (1607). 'In the churchyard there is erected a Crosse about 20 foote high, all of one entier four square stone, very artificially cut and engraven, but the letters are so worne and gone that they cannot be red.'
11 George Smith, *Gent. Mag.* xii (1742), 529
12 For Bewcastle see David Thomson, Bishop of Ely, 'Bewcastle Cross', www.bewcastle.com; Fred Orton & Ian Wood with Clare A. Lees, *Fragments of History: Rethinking the Ruthwell and Bewcastle Monuments* (2007); Hyde, *Cumbria*, 153–5
13 Lonsdale, 206
14 R. Tweddell (ed.), *The Remains of John Tweddell* (1815), 268, 317
15 H. B. Bullen, 'Sara Losh: architect, romantic, mythologist', *Burlington*

Magazine 1184, cxliii, November 2001; citing JLD 4, 6, 7 April 1827

16 See *Transactions of the Linnean Society* 12 (1818), 'On the rocks of Attica', *Geological Transactions* 1 (1824), 170–2, and *Letters of an Architect from France, Italy, and Greece,* 2 vols (1828), illustrated by the author

17 Information from June Holmes, NHSN. Manuscript Members book: James Losh, founder and committee member, joined 19 August 1829 (1829–33). W. S. Losh, founder, joined 19 August 1829, resigned in 1832. Robert Losh joined 20 November 1829. William Losh joined 2 January 1830. The lists of donations are in the society's *Transactions.*

18 Megan Aldrich, 'Thomas Rickman's Handbook of Gothic Architecture and the Taxonomic Classification of the Past', in *Antiquaries and Archaists,* ed. Megan Aldrich and Robert J. Wallis (2009)

19 Paul Frankl, *The Gothic: Literary Sources and Interpretations through Eight Centuries* (1960), 512

13 Broken Glass

1 HRO JL to James Thain, DE/MI 86374/41

2 JL to Henry Brougham, 18 August 1830, *JLD* Surtees, II 184

3 Elizabeth Stevenson (Gaskell) to Harriet Carr 18 June 1831, John Chapple and Alan Shelston (eds), *Further Letters of Mrs Gaskell* (2000), 3

4 JL to Brougham, 18 July 1833, *JLD* Surtees, II 227

5 CRO DX 11/47, also quoted in Henry Summerson, *'An Ancient Squire's Family': The History of the Aglionbys, c. 1130–2002* (2007), 130

6 *CJ* 13, 20 November, 4 December 1830; Katrina Navickas, 'Captain Swing in the North: the Carlisle Riots of 1830', *History Workshop Journal* 71 (January 2011), 13

7 Thomas Carlyle, 'Signs of the Times', in *Critical and Miscellaneous Essays* (1858), 188

8 Carlyle, 'Signs of the Times', 193

9 Lonsdale, 133

10 Kemp, 59

11 William Farish, *Autobiography: the Struggles of a Handloom Weaver* (1889), cited in George Topping and John J. Potter, *Two Carel Lads, Memories Of Old Carlisle* (1922)

12 Henry Brougham to JL August 1831, *JLD* Surtees, II

13 Quoted in June C. F. Barnes, 'The trade union and radical activities of the Carlisle handloom weavers', CWAAS lxxviii, 158. See also Farish, *Autobiography,* 14

14 JLD 21 March 1833

15 JLD 30 May 1831

16 Lonsdale, 222

17 JLD 4 May 1833

18 JLD 25 June 1832
19 Laurie Kemp, *From Carlisle to Old Cumberland* (2008), 24–31
20 JLD 23 May 1833
21 JLD 7 August 1833
22 Woof, 31
23 Robinson Library, 'A Brief Memorial of the Late James Losh', Newcastle 1833
24 Robinson Library, Newcastle Press, 9 November 1833

14 A Thousand Ages

1 Charles Lyell, 'Memoir on the Geology of Central France', review, *Quarterly Review* 36 (1827), 437–83
2 'Theory of the Earth', *Transactions of the Royal Society of Edinburgh* i (1788), 304: Nikolaas A. Rupke, *The Great Chain of History* (1983), 55. See also Rupke's '"The End of History" in the Early Picturing of Geological Time', *History of Science* 36 (1998), 61–90
3 Neville Haile, 'William Buckland', *ODNB*
4 *The Role of Women in the History of Geology*, ed. Cynthia V. Burek and Bettie Higgs, Geological Society of London (2007), 160–2
5 Letter of 1834, Sarah Hennell, *A Memoir of Charles Hennell* (1899); Jenny Uglow, *George Eliot* (1987), 33
6 George Eliot to Martha Jackson 4 March 1841, *Selections from George Eliot's Letters*, ed. Gordon S. Haight (1985), 16–17
7 'On the discovery of a New Species of Pterodactyle', *Transactions of the Geological Society* iii (1835), 217–18; Rupke, *Great Chain of History*, 139
8 Rupke, *Great Chain of History*, 143
9 Tennyson, 'The Princess' (1847), ll. 250–4, quoted in Virginia Zimmerman, *Excavating Victorians* (2008), 83
10 William Buckland, *Geology and Mineralogy* (1836), I 403; Rupke, *Great Chain of History*, 245
11 John Lindley and William Hutton, *Fossil Flora of the British Isles* (1833–7), I 17
12 Lindley and Hutton, *Fossil Flora*, I 26–30. These include the lepidodendrons, the 'scale trees', and ferns like *Pecopteris lobifolia* and *Sphenopteris furcata*, found in the Bensham coal seam at Jarrow. With thanks to June Holmes and Sylvia Humphrey.

15 Mourning

1 Lonsdale, 220
2 *CJ* 28 Feb 1835
3 WT E761 Red Book I, Blamire MSS
4 Cassandra Austen to Fanny Knight 20 July 1817, *Jane Austen's Letters*, ed. Deirdre Le Faye (1995), 344

5 In 1887, *Building News* reported the inscription over the garden entrance, written by the Rev. T. Lees, noting that Sarah stopped work in 1835, interrupted by the death of her beloved sister'. The work was completed by James and Isabella Arlosh in 1878.

6 *CJ* 17 October 1835

7 Curwen's visit was in 1813, described in his *Observations on the State of Ireland* (1818)

8 *CJ* 24 October 1835

9 CRO D/Ay 620, Francis Aglionby to Jane Aglionby 19 November 1835. Henry Summerson, *'An Ancient Squire's Family', The History of the Aglionbys c.1130–2002* (2007), 130

10 *The West Briton*, 15 September 1835. The heads are now in Truro Museum.

11 Michel's notes, Museum of the Royal Institution, Truro, quoted by Bullen in *Cross-Currents*, 72n. See also E. W. F. Tomlin, *In Search of St Piran* (1982)

12 Rev. C. Trelawney Collins, *Perranzabuloe, the Lost Church Found* (1836), 279

13 'Church of Perranzabuloe, Cornwall', *Gent. Mag.* n.s. IV (1835), 539–40

14 Collins, *Perranzabuloe*, 2

15 Collins, *Perranzabuloe*, 23

16 Collins, *Perranzabuloe*, 227

17 William Haslam, *Perran-Zabuloe* (1844), 89

18 Matthew Hyde, talk at Wreay church, September 2011. The Dublin church was designed by John Hungerford Pollen, inspired by the rebuilding in the 1840s of S. Paolo fuori le Mura in Rome in its original Constantinian style.

19 CRO PR 118/30 Jackson Notebook. See the letters of Henry Lonsdale and G. G. Mounsey (Mayor of Carlisle), to W. A. Mackinnon MP, on overcrowded cemeteries. 23 and 24 April 1842. *SLJ* 1 (2011), 141–2

20 See Kemp for Margaret Losh, will, 1679. With thanks to F. H. Stirling and Denis Perriam for information about High Hesket records. Hindson information: www.telusnet/Hindson/Family; Lorton & Derwent Fells Local Family History Society *Journal* 40 (August 2007). Also CRO D/X 92 and 1841 Census.

16 Extraordinary Power

1 *CJ* 17, 21 September 1833

2 Kenneth Smith, *Carlisle* (1984), 52

3 Report of Durham Spring Assizes, *Newcastle Journal* 19 March 1836

4 CRO D/X1314/21. Robinson Day Book, 1838

5 CRO DRC /8/ 202 Tithe commutation 1839–40. The meeting was advertised in *CJ* 10 March 1838.

6 *CJ* 24 June 1837

7 *CJ* 1 July 1837

8 *CJ* 7 Jan 1839. For the shipwreck, see *Cumberland Paquet and Ware's White-haven Advertiser* 8 January 1839

17 Not in the Gothick Style

1 Jane Stevenson, 'A Woman's Touch in Stone', *Guardian* 20 August 2005. The Institute of Architects, founded in 1834, was for men only; the first woman to qualify was Ethel Charles in 1898 and women were admitted to RIBA in the early twentieth century. See Lynne Walker, 'Golden Age or False Dawn? Women Architects in the Early Twentieth Century', available via www.english-heritage.org.uk

2 Jim Cheshire, 'Elizabeth Simcoe and her daughters: amateur ecclesiastical design in the 1840s', in M. Hall and R. Hill (eds), *The 1840s: Studies in Victorian Architecture and Design* (2008), 87–95

3 Hyde, *Cumbria*, 34

4 Whewell on Rickman, *ODNB*

5 Hyde, *Cumbria*, 606; Gilpin, II 124

6 Jefferson, *Carlisle*, 290–1. The building was opened in 1831.

7 Pugin to E. J. Willson, 6 November 1834

8 Hill, 52

9 J. A. Froude, 'Thomas Carlyle', *Leader* VI (27 October 1855), 1034–5

10 Rosemary Hill, 'Sarah Losh', *SLJ* 1 (2011), 15

11 Hill, 243

12 Hyde, *Cumbria*, 662

13 Paul Frankl, *The Gothic: Literary Sources and Interpretations through Eight Centuries* (1960), 556

14 Chris Brooks, *The Gothic Revival* (1999), 246

15 Hill, 214

16 Kenneth Clark, *The Gothic Revival* (1928; 1950 edn.), 191

17 See subscription list to *A Library of Fathers of the Holy Catholic Church*, also, within this series, *Tertullian* (1842), *Epistles of St Cyprian, Homilies of St John Chrysostom*, and, outside the series, George Bull, *Harmonia Apostolica* (1842) and Lancelot Andrewes, *Ninety-six Sermons* (1841)

18 *Novum aedificandi genus*: see T. Cocke, 'Rediscovery of the Romanesque' in the exhibition catalogue, T. Holland, J. Holt and G. Zarnecki, *English Romanesque Art, 1066–1200*, 360

19 Bullen, *Cross-Currents*, 40; Thomas Kerrich, 'Some Observations on Gothic Buildings Abroad, particularly those of Italy', *Archaeologia* 16 (1812), 293. For coinage of 'Romanesque' see William Gunn, *An Inquiry into the Origin and Influence of Gothic Architecture* (1819), 6

20 See Gunn, *Inquiry*, 80; cited by Cocke, 'Rediscovery of the Romanesque', 362. Also J. B. Bullen, 'Sara Losh: architect, romantic, mythologist',

Burlington Magazine 1 November 2001, quoting T. Waldeier-Bizzarro, *Romanesque Architectural Criticism: A Prehistory* (1992), 143

21 Cocke, 'Rediscovery of the Romanesque', 362

22 Cocke, 'Rediscovery of the Romanesque', 363

23 J. A. Picton, 'A Few Observations on the Anglo-Norman Style of Architecture and its Applicability to Modern Ecclesiastical Edifices', *Architectural Magazine* I (1834), 290: quoted by Bullen, 'Sara Losh'.

24 Hyde, *Cumbria*, 217

25 Thomas Hope, *An Historical Essay on Architecture* (1835), I 199

26 Hope, *Historical Essay*, I 250; Bullen, *Cross-Currents*, 59

27 J. B. Bullen, *Byzantium Rediscovered* (2003), 112, citing *Ecclesiologist* 2 (1842), 5–16

28 This interest accompanied the Romantic movement across Europe. Arguments arose when Creuzer identified the origin of monotheistic religions with Indian symbolism.

29 The link to Payne Knight is made strongly by Bullen in *Cross Currents*, 74–8

30 Richard Payne Knight, *Inquiry into the Symbolical Language of Ancient Art and Mythology* (1818), 39–40, 160, 32, 124

31 Peter A. Schouls, *Descartes and the Enlightenment* (1989), 155 (art. 34); see the definition of 'the Pineal Gland' in Aitken, *Elements of Physiology* (1838)

18 Stone by Stone

1 CRO D/X 1314/22 Robinson Day Book, 1841

2 CRO PR118/30 Jackson Notebook 61, 25 March 1841

3 CRO D/X 1314. Robinson Day Book 1838–42

4 CRO PR118/30 Jackson Notebook

5 All quotations for Sarah Losh in this chapter are from CRO PR 118/30 Jackson Notebook.

6 *CJ* 22 and 25 May 1841

7 Lonsdale, 217

8 Francis Aglionby died in 1840; Henry Aglionby, previously Bateman, changed his name on being made heir to the estates of his aunt Sarah Lowthian (nee Aglionby) at Newbiggin in 1822. Henry Summerson, *'An Ancient Squire's Family', The History of the Aglionbys c. 1130–2002* (2007)

9 Hall, 74

10 Matthews, 10. The original was removed as dangerous in 1997: current copy by the York sculptor Dick Reid.

11 Lonsdale, 217

12 Hall, 86

13 CRO PR 118/30 Jackson Notebook, Committee Minutes 1 September 1841

19 Jubilate

1 Bell Scott, I 188

2 Bouet's father was in the train of the Comte d'Artois, the brother of Louis XVI, whom George III allowed to live at Holyrood Palace. Bouet taught drawing and French, painted portraits and produced drawings for engravings of local topography. David Cross, 'William Septimus Losh and the Artist Joseph Bouet', *SLJ* 1 (2011), 28. The Losh sketch is not of William Septimus Losh, as Cross suggests, but his father James Losh (BL Add MS 1300 no. 119). In 1856, Bouet left his 'old friend and pupil W. S. Losh of Wreay Syke, near Carlisle, a gold ring of the value of five pounds sterling' and an identical ring to his wife.

3 CRO D/MBS/5/22 Mounsey, Bowman & Sutcliffe of Carlisle, 1838, 1840: lease renewed by William James of Barrock Lodge to James and Mark Thomson.

4 Named by Lonsdale: see John Lindley and William Hutton, *Fossil Flora of the British Isles* (1833–7), I 142–4, 112–14, 115–20, 85–7

5 With thanks to J.patricia.art@gmail.com. For the connection with San Vitale, see Jane Stevenson, *Guardian* 20 August 2005

6 Hugh Wright, 'Wreay Church – Aspects of Craftsmanship', *SLJ* 1 (2011), 149

7 CRO PR 118/30 Jackson Notebook

8 CRO PR 118/30 Jackson Notebook

9 Lonsdale, 228–30, citing Walcott's *Archaeologia* on pedalia or footcloths in front of the altar in 1092

10 Lonsdale, 228. This is now in the cathedral treasury, with the Verona inkstand, left in her will. Other items mentioned by Lonsdale that have since disappeared include an Italian lamp above the pulpit, an Italian *scaldino* or chafing dish, figures of lions near the pulpit, and another antique stove.

11 This is suggested by Rosemary Hill in 'Sarah Losh', *SLJ* 1 (2011), 11–12.

12 CRO D/X 1314/22 Robinson Day Book 1841–2

13 Lonsdale, 226

14 Hall, 83

15 Hall, 82

16 Hall, 76

17 Lonsdale, 226

18 Pevsner, *Architectural Review*, 65–7

19 Lonsdale, 229

20 In 1869 John Purchas, perpetual curate of St James's, Brighton, was arraigned before the ecclesiastical Court of Arches on thirty-five counts. More cases followed the Public Worship Regulation Act in 1874, and four clergymen were imprisoned. Nigel Scotland, 'Evangelicals, Anglicans and Ritualism in Victorian England', *Churchman* 111/3 (1997)

21 1 Kings 6:29

20 Remembering

1 HRO DE/MI/86502-86512 William Thain to Sophia Thain, from Meerut, Mulgan, Chenab, Yellalabad, Cabul.

2 HRO DE/MI/86506 Camp between the Chenab & the Jelum (Acesines & Hydaspes) 16 February 1841

3 Jules Stewart, *Crimson Snow: Britain's First Disaster in Afghanistan* (2008), 159

4 Lady Florentia Sale, *A Journal of the Disasters in Afghanistan: A Firsthand Account by One of the Few Survivors* (1843)

5 For attempts to identify the tree, thanks to Tony Flowers' unpublished paper, 'Thain's Tree'. A conifer is just visible near the mausoleum and cross in a sepia photograph of the 1880s, CL, Arlosh correspondence, B202

6 CRO Tithes and Registers, Register C, PR 118/4 1813–73 Baptisms, December 1842

7 CRO PR 118/30 Jackson Notebook

8 CRO PR 118/30 Jackson Notebook

9 Matthew Hyde, personal communication and *SLJ* 2 (September 2012)

10 The Latin runs: *Jehovah lux mea et salus mea est* (Ps. 27); *Gratiam fac mihi: Deus, gratiam fac mihi; nam ad te se receptit anima mea: et ad umbram alarum tuarum me recepturus sum* (Ps. 57): translation from King James Bible. At the base, on the west: *Inumbret hoc signum consolationis sepulchrum Joannis Lossii et uxoris Isabellae. Salvi eatis, animae carissimae, per mediam umbram mortis. Avete in tempora refrigerii a conspectu Domini.* Translation by Lonsdale.

11 See Matthews, 91. For Wordsworth, and another reading of death as return to earth, see Michael Wheeler, 'The Grave, and the Analogy of Nature', in *Death and the Future Life in Victorian Literature and Theology* (1990), 47–68

12 'Newton Arlosh', visitcumbria.com

13 Hyde, Cumbria, 334. Also [D. R. Perriam], English Heritage List entry 1212611, citing Licence to crenellate, 11 April 1304. The defensive church was built after Robert the Bruce's raid in 1322. See Bulmer's *History and Directory of Cumberland* (1901); J. F. Curwen, *Castles and Fortified Towers of Cumberland and Westmorland* (1913), 328–30; D. R. Perriam and John Robertson, *The Medieval Fortified Buildings of Cumbria*, CWAAS (1998)

14 Walter Scott, *Harold the Dauntless* (1817)

15 Lonsdale, 234n.

16 Her design is now swamped by later renovations in 1894.

17 14 July 1849: From: 'Records: The Church of the Reformation', *Register & Records of Holm Cultram* (1929), 176–90, available via http://www.british-history.ac.uk

21 Living On

1   1841 Census, Wreay and Petteril Crooks

2   For the auction see *CP* 14 November 1841. For the petition see Hughes, 363–5

3   *CJ* 20 January 1844

4   Lonsdale, 236–7

5   James Arlosh, 'The Museum and its Relation to the Natural History of the District', 4 February 1880, *Cumberland and Westmorland Association Transactions*, Part 5 (1879–80), 129–41

6   Hall, 16

7   *CJ* 10 January 1839

8   NA RAIL 346/1, Lancaster and Carlisle Railway Company, Minute Book, 6 December 1843

9   The Grand Junction subscribed £250,000, the London and Birmingham £100,000, and the North Union and the Lancaster and Preston Junction £65,000 each. *Regional History of the Railways of Great Britain*, vol. 14, David Joy, *The Lake Counties* (1983), 24. For the L&C see also articles by Denis Perriam, *CN* 20 December 1996, 16 March 2007, 9 February 2009, 19 November 2010. Locke gave the contract to Thomas Brassey and his partners William Mackenzie and John Stephenson, the largest railway contract yet.

10 *CP* 15 November 1844; Lancaster and Carlisle Railway navvies' strike, February 1846: CRO D/Hud 4/44 1846, 'Strikers' depositions and notes of the events' See also Dick Sullivan, *Navvyman* (1983), 130–2; 'Ewanian', *History of Penrith* (1894), David Joy, *Main Line over Shap* (1967), 28–31, and Jean Scott-Smith, 'Shap and the Railway', *Cumbrian Railways Journal* 9 (August 2008).

11 *CP* 27 February 1846

12 *Illustrated London News* 19 and 26 December 1846; see also Denis Perriam, 'The first train from Carlisle to Penrith', *CN* 20 December 1996

13 Informal note attached to enquiries about Alicia Losh, from editors of the Fredeman edition of *Letters of Dante Gabriel Rossetti*.

14 William Fordyce, *The History and Antiquities of the County Palatine of Durham* (1857), 191

15 Information from Marie McCulloch. According to census data the three children, James (b. 1845), Mary and John, kept the surname Brown until the 1880s, when all three changed their name to Losh. See also the elaborate will of James Losh, made in 1854, appointing John Joseph and William Septimus as trustees. Probate 3 November 1858, Newcastle.

16 James A. Secord, *Victorian Sensation* (2001), 1

17 Secord, *Victorian Sensation*, 331

18 Lonsdale, 214

19 *New York Times*, 29 November 1880; nytimes.com/gst/abstract. Gavazzi,

who later converted to Protestantism, went on to lecture in Canada, and in the United States, returning there for a third time in his seventies, in 1880.

20 *Letters of Mary Wordsworth, 1800–1855*, ed. Mary E. Burton (1958), 310

21 Bell Scott, I 221. Denis Perriam, 'Carlisle cathedral cupboard reveals its vested interests', *CN* 25 July 2011; see also Simon Swynfen Jervis, 'Antiquarian Gleanings in the North of England', *Antiquaries Journal* 85, 2005

Epilogue

1 Bell Scott, I 221

2 Wordsworth, Preface, *Lyrical Ballads* (1800). See Rosemary Hill in 'Romantic Affinities', *Crafts* 166, and 'Sarah Losh', *SLJ* 1 (2011).

3 *Local Collections or Records of Remarkable Events* 15 (1853), 32; also *SLJ* 1 (2011), 138

4 Handwritten will, 23 December 1851; codicil 4 September 1852, CRO PR118/38; Probate will, 1853, NA PROB 11/2174. Frances Hutchinson was left £2,000 and an annuity, and John Warwick £2,500.

5 Jan Marsh, 'The Topsaic Tapestries and Penkill Castle', *Journal of William Morris Studies* 13.4 (Spring 2000), 36, and 'The Letters of Pictor Ignotus: William Bell Scott's relationship with Alice Boyd, 1859–1884', *John Rylands Library Bulletin* 58 (Autumn 1975, Spring 1976). Penkill Papers, University of British Columbia, Vancouver.

6 Marsh, 'The Topsaic Tapestries', 39; quoting Norman Kelvin (ed.), *The Collected Letters of William Morris* (1987), II 759–60

7 Michael Hall, *Country Life* 21 March 1991, 118

8 Bell Scott, II 108–11

9 Rossetti to his mother August 1869, O. Doughty and J. R. Wahl (eds), *Letters of Dante Gabriel Rossetti* (1967), II 716

10 Rossetti to Jane Morris 23 August 1869. J. Bryson (ed.), *Dante Gabriel Rossetti and Janey Morris: their correspondence* (1976), 24

11 'Rossetti and Miss Losh', *Three Rossetis: Unpublished Letters to and from Dante Gabriel, Christina, and William*, collected and edited by Janet Camp Troxell (1937), 80–108

12 Alicia died after an operation for cataract, while staying with James Arlosh's sister in law at Abbotsleigh, Upper Norwood. She left Ravenside to her niece Frances Pennell, née Hutchinson, wife of Admiral Follett Walrond Pennell (1804–76). The Pennells stayed in Langarth House, while Robert Losh moved to Ravenside.

13 *Three Rossetis*, 84–5. See Helen Rossetti Angeli, *Dante Gabriel Rossetti: His Friends and Enemies* (1949), 153–4.

14 Will of James Losh, dated 1854, Probate 3 November 1858, Newcastle

15 Woodside lodgers included a Mr Malthus, whose daughter set her sights

on James: in 1859, however, he married Isabella Benn, daughter of a naval captain, with connections to the Spedding family. The 1861 census shows Commander Benn at Woodside. For name change see *The Times* 2 August 1870, recording change by deed poll, 30 June 1870.

16 Henry Lonsdale, letter to the editor, *CJ* 30 July 1856.

17 F. R. Leach, appointment diary and tradecard, listing churches he worked on, including 'RHEA', the phonetic version of Wreay: Leach Archive, courtesy of Ric Leach. See *CJ* 25 September 1885; J. Uglow, 'The Apse Wall-paintings', *SLJ* 1 (2011), 16–19. With thanks to Rosemary Hill and Michael Hall.

18 See Raymond Whittaker's article on the restoration, *SLJ* 1 (2011).

19 Pevsner, 210–13, and Pevsner, *Architectural Review*

20 John Ruskin, *Seven Lamps of Architecture* (1849), 65, 173; for Ruskin, the Bible and Solomon in the 1830s, see Michael Wheeler, *Ruskin's God* (1999) 3–51

21 Jane Stevenson, 'A Woman's Touch in Stone', *Guardian* 20 August 2005

22 Hill, *Crafts*, 39

23 Transcript of meeting at the Plough, 9 May 2011. *SLJ* 1 (2011), 29–41

List of Illustrations

[315]

Photography credits: Claire Storr 1, 2, 8, 9, 10, 11, 16, 17, 18, 19, 24, 28, 30, 35, 36; Raymond Whittaker 13, 15, 21, 22, 28, 31, 33, 37, 38; Sara Crofts 25, 26, 29, 32, 34; Phil Rigby 12, 23; Steve Uglow 14; Tom Uglow 20.

Illustrations in the text

Part-title vignettes are details from the engraving of the 'Ancient Obelisk in Bewcastle Churchyard', from Daniel Lysons and Samuel Lysons, *Magna Britannia* (1784), vol. 4, *Account of the County of Cumberland* (1816). The title page and all the chapter-head vignettes in pen and wash are by Ray R. Nichol, 2011.

Index

Blamire, William, 113, 163, 194
Blamire family, 12, 30, 65, 84
Bland, Robert, 81
Blaylock, Jane, 138
Blaylock, Josiah, 138
Blaylock, Nanny, 123
Blaylock family, 144
Bonaparte, Joseph, 110
Bonner, Ann (SL's aunt): in Brisco, 76, 182;
    death, 254; finances, 65, 138; gifts for
    church, 236; gravestone, 254; relationship
    with Woodside family, 92
Bonner, Robert (SL's uncle), 17
Bonner, Sarah (SL's aunt), 182
Bonner, Thomas, 17
Bonner family, 50
Border Antiquities of England and Scotland, 150
Borthwick, William, 128
Bouch, William, 259
Bouet, Joseph, 231
Boulton, Matthew, 53
Bowman, Mr (surveyor), 143
Bowman, William, 234
Boyd, Alice, 266, 277–8
Boyd, Margaret (Losh, SL's cousin), 130,
    157, 266
Boyd, Spencer, 130, 157
Boyd, Spencer (son of above), 266, 277–8
Brand, John, 269
Brandling, Fanny, 127
Bridekirk, 38, 147–8, 149
Bridgewater, Francis Egerton, Earl of, 172
Bridgewater Treatises, 171–2
Brisco: Ann Bonner in, 76, 182; enclosure,
    42; Hutchinson family in, 265–6, 267;
    Losh lands, 9, 137–8; railway station, 265;
    St Ninian's Lane, Plate 7; St Ninian's well,
    37, 268
Brisco Hall, 190
Bristol, 63–4, 65, 114–15
Britannia (Camden), 33, 152
Britton, John, 115, 201
Brougham, Henry, 120, 125, 126, 158, 163–4,
    182
Brougham Hall, 264
Brown, John, 139–40, 142–3, 190
Brown, Mary Lindsay, 267
Brownrigg, William, 66
Bruce, John, 93, 98
Bruce, John Collingwood, 269

Brydon, William, 245
Buckland, Mary, 174, 176
Buckland, William, 172–3, 174, 175–6, 199, 227
Buffon, Comte de, 171
Building News, 118
Buildings of Britain (Pevsner), 2
Burdon, Rowland, 67, 74
Burke, Edmund, 27–8
Burne-Jones, Edward, 148, 279, 280
Burns, Robert, 62
Butler, Alban, 269
Butterfield, William, 203
Byron, Lord: in Athens, 70; on fossils, 172–3;
    in Italy, 104, 105; response to *Anastasius*,
    209; Sarah's reading, 137, 274

Calder Bridge, 208
Caldew, river, 20, 49, 72
Caledonian Railway, 264
Camden, William, 33, 149
Camden Society, 205, 206
Carew, Nicholas, 185
Carlisle: Academy, 122, 126–7, 136, 166,
    190, 191; architecture, 154, 156; Assembly
    Rooms, 191, 264; assizes, 69, 77, 84, 114;
    banks, 50–1, 74–5, 128–9, 193; booksellers,
    120; Botchergate, 81, 154; Caldewgate,
    154, 160, 164, 192; canal, 133; cathedral,
    21, 22, 35, 38, 216, 218, 229, 272, 281;
    cholera, 164; Citadel, 22, 81–2, 154; Court
    House, 81–3; elections, 126; fairs, 19;
    floods, 128; gale damage, 196; Gas and
    Coke Company, 134; Harmony Lodge
    of Masons, 81–3; Harriers, 73; Hunt,
    76; immigrants, 21, 132; industry, 19–21,
    81, 192–3; Jacobite rising (1745), 39–40;
    Losh family in, 12, 18, 19, 50–1, 73–4,
    76, 83, 114; market, 19, 84, 137–8, 194;
    mayors, 24, 26, 80; Mechanics Institute,
    166; parliamentary representation, 26,
    126, 159–60; Patriotic Club, 28; patron
    saint, 37; Pitt Club, 100; plan in 1822,
    22; population, 21; port, 19; races, 73,
    136; railway lines, 134, 141, 143, 159, 165,
    195–6, 260–3; railway stations, 195, 264;
    Reading Rooms, 200; reform movement,
    160–1, 163; roads, 19; robberies, 84, 132;
    Roman fort, 145; St Cuthbert's Church,
    12, 282; St Mary's Abbey, 8; St Mary's
    priory, 33; society, 12, 21, 60, 65–6, 76,